DATE DUE			
Apr18 '83			

THE LONG TRAIL

HOW COWBOYS
& LONGHORNS
OPENED
THE WEST

By Gardner Soule

Other books written by Gardner Soule

Men Who Dared the Sea
Remarkable Creatures of the Seas
New Discoveries in Oceanography
Surprising Facts
Strange Things Animals Do
Wide Ocean
The Greatest Depths
Under the Sea
Undersea Frontiers
UFOs and IFOs
Trail of the Abominable Snowman
The Ocean Adventure
Sea Rescue
The Mystery Monsters
Gemini and Apollo
Tomorrow's World of Science
The Maybe Monsters

THE LONG TRAIL

HOW COWBOYS & LONGHORNS OPENED THE WEST

By Gardner Soule

McGraw-Hill Book Company

New York   St. Louis   San Francisco
Düsseldorf   London   Mexico   Sydney   Toronto

123456789 DODO 79876

Library of Congress Cataloging in Publication Data

Soule, Gardner.
The long trail.

Bibliography: p.
Includes index.
1. Cowboys—Great Plains.   2. Longhorn cattle.
3. Great Plains—History.   I. Title.
F596.S74   976.4'8   76-16168
ISBN   0-07-059765-0

The Frontispiece sketch, drawn by Harold D. Bugbee, is used by
courtesy of Mrs. Olive Bugbee. The original of this, and other of
Mr. Bugbee's drawings, are in the collection of the Panhandle-
Plains Historical Museum, Canyon, Texas.

To a Texas family:

Fred Holmes, Lois (Simmons), and Cliffie Alexander;
Frederick D., Debbie, Christopher, and Troy Alexander;
Henry Paul and Bernice (Bootie Alexander) and Annette Marie
Arboneaux.

And a Kansas family:

Paul and Mildred Lee Ward; Dean and Virginia (Ward) and Gina and
Paula Graves; William Paul and Kathy, Laura, Wendy, Russ, and
Ann Ward.

And a Kansas-Missouri family:

Wade Hampton and Grace Frances (Hipsher) and Ardith Grace
McDowell; Wade Edward, Loretta (Fichino), Theresa Lynn, and
Wade Edward (Jr.) McDowell; Warren A., Dorothy Ann
(McDowell), and Warren A. (Bud) Gresham; and Mr. and Mrs.
Paul John Pfister (Amelia Ann—Amy) Gresham.

Acknowledgments

WITH MY THANKS

I have tried to tell the story of the cowboy—and what he means to us today: Who he was, where he came from, what he did, why he did it, why he could do it, who helped him, who didn't, and what his effect was on the world of his time, and what his effect has been on the world of our time, yours and mine.

The Old Trail Drivers of Texas is an organization originally formed by the cowboys, today composed of their descendants; over fifty years ago, the Trail Drivers issued a collection of first-person experiences of cowboys that is the most authoritative source of information, *The Trail Drivers of Texas,* edited by a newspaperman of Bandera, Texas, J. Marvin Hunter. I have used it for information, for dozens of stories, and whenever I have checked a fact I have accepted this book's word as final. Recently, the Old Trail Drivers and their directors, and Horace Probst, their president, have kindly furnished me more information, plus photographs, unobtainable elsewhere, of men who drove longhorn cattle north from Texas.

There are many helpful books on cowboys and longhorns; some of them I list in the Bibliography.

For a steady flow, over many years, of lore about cowboys and longhorns, I am indebted to my cousin, Mrs. Ben Earl (Mary Elizabeth Perfect) Grimes of Dallas and her son, Billy; Mrs. Grimes on my behalf checked with the DeGolyer collection at Southern Methodist University for photographs.

My other helpful searchers for pictures include my niece, Mrs. Linda Biesele Hall, a teacher of cowboy history at Trinity University in San Antonio; Mrs. Elbert (Eretha Lois) Turner of the *Houston Post* (I also owe her thanks for a few steak and roastbeef dinners along the way); Mrs. Richard (Mary Patricia Flynn) Kollings, one of the editors of the magazine *The American West.* Those who have given their time and taken their trouble to provide or suggest illustrations include Mrs. Claire R. Kuehn, archivist-librarian, The Panhandle-Plains Historical Museum, Canyon, Texas; Jerry L. Kearns, head, Reference Section, Prints and Photographs Division, the Library of Congress, Washington, D.C.; Mrs. Eric Steinfeldt, curator of decorative arts, Witte Memorial Museum, San Antonio; Mrs. Gilard Kargl, acting director of the Witte Museum; M. D. Monaghan, O.D., curator, Southwest Railroad Historical Society, of Garland, Texas; Joe R. Thompson, a photographer of Jayton, Texas; Fritz Toepperwein of the *Highland Press,* Boerne, Texas; Mary S. Carnahan, curator of collections, Texas Memorial Museum—the University of Texas at Austin; Mrs. Marjorie A. Morey, curator of photographic collections, Amon Carter Museum of Western Art, Fort Worth; Ron Tyler, curator of history at the Amon Carter Museum; Bill Wilson, director of public relations, National Cowboy Hall of Fame and Western Heritage Center, Oklahoma City; Mrs. Charlie (Verna Anne) Wheeler, director, the Crosby County Pioneer Museum.

For photographs of cattle towns and early railroads, I thank Bill Burk, vice-president, The Atchison, Topeka and Santa Fe Railway Company; and Barry R. Combs, director of public relations, Union Pacific Railroad Company.

For everything, I am indebted to my wife, Janie.

For all the help an editor can give, I thank mine, Mrs. Lou S. Ashworth of McGraw-Hill.

For special assistance when I needed it, my appreciation to Mrs. Roland Tisinger of the Roland Tisinger Memorial Library, Shepherd, Texas.

For patient listening and encouragement and inspiration and strength and sustenance, my thanks to E. C. and Annabel Murray Thomas and their daughters, Margaret Ann and Frances Claire; Joe Weldon and Margaret Murray Bailey; William Paul and Frances Louise Mueller Danforth, and their sons Billy, Donald, and Douglas; Phillips and Elaine Brooks, and their youngsters, Denise and Steven; Mrs. Bernice Ikins; Curtis and Connie Burge; Jerry, Anne Simmons, Johnny, and Kathy Schwartz; Mrs. Margaret Seale Biggerstaff; Barbara and Gus Roesch; Hy and Mary Jane (Janey) Toom Parkinson and Nancy; Lynn and Marjorie Holmes Mighell; Hoke, Grace, Sally and Meg Brissenden; Arik, Sally, Mark, Kira and Noel Brissenden; Paul and Anna Brissenden and their daughters Jeree and Debbie; Lucy Arant; Mrs. Anna Biesele; Rudy L. and Peggy Soule Biesele; Luis, Patricia, and Eric Villegas. Most all of these people have been with me on the long, long trail.

My Dad, Edgar Soule (1886–1971), put me on the track of much of the history in this book. My Mother, once Floy De Vore Perfect, is the writer I wish I were, and when I was small, she was a Mother who read to me.

—Gardner Soule.
Morningside Heights
New York City
February 26, 1976

Contents

1   A nineteen-year-old overhears men talk   1
2   Men drive the longhorns north   7
3   The longhorns came over the ocean   11
4   Some Texians fight a short war   19
5   A sixteen-year-old dreams up a gun   25
6   A vast land changes hands   31
7   Men head for the first roundups   35
8   Fathers and sons and brothers together fight Indians   45
9   A bullwhacker, thirty, improves a wagon   49
10   A herd crosses the Pecos River country   53
11   Two men sit on a pile of lumber   61
12   The trail gets crowded   65
13   A trail boss, twenty-two, completes a trip   69
14   A man who didn't drive the trail   75
15   "A thousand steers swimming . . ."   79
16   A steamboat man locates a ranch   85
17   At home, things were difficult   89
18   Men on horseback ride a long way   99
19   The men on the trail were boys   111
20   The trail to Wichita, Wyoming, Utah, Idaho   119

21 A day on the trail   125
22 All sorts of things kept happening   135
23 "I was barely 17 years old"   143
24 A woman travels the Long Trail   149
25 Men, women, and horses keep trying   155
26 The cowboy obtains a better Colt   163
27 Barbed wire holds the longhorns   167
28 A Long Trail to many places   171
29 A trail driver sets up as a rancher   175
30 The rattlesnake and other neighbors   179
31 Some cowmen visit a world's fair   189
32 The trail to Wyoming   195
33 Conversation on the Long Trail   199
34 More and more Texas ranches   203
35 He never got away from the birds   209
36 The superest cowboy who never lived   217
37 All kinds of weather   219
38 Lost—and dying of thirst   223
39 The longhorns graze on Northern ranches   229
40 The day he wasn't killed   237
41 A wild white mustang forever roams free   241
42 Hail on July 4—and other items   243
43 A cowman handles cow thieves   249
44 The entire midcontinent changes   251
45 The terrible winter   259
46 The cowboy with no bad habits   261
47 When cowboys rode trains   265
48 The cowboy marries the farmer's daughter   269
49 Nearing the end of the trail   277
50 A young man picks ticks off cattle   281
51 Heroes on various fronts   285
52 Some of the last of the cowboys   291
53 Some of the things they got done   297
54 A vanishing animal makes a comeback   303
55 After the trail was over   307
56 Postscript: Memories and Reminders   317
Annotated bibliography   327
Index   333

1

A nineteen-year-old overhears men talk

1866, NINETY YEARS after the American Declaration of Independence: It was the first full year of peace after the War Between the States, the Civil War. Down in Texas, dirt-poor Americans were scrounging for a way to make a living. They could not help but see around them wild cattle—longhorns—that roamed free in almost every county. There were also some wild horses—mustangs. Desperate for a fairer shake for their women and children and themselves, a few men caught and tamed some of the mustangs, and then, on horseback, hunted and captured longhorns and drove them north. Often riding the mustangs they themselves had tamed and trained, they traveled through unknown, unmapped, Indian country with no definite place to go—just in the hope they would find some Northern people who would buy the cattle.

Meanwhile, AROUND THE WORLD: Far away, in Newfoundland, at a harbor called Heart's Content, the dream of one American came true: On July 17, Cyrus W. Field's cable beneath the Atlantic Ocean finally was complete. The cable would transmit messages across the sea in minutes instead of the two weeks or more a sailing ship required. On land, railroads were being built, but the basic form of transportation was on foot—or as it had been for thousands of years, on horseback. A man or woman, accordingly, rarely traveled over 100 or 150 miles from his birthplace.

James M. Daugherty listened, as calmly as he could, to the men discussing how best to end his life. What he overheard was a conversation on whether to hang him or to horsewhip him to death.

He was nineteen years old. He was tied to a tree.

On horseback, he had driven a herd of cattle north, one of the first herds, north to Kansas—where he hoped he could sell it. He was one of the first people to open a trail, a trail from Texas north, a trail that eventually would itself open the almost-unknown mid-continent of North America.

"In the spring of 1866," said Daugherty, in a book, *The Trail Drivers of Texas,* "I made my first trail drive. Starting from Denton County, Texas [not far from today's Dallas and Fort Worth], with a herd of about 500 steers and five cow hands and myself, I crossed Red River at a crossing known at that time as Preston." The winding Red River forms much of the boundary between Texas and Oklahoma.

"From Preston," Daugherty continued, "I drove to Fort Gibson, Indian Territory [today Oklahoma], and from Fort Gibson, I drove to Baxter Springs, Kansas, close to the Kansas and Indian Territory line." (Baxter Springs is at the very southeastern tip of Kansas.)

He had hoped to reach Sedalia, Missouri, where he thought he could ship the cattle to St. Louis over one of the first U.S. railroad lines.

At Baxter Springs, Daugherty heard that several herds had been ahead of him. They "had been disturbed by what we called at that time Kansas Jayhawkers, and in one instance the Jayhawkers had killed the owner, taken the herd, and ran the rest of the cowboys off. This herd belonged to Kaynaird and was gathered in the southern part of the Choctaw Nation in the Indian Territory."

The Jayhawkers asserted that the Texas cattle would infect their own cattle with Texas (tick) fever, a disease little understood at the time.

The Kansans' fears, based on experience, were justified. Before Jim Daugherty's drive, even before the War Between the States, some Texas cattle marched to Kansas and Missouri had infected the domestic cattle of early farmers in those states. This was a serious matter. The sick animals usually died from the Texas —also called Spanish—fever.

The settlers in Kansas and Missouri were poor; if their one or two milk cows died, their women and children would be without milk—maybe without food. So Kansas farmers formed armed bands to halt Texas cattle.

The situation was just as serious for the Texas drivers. They too were poor. The longhorns were the only property they had to sell. If they did not somehow make a connection with a buyer, their women and children back home would go without food and clothing and other necessities. And they had driven the cattle hundreds of miles through a wilderness to seek what looked like the only chance for their families' survival.

To look for a purchaser for his steers, Jim Daugherty rode alone, ahead of the herd. At Fort Scott, Kansas, about fifty miles north of Baxter Springs, Daugherty met a man named Ben Keys. Keys offered to buy the cattle if they could be delivered at Fort Scott. Daugherty returned to his herd and began driving to Fort Scott. He moved north along the Kansas-Missouri border, weaving back and forth across the border. "We were," he said, "always on the lookout for trouble."

It came about twenty miles south of Fort Scott, when fifteen or twenty Kansans met the herd. "One of my cowboys, John Dobbins by name, was leading the herd and I was riding close to the leader. Upon approach of the Jayhawkers John attempted to draw his gun and the Jayhawkers shot him dead in the saddle. This caused the cattle to stampede and at the time they covered me with their guns and I was forced to surrender. The rest of the cowboys stayed with the herd, losing part of them in the stampede."

The Kansans took Daugherty away from the herd and lashed him to the tree with his own rope.

They accused Daugherty of driving cattle infested with ticks into their country. "I was," said Daugherty, "found guilty without any evidence." They did not have even one of his cows on hand to inspect.

The Jayhawkers argued over what to do with the nineteen-year-old. "Some wanted to hang me while others wanted to whip me to death. I being a young man in my teens and my sympathetic talk about being ignorant of ticky cattle of the south diseasing any of the cattle in their country caused one of the big Jayhawkers to take my part. The balance were strong for hanging me on the spot, but through his arguments they finally let me go."

Then a Texas cowman, who had migrated from Missouri, Dr. J. W. Hargus, came along with his cattle. He had driven north from Martindale, between San Antonio and Austin. He had passed through Austin, Waco, Dallas, and Sherman, and had crossed the Red River near Denison, Texas—later the birthplace and home for the first years of Dwight David Eisenhower.

Dr. Hargus had with him a cowboy who wished to hide his identity. He called himself Porter. Later he turned out to be a famous Confederate guerrilla of the Civil War, Capt. William Clarke Quantrill.

At the Red River, Hargus' cattle had caught up with others belonging to men named Millett, Lane, and Col. J. J. Meyers. The river was swollen. It was 300 yards wide, and the waves were high. But Hargus' cattle led the others across.

Hargus himself had tried to swim his horse across it: the horse drowned. He tried a second horse, and he and another man, R. C. Farmer, made it across the river. No other cowboys had. "We two had our hands full, as we had to sing to about six thousand head of cattle in order to keep them together. It was midnight before any of the others could cross over. This was a pretty cool job, as it was the early part of April and we had on only our shirts."

There was no further difficulty till Hargus reached the Kansas-Missouri line—and found Jim Daugherty.

Here Hargus learned that there was such a thing as Texas fever. "This," he said, "was the first time I had ever heard of this." Hargus drove his cattle to Jasper County, Missouri, and near Joplin, where he kept them all summer.

Hargus, after the Jayhawkers had left, untied Daugherty and set him free.

Said Jim Daugherty: "After I was freed and joined the herd, two of my cowboys and I slipped back and buried John Dobbins where he fell. After we had buried him we cut down a small tree and hewed out a head and footboard and marked his grave."

The Kansans who had captured him, he said later, were a band of thieves.

"They were nothing more than a bunch of cattle rustlers and were not interested about fever ticks coming into their country but used this just as a pretense to kill the men with the herds and steal the cattle or stampede the herds."

Daugherty found that he had lost 150 cattle in the stampede caused when the Jayhawkers had shot John Dobbins.

Daugherty obtained a guide from prospective buyer Ben Keys, and with the guide Daugherty drove the herd at night, rested it in secluded spots by day, and after five days and nights reached Fort Scott. At daylight, he penned the cattle in a high, board corral, adjoining a livery stable, so they were hidden from public view. Purchaser Ben Keys paid for the cattle. "Then," said Daugherty, "we ate our breakfast and slept all day."

"When darkness fell we saddled our horses and started back over the trail to Texas. I returned to Texas without any further incident worth noting, and continued to drive the trail, rarely missing a year that I did not make a drive."

Daugherty, at age nineteen, in 1866 had met disaster, discouragement, and the death of a comrade. He was one of the first to encounter the same things many others would meet on the trail from Texas north.

He also encountered something else: success.

He got his cattle through. He sold them.

As Cyrus Field had for his dream the laying of a cable across the Atlantic ocean, so Jim Daugherty had for his dream following— with his longhorns—a trail north to market. One of the first of the trail drivers, Daugherty really meant it when he said he "continued to drive the trail." In spite of the loss of John Dobbins and the threat to his own life on his first trip, Jim Daugherty would drive cattle up the trail from Texas in most of the next twenty-one years, or till 1887. Those years would make Daugherty one of the most capable and successful of the men on the trail north.

2

Men drive
the longhorns north

Men, BEFORE or since, have never done anything remotely like what they did next. From 1866 through 1895, men drove almost ten million cattle, maybe far more, each one plodding on its own four legs, from the Gulf Coast state of Texas north to Kansas and beyond. Beyond as far as Nebraska, Montana, Wyoming, the Dakotas, California, Canada.

It was by far—incomparably—the hugest movement of animals in all history that men have caused and directed.

It couldn't be done. Men did it.

The cattle were driven across a then-unknown land—an unmapped land—a largely uninhabited land—the middle of the North American continent.

Jim Daugherty, Dr. Hargus, Colonel Meyers and others in 1866 pointed the way.

The spreading, sharp horns of the cattle the men drove north gave them their name: the longhorns. The horns, in shape and size, were as varied as could be. Some horns extended almost straight out from the head. Others spread. Some horns corkscrewed. A longhorn reached its full growth at about ten years of age, but its horns grew and spread as long as the animal lived. They grew up to 7 feet 9 inches between the tips. The horns of one steer named Champion, exhibited over the United States, were said to measure from tip to tip 9 feet 7 inches. A longhorn steer as late as 1941 had his horn-spread measured: 8 feet 7⅜ inches.

Both bulls and cows possessed the long horns, and knew how to use them against wolves or other attackers. One experienced hunter said the longhorns were fifty times as dangerous to a man on foot as the fiercest buffalo.

In size, the longhorns at first were small, six or eight hundred pounds, but they grew larger as the years passed and as cowmen learned to take care of them and to fatten them. In color, the longhorn could be brown, dun (a dingy or murky brown), red, yellow, black, white, sometimes even blue, and more combinations than you can imagine. "They were good colors because they were all colors," said J. F. Ellison, Jr., of Fort Cobb, Oklahoma, about a herd of longhorns.

Many of the longhorns roaming Texas had wandered away from private owners. Others never had been anything but free. It was their ancestors that had strayed. Generations of their calves had reverted to the wild and had multiplied.

The longhorns were wild animals.

They had survived as wild animals because they could take care of themselves. The longhorns could locate water—smell was one way—as much as fifteen miles away. They protected themselves: a small herd of cows actually would put out two cows to stand guard while the others went to a watering place.

The longhorn foraged by night, and hid—when it could—in thickets by day. Grazing on the prairie after dark, the longhorn would work back so that by dawn it would again be near its hiding place—often a thicket of thorn and bush known as chaparral. Or it might hide among trees festooned with gray Spanish moss, collect the moss on its long horns, and so be called a mossyhorn.

A longhorn could live on only grass and water. In the winter, the longhorns—and horses as well—ate the bark of the cottonwood tree. The tree, whose cottony, white seeds fall about the middle of June, is a sign that water is nearby.

When grass was scarce, a longhorn could put its front hoofs against a large tree trunk and stretch up to eat tree leaves. The longhorn ate leaves of the small, thorny tree known as the mesquite.

Because the longhorn, as wild as the buffalo, could survive so well, it had prospered. There were thousands of longhorns in Texas in 1866. Hundreds of thousands. Millions. They teemed like the buffalo herds.

There were so many that they would be able for some years to support the men, women, and children of Texas. There is perhaps no other case in history where a civilized people depended so greatly, for so much, on a single wild animal.

3

The longhorns came over the ocean

THE EARLY American settlers in Texas had another name for the longhorns: Spanish cattle. They were cattle whose ancestors first had arrived hundreds of years earlier, with Columbus, with the Spaniards. For centuries, on the plains of Andalusia in Spain, the Moors had raised longhorns, and later the Spaniards had done so. When, starting in 1492, Columbus and Spanish sailors discovered and then opened up the Caribbean Sea area, the only way to take along a supply of fresh milk and meat was to carry live cattle in the holds or on the decks of small sailing ships. Christopher Columbus on his second voyage to the New World in 1493 brought cattle to the island of Santo Domingo.

In 1513, Ponce de León, for Spain, reached Florida—the first European definitely known to have reached what is today's United States. The Spaniards, twenty-one years after Columbus' first trip, were gaining experience every year. They were learning how to explore new lands. Everywhere they went, they took along, turned loose, and left behind, horses, cattle, hogs, and sheep. These, of course, all ran free and became wild. The horses would help and the other animals would feed any Spaniards who might follow along later.

The explorers for Spain, besides reaching the West Indies and the United States first, would also be first in Central America, and first in most of South America.

In 1519, Alonso Alvarez Piñeda, for Spain, became the second European commander to reach the shores of what is now the United States. He discovered Texas. As had Columbus, he was seeking a route by sea from Europe to Asia. As had Columbus, he had cattle with him. He explored what is today the Gulf Coast of the United States from Florida to Mexico and continued to explore on to Yucatán, Mexico. He may have discovered the mouth of the Mississippi River.

At any rate, Piñeda and his men were the first Europeans to reach the Gulf Coast. This they did 88 years before John Smith landed in Virginia and 101 years before the Pilgrims reached Massachusetts.

Piñeda named a bay in Texas Corpus Christi (body of Christ) —the name the city uses today. He charted Las Islas Blancas—the White Islands, in other words—and Padre Island off Corpus. Piñeda claimed both the islands and the island region beyond the bay for the King of Spain.

At the mouth of the Rio Grande, Piñeda explored the country for forty days while his ships were being repaired. He made the first map of the Texas coast. His expedition was the first to penetrate the interior.

A contemporary of Piñeda's, another Spaniard, Hernando Cortez, at the same time (in 1519) was conquering Mexico. After Cortez' conquest, Gregorio de Villalobos brought longhorns—descended from Columbus'—to Mexico, and therefore to the mainland of North America. Some of them escaped and ran wild. In 1520 and 1523, a man who had been a companion of Christopher Columbus, Francisco Garay, brought ships to the Rio Grande River, discovered by Piñeda. In 1527 Nuño de Guzman visited the area.

In 1528, some members of Spain's Narváez expedition, moving along the shore from Florida to Texas, were struck by a hurricane. In battered vessels—using shirts for sails and their horses' tails for rigging—they were washed ashore near Galveston. One of them was Cabeza de Vaca (a Spaniard whose name meant Head of a Cow), who explored Texas into Mexico. De Vaca took cattle with him, and branded them with a cow's head. De Vaca and his companions were the first Europeans to see and report a large, shaggy, strange beast related to cattle: the buffalo.

Francisco Coronado, with a large number of cattle, in 1541 marched overland from Mexico perhaps to the land that would become Texas. He was looking for legendary cities of gold. On St. Augustine's day in 1565, a sailor for Spain, Pedro Mendes de Airles —Pedro Meléndez—established in Florida St. Augustine. The town has been continuously occupied ever since and is the oldest in the United States.

In April 1598, a Spanish explorer from Mexico City, Juan de Oñate, reached the Rio Grande. He had 400 men, many with families, and also had along what would become the first permanent herd of longhorns north of Mexico. Oñate crossed the Rio Grande at the ford of El Paso, took possession of a land he named New Mexico, and explored onward into today's Kansas.

In 1685, a Frenchman, La Salle, landed at Lavaca Bay in Texas with cattle he had taken aboard at Santo Domingo. In the 1600s, Spanish missionaries and explorers brought other cattle up from Mexico. Mexican General Alonso de León brought cattle and horses on four trips across the Rio Grande; on the last, he is said to have left behind, at each river he crossed, a stallion and a mare, a bull and a cow. In 1690 de León and Father Damién Massanet took 200 cattle to Texas. In 1691, the governor of a new province of Mexico, Domingo Terán los Rios, arrived with horses and cattle to govern his domain. The new province began to be called by the name Texas.

In Texas, cattle—and horses also brought by the Spaniards— were from the first continually escaping their owners and returning to the wild. A French trader, Louis Juchereau, in 1715 remarked on how many wild cattle and horses there were. Their number, he said, had "increased to thousands of cows, bulls, horses, and mares, with which the whole country is covered."

In 1718, the Spanish governor of the province of Texas, Don Martin de Alarcón, arrived with 72 settlers, 200 cows, 1000 sheep, 548 horses, and 200 oxen.

From 1718 to 1725, under the Spanish Empire, in the vast brush country to the south and west of the San Antonio missions, the wild cattle attracted settlers who could live off the longhorns, capture them, and begin to raise them. These things they did, and cattle raising began—the first industry in Texas.

In 1779, when the American Revolution was under way, Gil Ybarbo, a Spanish cattleman in Texas, brought along a few cattle when he established what today is the town of Nacogdoches.

Spaniards in Texas, in Gil Ybarbo's day, had laws against smuggling. These laws they broke by driving cattle into Louisiana. The goods they smuggled walked on four feet. The fact that transportation was all but nonexistent made cattle of special value to Texans, then and later on.

The cattle were a raw material. But they were that rare thing— a raw material that needed no transportation, but that could move itself to where it was wanted.

In 1799, a boy drove cattle 400 miles from Tennessee into Virginia. And twenty years later a man drove horses from Tennessee into southern North Carolina. These two drives, of cattle and horses, were among the early efforts of Americans to move herds of cattle and horses—they helped teach Americans how to do the job. The boy who drove the cattle and the man who drove the horses were one and the same person, a famous name in United States folklore and history: Davy Crockett.

While Texas was still a part of the Spanish Empire, and the numbers of cattle and wild horses were increasing, another man back on the East Coast demonstrated something that was breathtaking. And that one day would have a profound effect on horses and men's use of them. Down the streets of Philadelphia in 1805, Oliver Evans operated the world's first steam traction engine, a wagon that moved by itself—without a horse, ox, or mule in front of it. No man, woman, or child on the American side of the Atlantic Ocean had ever seen any such thing. Evans' trundling wagon had a body that made it also a dredge: the device could enter the river and there, while citizens gaped, the same steam engine propelled it along.

Oliver Evans could see that one day steam power would provide transportation for men. To the demonstration of his self-propelled wagon-or-dredge, Oliver Evans added a startling prediction: "The time will come when people will travel in stages moved by steam engines, from one city to another, almost as fast as birds fly, from fifteen to twenty miles an hour.''

Oliver Evans was foreseeing the day of the railroad.

In the year 1819, before there were any Americans to speak of in Texas, a man named James Taylor White established a ranch southeast of today's Houston. He is said to have reached over parts of modern Polk, Liberty, and Jefferson counties, and over all of Chambers County (on the Gulf of Mexico). His headquarters was on the Trinity River, near Turtle Bayou, near Anahuac, and near Louisiana. White started with some cattle he had brought in, added some longhorns, and became one of the first Americans to drive his cattle to market on their own four legs—to Louisiana.

A few other men set themselves up as ranchers in east Texas. They sometimes drove cattle to New Orleans over what they called the Old Beef Trail.

Moses Austin, who had been born in Durham, Connecticut, went to Texas in 1820 and received a grant of land from the Spanish government. Many of Austin's first settlers took up raising cattle for a good and sufficient reason. Cattle need lots of grazing land, 10 to 15 acres apiece usually, up to almost 50 acres in the sparse grass land of west Texas. Under Spanish law, a farmer was given 107 acres of land. But a cattleman was granted, in addition to that, one square league, or 4,428.4 acres more.

In 1821 Mexico—which then included Texas—won her independence from Spain.

During the fighting more longhorns escaped from ranches.

Pioneer cattle drivers Abner, Joseph, and Robert Kuykendall brought more cattle into Texas in 1821. They drove them from Natchitoches, Louisiana, to the east banks of the Colorado River.

In 1822, Daniel Shipman began ranching in Brazoria County—an activity he would continue for over sixty years, or until his death in 1883.

In 1822, Stephen Fuller Austin, the son of Moses (the boy had been brought up largely in Missouri), settled the first American colonists in Texas and established a town that would be known as Austin.

A cowman, J. E. Pettus of Goliad, Texas, much later remembered: "My father came to Texas with Austin's colony in 1822."

The first American colonists in Texas brought with them British cattle, some of them descendants of Warwick longhorns bred in Britain and Scotland since time immemorial. Of all cattle alive today, the Warwicks are believed to have been most similar to the original cattle from which all are descended—the large, black, buffalolike wild oxen of Europe, the cattle mentioned before Christ by Julius Caesar and known to the Romans as the aurochs.

In the vast, open, often flat land of Texas—there is a total of 167,732,160 acres of land in the state—60 percent of it suitable for grazing, the American settlers' Warwick longhorns often escaped and joined the cattle already running wild. They were equipped to do so; originally the auroch was the wild European bison.

Some of the aurochs themselves had had long horns.

More cattle arrived in Texas in 1824 when the town of Victoria was established by a man who once had lived in Spanish Texas, Martin de León.

Meanwhile, back in the eastern United States, a man took another step in the development of the Iron Horse. In 1825, John Stevens, seventy-six, on the lawn of his Hoboken, New Jersey, home, was operating, on a circular track, a small, model self-propelling engine, driven by steam. Stevens thought that one day self-propelled vehicles would open up the North American continent. It is hard to grasp in the 1970s, but Stevens' engine of 150 years ago was only the second self-propelling vehicle ever seen in North America. Oliver Evans' steam wagon-dredge was the first.

A hundred and fifty years ago amounts to only a short time—the lives of two 75-year-old folks would cover the span. Yet it was a long time back as American history goes: not till 1826 did anyone manage to travel across land all the way to California. That year Jedediah Smith and fifteen other persons left Great Salt Lake for California. And they made it. Smith, twenty-eight, was known for his ability to survive in the wilderness. He needed all his skills. His party ran out of supplies. Their horses failed. Game was scarce. But they crossed the Sierra Nevada mountains and, gaunt and ragged, on November 26 reached the Mission San Gabriel, in today's Los Angeles County. The significance: At a time when cattle and some ranchers already were established in Texas, Jedediah Smith and his people had traveled by land to California and had helped to open the way for both gold seekers, the forty-niners, and for Texas cattle to follow.

On August 6, 1829, the first full-size steam locomotive was seen in America—the Stourbridge Lion, imported from England by Horatio Allen, and run on a short stretch of track in Pennsylvania. In 1829-30, for the Baltimore and Ohio Railroad, Peter Cooper built a locomotive, the Tom Thumb. The Tom Thumb, which weighed one ton, raced against a horse drawing the same load on a parallel track. The steam-driven Tom Thumb pulled ahead. Then it failed, and the horse won. The horse thus, for about the last time, outran an engine.

Horatio Allen next designed his own locomotive, the Best Friend of Charleston. On Christmas Day, 1830, it hauled four cars containing forty passengers at twenty-one miles an hour. It was to be the first locomotive in America to explode. But its line, the South Carolina Canal and Railway Company, would become North America's first successful railroad.

4

Some Texians
fight a short war

BY 1830, the longhorns are believed to have been roaming in far-west Texas—around Presidio and El Paso. We cannot be sure, but one estimate is that, besides the wild cattle, there were then 100,000 domesticated cattle in Texas.

On October 17, 1835, a small force—sixty men—was organized to patrol the wide, almost limitless land of Texas: the Texas Rangers.

The people settling in Texas, having nothing else to sell, gathered some wild cattle and before 1836 had followed in the hoof-prints, to New Orleans, of James Taylor White's cattle, and had established to that city what was called the Beef Trail.

Then in 1836, Texians—Texans, that is, who had arrived from all the then-existing United States and from much of the world— fought and won a brief war of independence against Mexico.

Exactly as other English-speaking men have done in so many wars, the Texians lost the first battle—at Goliad. Then they holed up in a Spanish mission in San Antonio named the Alamo. A Mexican army besieged them. There were about 150 Texians together in the Alamo. One was the cattle- and horse-driver from Tennessee, David Crockett. Another, a South Carolina lawyer, was Col. William Barret (Buck) Travis. Another was a frontiersman from Louisiana, James Bowie. His brother—or a blacksmith working with his brother—had invented a sheath knife with a guarded hilt and a strong nine- or ten-inch blade, the Bowie knife. James Bowie himself had made the knife lighter and keener—he had its cutting-point sharpened on both sides and made longer. The knife became useful up and down the Mississippi River frontier. Much later, almost every cowboy carried one. A dangerous weapon, the Bowie knife was made illegal by some states. Its manufacturers gave it other names and kept right on providing it.

On March 2, 1836, at Washington-on-the-Brazos, near today's Houston, with the Texians already holed up in the Alamo, Texas declared her independence.

A newspaper, *The Telegraph and Texas Register,* supported the Texians. It was partly owned by Gail Borden—who, some fifteen years later, would invent condensed milk.

A messenger who managed to slip into the surrounded Alamo several times was George Webb Slaughter, twenty-five, from Mississippi. Later he would be a cowboy and cowman and would drive thousands of cattle from Texas to the north. Slaughter on one occasion arrived with a message from Sam Houston ordering Colonel Travis to retreat from the Alamo.

Houston, a Virginian who had been brought up on the tough Tennessee frontier, was commanding the Texian so-called army.

Colonel Travis gave his men the message. With his sword he drew a line and asked all who were willing to stay with him and to fight alongside him to cross the line. All but one man did. That man was let down outside the walls and escaped.

Some people assert that the tale of Colonel Travis drawing the line is a legend. There is no doubt what happened afterward.

A blood-red flag—which meant no quarter—was hoisted by the Mexican general, López de Santa Anna. He had his buglers play the *deguello*—the no-quarter call of Spain.

Several thousand Mexicans—one figure is 4,000—overwhelmed the Alamo, and to the last man, the Texians, Crockett, Travis, Bowie, and the rest were killed. Among their booty, the Mexicans collected James Bowie's knife.

George Webb Slaughter made a later trip to the Alamo, after the Mexicans had captured it. He met a woman, Mrs. Susanna Dickerson (sometimes spelled Dickinson or Dickenson), her baby, and a Negro slave. The Mexicans had told them to take the word of the massacre at the Alamo to Sam Houston.

Santa Anna's army and Sam Houston's ragtag army marched till they came close to each other at a place near the San Jacinto River and Buffalo Bayou, not far from today's Houston. Here some of the Mexicans saw, and were amazed by, a startling new machine—a sawmill. Some thought the noisy, whirring thing would catapult its logs at the Mexican army.

A scout for Houston, Erasmus (Deaf) Smith, led a group of men who destroyed Vince's Bridge and thus cut a possible escape route.

On April 21, 1836, the Texians sneaked up on the Mexicans— through what was to play a great part in Texas history, tall grass, and through elms, cypresses, pines, live oaks, and eighty-foot-tall magnolias. Sam Houston made a sixteen-word speech: "Victory is certain! Trust in God and fear not! And remember the Alamo! Remember the Alamo!"

Sam Houston waved a battered hat at his seven or eight hundred soldiers—not in uniform, but in homemade clothes or rags.

As the Texians drew near, one man played a fife. Others sang, "Won't you come to the bower with me?"

The Texians wielded Bowie knives and fired muzzle-loading, single-shot long rifles. The Texians won the battle of San Jacinto from General Santa Anna and about sixteen hundred Mexicans, and with it the war.

Texas was independent of Mexico.

The morning after the battle, the woman who owned the land on which it was fought, Peggy McCormick, walked up to Sam Houston. Three times she said to him to "take your men off me legge [league of land]."

After the battle, George Webb Slaughter took time off and married his fiancée, Sarah (Sallie) Mason—the first marriage in independent Texas.

J. E. Pettus said his father (who had come to Texas in 1822) had fought in the Battle of San Jacinto. Pettus himself later would drive cattle to Kansas and on to Ogallala, Nebraska.

Within hearing distance of the Battle of San Jacinto, there was camped a woman who would become the mother of cowman W. F. Cude of Pearsall, Texas. "The first news she had from the battle-field," said Cude long afterward, "was to the effect that General Houston's forces were all killed, but in a little while word came that the Mexican army had been defeated and utterly routed."

One hundred miles from the Battle of San Jacinto, which they heard about, were Benjamin and Minerva Slaughter. They were migrating from Mississippi to Texas. They had with them a son, William James Slaughter, who had been born on November 8, 1835. The father, Benjamin, who hoped to join the Texian army, instead served for ninety days as a Texas Ranger. Then he and Minerva returned to Mississippi.

But "Uncle Ben has got a taste of Texas and can't get rid of it," someone said afterward. Four years later, Ben and Minerva were back in east Texas. Their son, William James, would grow up to be a cattleman, would drive herds to Kansas, and would own one of the biggest ranches in west Texas.

The men at San Jacinto obtained, with their victory, a nation. Texas would be an independent republic for ten years, until admission to the United States. In 1837, the new nation, Texas, was recognized by Britain, Belgium, France, and the United States. Houston was its first president. Mirabeau Buonaparte Lamar, who had been a commander at San Jacinto and who was a poet, was the second president.

The republic in 1839 adopted a flag: A blue vertical stripe, next to the flagpole, with a white star upon it—the Lone Star; next, two horizontal stripes, the upper white, the lower red. Today nobody seems able to prove where the Lone Star came from. One idea is that it was based on a flower of the cypress. Another idea is that a Mrs. Venson or Vinson placed it on a flag of a Texas regiment. Another is that a Georgia woman, Johanna Troutman, put an azure star on white silk on the banner of a Georgia battalion that fought in the Texas revolution. Another is that a provincial governor of Texas, Henry Smith, had no official seal and so he stamped documents with a brass button from his coat—the button made the impression of a star. Later, the Lone Star of Texas contributed to the idea of the single star on the California state flag, and to the single star on what was called the Bonnie Blue banner of the Confederate states. At Chapel Hill, Texas, the star decorated the front of Stagecoach House. Wherever it may have come from, the star in time went onto boots and saddles, bridles and chaps. It was to become a standard ornament of a cowboy's outfit. In time, it became popular on a cowboy's gloves. And if he wore those gloves all the time they were a badge of honor: they showed he was so good at riding and roping that he had to do no other work.

Texas' is the only state flag that once was the flag of an independent country, the Republic of Texas, recognized by other nations. This independent country would receive settlers—immigrants—from many other nations. Immigrants to the northern United States were likely to go on west in covered wagons. Immigrants to Texas were more likely to become men on horseback—the cowboys.

5

A sixteen-year-old
dreams up a gun

THE TEXIANS at the Alamo and at the Battle of San Jacinto had no six-shooters. They had not been invented. After they were, they would influence a great many events in the West.

In the 1840s, less than 135 years ago, Texians and Americans, armed only with guns that would fire a single shot, were fighting on the North American continent an enemy superior in weapons—the mounted Plains Indians.

The Indians captured their horses from wild-horse herds descended from Columbus' and Cortez' stock. While riding horseback, a Plains Indian could shoot from twenty to thirty arrows from his bow, with accuracy, in the same time it took an American, who had to dismount to load his single-shot gun, to get off only one shot. (The expert English archers of the Middle Ages, who won, among other battles, the Battle of Agincourt, had been able to shoot ten arrows a minute.)

The Indians, on horseback, could chase the frontiersman; the frontiersman, crouching behind his horse, had to remain still and often had to lie flat on the ground to fire back his one shot.

Indians won battle after battle from the pioneers.

From Texas to Canada, the bodies of Americans—riddled by arrows—were called pincushions.

A lad from Connecticut would change all that.

Samuel Colt, as a youngster, had heard about how soldiers in the American Revolution had been handicapped by single-shot guns, and had needed double-barreled shotguns.

At Amherst Academy in Massachusetts, Colt set off fireworks that made him unpopular with the faculty. At sixteen years of age he went to sea. There, in 1830, he had a better idea. On a brig, the *Corin,* en route to Calcutta, India, he watched the ship's wheel turn. He thought of a gun with a cylinder that might hold five or six bullets and would revolve to put each bullet into firing position. A repeating gun or pistol.

Sam, a slender, six-foot, hazel-eyed, curly-headed young sailor, whittled a wooden model. Home after his sea voyage, he wanted to quit being a sailor. Asked his father, "Have you brought home a fortune that you are ready to quit the sea?" Sam answered "Yes."

In 1836, the year of the Alamo and of San Jacinto, President Andrew Jackson signed one of the first United States patents under the present system for the twenty-one-year-old Colt. For years, however, Sam found no buyers for his Colts in the army, navy, or elsewhere, even though he gave away free samples.

One day a stranger bought some of Sam Colt's guns. He turned out to be Sam Walker, a captain in the small force of peace-keepers that were then called the Republic of Texas Rangers.

Walker was a frontiersman who well understood how many arrows a mounted Indian could fire at a man—while only one shot was fired at the Indian.

Walker took some of the Colts back to Texas.

On June 8, 1844, Walker was with fifteen other Texas Rangers near the Pedernales River, which flows into Texas' Colorado River west and slightly north of today's Austin, not far from Lake Travis.

The sixteen Rangers were charged by eighty Comanche Indians.

The Comanches expected the Rangers to have to dismount and hide behind their horses to load single-shot weapons.

The Rangers did not climb down off their horses.

The Comanches expected each Ranger to fire only one shot at a time.

The Rangers, with their new Colts, untried in battle, were apprehensive of their unproved weapons.

The Colts worked. Instead of firing only one shot, each Ranger pistol got off one after another. And the Rangers, far from dismounting, charged right back at the Comanches.

The Indians, to save themselves, had to race away. Even so, thirty-three of them were killed.

Each of the Rangers' repeating pistols had fired five shots. Long after the battle on the Pedernales, a Comanche chief, who had survived it, said the Rangers fired shot after shot—one for every finger upon his hand.

Colt made a special model for stagecoaches, the Wells-Fargo Colt. It also was a five-shot.

Later models fired six shots.

Americans, armed with Colts, for the first time could pursue the Indians.

American frontiersmen began to win battles in the West. Soon a $25 Colt, out West, would fetch $200.

That price was partly because Colt, even after the Battle of the Pedernales, still could not peddle enough of his pistols to the army or navy so that they became plentiful.

After the Alamo and San Jacinto and during the years Texas was a separate nation, some young men, including some who had lost their fathers in these battles and others in the Texas revolution, drifted into west Texas near the Rio Grande and Mexico and lived as best they could. Here Spaniards and Americans once had had huge ranches. Here the longhorns had returned to the wild. Said Frederick R. Becholdt: "They roved the prairies and browsed in the timber, shy as the antelope which wandered in the hills, lean-bodied, swift as mustangs." The newly arrived, often-fatherless young men used bright moonlight nights to hunt through thickets for the night-prowling, night-foraging longhorns. They ate the beef and they made what they wore largely of leather. A group of them were led by a man called Ewen Cameron and became known as Cameron's Cowboys. In time, people began calling all of them by a new name: the cowboys.

Meanwhile, other Texans, poor as any pioneers, were beginning to peddle what they had to sell—the longhorns. Some cattle were trailed to New Orleans in 1842.

And some Texans were making the very first beginning of efforts to provide higher education to youngsters. At the University of San Augustine in 1842, a university no longer in existence, the first laboratory work in science in Texas was done—a remarkable thing for the wild, primitive, frontierlike time and place. Just such work contributed over the next hundred years to ending hunger and poverty for millions.

Other struggling efforts to provide education led in 1845 to the establishment of Waco University. Still located in Waco, it today is known as Baylor University, and is Texas' oldest.

On Lavaca Bay (*la vaca* is Spanish for "the cow"), off Matagorda Bay, the port of Indianola during the days of the Republic of Texas received thousands of Irish, Polish, German and French immigrants.

(The town of Indianola later was to have a tragic history. Cholera in 1846 would pile unburied dead in its streets. In 1875 and 1886 hurricanes wiped Indianola out of existence. Ruins of houses, cisterns, graves, bits of pottery, glass, china, and an occasional article of pewter mark the site now.)

The admission of Texas, in 1845, as the twenty-eighth of the United States—the only state ever to come in, as an independent nation, by treaty—led, in 1846, to a war between the United States and Mexico. In that war, when James Knox Polk was President, the soldiers sang, "Green grow the lilacs for the red, white and blue." Ever since, according to some folks on the Texas-Mexico border, Americans have been gringos (which is what "green grows" sounds like to Mexican ears).

When the war came, Sam Colt, now broke, owned not a single pistol, not even a model. Some Colts, however, were manufactured by the cotton-gin inventor, Eli Whitney. They reached U.S. soldiers. They were highly effective, one historian has written, in "emptying Mexican saddles." A good horse and a six-shooter,

Frank Hamer of the Texas Rangers was to say, "just run together like molasses."

The Colts made their reputation. And they made Colt rich.

Most handguns, before Colt, had been horse pistols or derringers and fired only a single ball or two. Sam Colt made the pistol, for the first time, an important weapon.

A small machine in its own right, the Colt would help to bring the mechanical age to the West.

It would also even up the odds in the fights between the cowboys and the Plains Indians.

6

A vast land changes hands

IN 1846, a lieutenant in the war with Mexico, Ulysses Simpson Grant, and his soldiers one day in southern Texas saw animals other than longhorns running wild on the plains—wild horses: "As far as the eye could reach, the herd extended. There was no estimating the animals in it."

A little later, another young army man, Robert Edward Lee, gazed over the Texas plains and thoughtfully remarked to a companion: "I am thinking of the footsteps of the coming millions."

In 1846, a man named Edward H. Piper drove cattle from Texas to Ohio. C. P. Vance, eighty-nine years old in 1916, remembered the beginnings of the cattle drives. Said he, "I drove one of the wagons when the soldiers went into Mexico. That was way back in '46." And then: "When I was a young fellow, we used to drive our herds out to New o'Leans." That would have been in 1848 or '49, a time, he remembered, when "I used to know 'bout everyone along the Colorado and Brazos rivers."

Also in 1848, T. J. Trimmer drove from Washington County—between today's Austin and Houston—to the California goldfields.

Other early cattlemen included Martin Hebert (Jefferson County), John H. Wood (San Patricio and Refugio counties), and

31

J. A. McFaddin (Refugio and Victoria counties), who trailed cattle for a while, and Willis McCutcheon, who became known as a trail driver.

The Colt in the hands of American soldiers had helped win the war with Mexico. In the hands of frontiersmen it was beginning to defeat mounted Indians. In the hands of cowboys it was to be used against Indians and cattle thieves.

The Spanish Empire that had started in 1492 with Columbus eventually had grown to include: all of South America except Brazil; all of Central America, including Mexico; today's United States from Texas to the Pacific; the West Indies islands, the Canary Islands, plus islands all the way to Guam and on to the Philippines.

When Mexico broke away from Spain, the area of much of today's western United States went along. Ending the war with Mexico, the treaty of Guadalupe Hidalgo (February 2, 1848) changed the ownership of more land than any other treaty in history.

For $15 million the United States acquired Texas, New Mexico, Arizona and California, and some of Idaho, Nevada, and Colorado from Mexico. Boundaries and claims running far back into the days of the Spanish Empire were so indefinite—and the land so inadequately surveyed—that parts of Oklahoma, Kansas, and Wyoming appeared to have been included in land the United States obtained. Spain's Coronado may even have reached as far north as Nebraska. In *My Ántonia*, Willa Cather mentions a stirrup and sword blade turned up by an early Nebraska farmer breaking sod. The sword had an inscription that stood for the city of Córdoba, Spain.

Had it not been for the Alamo, the Battle of San Jacinto, and the war with Mexico, Texas and the West might have remained what they were: part of Latin America. When the Texians won the Battle of San Jacinto, they won one of the decisive battles of history.

Immediately after the Mexican war, Milton Faver established a large ranch near Shafter. His cattle at one time ranged from the Rio Grande to the Pecos River.

John Davis was ranching on Alamita Creek.

In 1850, the tally book of Thomas O'Connor showed thousands of cattle from a start on land he had received as a colonist and later for his services at the Battle of San Jacinto.

He was by then a cattle king. His descendants at Victoria were to be among Texas' great ranch owners.

And by 1850, one estimate is, there were 330,000 domesticated cattle in Texas, plus countless wild ones. Another estimate is almost 400,000.

A few scattered packing plants had been established. Two men named King and Kenedy, who owned huge ranches, had packing plants on them. A cowman, Shanghai Pierce, had one on Matagorda Bay. A bone mill on Aransas Bay made fertilizer. There was no refrigeration. Some beef was salted. Some was pickled in barrels.

In 1851, Gail Borden, the newspaper editor who had supported the Texas revolution, visited a world's fair in London. He himself exhibited a meat biscuit—beef juices and whole wheat flour. He won a medal for it; it was called high in food value. But back in Texas he never could produce it successfully.

On his way home across the Atlantic, aboard a sailing ship, the weather became rough. Cattle, carried for fresh milk—as they had been ever since Columbus—failed to give it. Children cried. For the next few years, Borden struggled to develop a good-tasting condensed milk that could be canned and would last. He finally succeeded in 1857, and set up his first cannery in an abandoned mill in Burrville, Connecticut.

While Texians were becoming Texans and Americans, their wild cattle were becoming the Texas longhorns: an animal that was bigger than the original Moorish, Spanish, or Mexican ancestors, but that at around 800 pounds in weight still was not a large beast. In later years the longhorns' weight would double and their horns become shorter. But first the longhorns, wild as they were, dangerous to men as they were, had to be caught. That job would bring into existence a new event and new name for it, the roundup.

7

Men head for the first roundups

TEXIANS AFTER the War Between the States, just over a hundred years ago, were desperate—helpless victims of hunger and disease.

In much of the state there were few trees—and therefore no fuel to burn except the dried droppings of longhorns and buffaloes. There was little or no water in much of the state. No fuel plus no water is a compound headache. The scarcity of water meant that it was hard or impossible to irrigate the crops that were needed. Few rivers meant little fishing. Where there was fishing, perch or bass might be caught, or the whiskered, gray-mud-colored catfish, up to 20 or 35 or even 100 pounds, at least three species of which were eaten.

The children, women, and men of Texas had to eat.

It was not a question of a well-balanced diet; it was a question of getting enough to eat to keep a body alive. Weakened by insufficient food, men, women, and children died more readily under the scourges of the diseases that flourished on the Gulf Coast—malaria, yellow fever, scarlet fever, pneumonia, cholera, tuberculosis (which often passed into galloping consumption), polio, meningitis, jaundice (hepatitis), rheumatic fever, others—a vast number of diseases that included tropical ones and subtropical ones and

African ones and northern ones. Frontier medicine was primitive at best, and understanding of what caused many diseases was nonexistent.

Still other diseases included hookworm, from a worm in the soil whose larvae invaded right through the unbroken skin of bare feet. The worm then lived as long as ten years in a person's intestines. The hookworm caused anemia and weakness and sometimes impelled its victims to crave a diet of dirt.

There was pellagra, a disease caused by inadequate diet. It turns the tongue, the backs of the hands, and the back of the neck red; it can cause mental and nervous disorders, and diarrhea. It was prevalent in the southern United States whenever people had to live on only pork and corn meal—a common situation, especially before longhorn beef was available.

So many children died so young that the earliest photographers, traveling the primitive roads, often photographed the youngsters who had just died. The children often would be propped up and their pictures taken so their mothers and fathers would have something to remember them by.

A doctor, if any, would usually be called from fifteen or thirty miles away, and had to ride a horse or ride in a wagon to a patient. He was allowed by custom to charge mileage, $1 a mile, as part of his fee. The doctor stayed with his patient till the disease had run its course. "The physician," said Philip Paxton, "must make short work of the disease or the disease will of the patient."

When no cure was known, doctors sometimes tried anything and everything. For chills and malaria, Philip Paxton was given "calomel, rhubarb, senna, castor oil combined with spirits of turpentine, Cook's pills, quinine, and sundry other dainties."

He grew worse. One day his forehead ached; it "almost drove me mad," he said. Next, his temple, ear, and jaw ached. Then the back of his head ached violently. He became sicker and again received the anything-or-everything treatment. "For two months I rang the changes upon opium, morphine, quinine, laudanum, cinchona, myrtle tea, red pepper, cold baths, hard riding during the chill, chopping wood ditto ditto, strong coffee, brandy, and port wine."

A young man, if he reached twenty-one, might expect to live into his thirties.

A woman, if she somehow survived childbirth, might live into her thirties, sometimes longer.

An infant was fortunate to survive either the first or second summer. In west Texas with the U.S. Army, a Mrs. Vielé came upon "the little lonely grave" of a child. She remained in the area a few months. "There was another little grave beside it when I came away."

Food was the immediate problem, and the only possibility in sight in quantity was the teeming longhorns.

Into the mesquite thickets of southwest Texas the men would go—on what they called a cow hunt—often by moonlight, capturing the night-prowling longhorn either by lassoing it or by hog-tying its feet (tying its feet together). Another method was for a man on horseback to tail a yearling or a cow: he would ride up behind it, catch its tail, twist the tail around the horn of his saddle, jerk the animal to the ground, and tie it up before it recovered from shock. Yet another way to capture the longhorns was to drive a herd of tame cattle through the brush. The longhorns often came out with the tame animals.

Beside wild cattle, the domestic longhorns that had wandered off had to be recaptured, or, as the cowmen put it in a phrase that became part of the English language, "rounded up."

In Texas, where there were no fences, a cow might have wandered anywhere in an area about a hundred miles in diameter. There were newborn calves loose on the range to be rounded up, too.

As a youngster, L. B. Anderson of Seguin, Texas, who later drove cattle up the trail, went on cow hunts. Ten to twenty men set out, he said. Each had an extra pony and a hair or rawhide rope. Each brought some flour, cornbread, salt, coffee, and fat bacon. The men, when hunger forced them to, "would kill a fat yearling." Said Anderson: "On these trips I acquired my first experience at cow-punching."

Anywhere in Texas, at any hour of the day or night, men out
hunting cattle could call at any dugout or log cabin they came upon,
and ask that their flour be baked into bread. The woman or women
in the house would bake it. The cow hunters, when departing with
their bread, usually left half a sack of flour behind them.

If a cow hunter was taken ill, the woman and her daughters in
any house in the sparsely settled land would nurse him back to
health.

Jim Hough's wife, Philip Paxton remembered, was an early
pioneer woman in Texas when the first roundups were taking place.
One day Jim, with Paxton, came home to the Hough cabin where
his wife had been left with her small sons.

At the cabin the men were startled to see inside it the skin of a
large mountain lion (then called a catamount or a panther). She
had shot it and skinned it herself. She used what Philip Paxton
called "more than Spartan brevity" in telling the men what had
happened and thereby she helped give the pioneer woman her
reputation for calm and matter-of-factness.

"The boys see the varmint nigh the house," she said. "I called
the dogs and tuk [picked up] the gun; he tuk [climbed] a tree, and I
fetched him."

Once captured, the longhorns could be tied to domesticated
oxen that would guide them to a corral. Or it might be necessary, in
the case of a herd of wild longhorns, to drive them for several days
till they were tired out and could be managed.

They were marked with the only known marks that would not
wash off. Into each animal's hide the mark of an owner would be
cut with a knife or burned with a hot iron.

A cowboy's rope dragged a steer to the branding area. There
a cowboy might reach over the animal's back and grab the skin on
the opposite side. The cow would jump. While it was in the air, the
cowboy would twist it over on its side or even on its back. Or he
might bulldog it—twist the neck of the animal. Or tail it—jerk the
tail when the feet were in the air. In any case, the cowboy would
get the animal onto the ground. Then he would call out "hot iron"
or "sharp knife" and a red-hot branding iron or a knife would burn
or carve on the Lazy S or Flying U or some other brand—the sym-
bol of the owner.

Once they were branded, the longhorns belonged to someone
—they no longer were considered wild, however wild they might in
fact remain. As long as they did not wander off so far they could
not be retrieved, they could furnish milk, calves, leather, and beef.

Besides the wild cattle, wild horses were taken in the roundups.

The horses' ancestors, those the Spaniards had brought,
traced their ancestry back to the Moors or Arabs. In January 1494,
Columbus, on his second trip to Haiti, landed twenty-four stallions,
ten mares, and three mules. Hernando Cortez in 1519, when he
conquered Mexico, had with him sixteen horses—eleven stallions
and five mares, plus a foal.

North America had had its own native horses in prehistoric
times. They included the little cat-size eohippus, the four-toed (on
the front feet) ancestor of all today's one-toed horses. Eohippuses'
descendants may have crossed a land (or ice) bridge from Alaska to
Europe and so made their way to the Old World. But in North
America, horses are believed to have become extinct during the
last ice age (which ended about 11,000 years ago). The horses
brought from Havana to Mexico by Cortez were perhaps the first
on the North American continent since the ice age. And the Spanish horses, like their longhorns, escaped and ran free.

The Spaniards named their runaway horses *mestengos*—in
English, "strays," which became "mustangs." From the Gulf
Coast to the Columbia River in the Pacific Northwest, probably
two million horses (by the time of the Civil War) ran free. The stallions, battling for mares, screaming, neighing, striking at each other
with their hoofs, biting and tearing flesh with their strong teeth,
were among the fiercest fighters on the plains. Like the longhorns,
they were of all colors—palominos, bays, blues, sorrels, whites,
roans, and blacks. The Strawberry Roan of the song was of a white
or light gray color with a splotch of dark red upon it. They roamed
usually in small groups, once in a while in huge concentrations
such as Lt. Ulysses S. Grant had seen in 1846 during the war with
Mexico. The trampling of a great herd like that one sounded like
the roar of the surf.

The wild horses, from Texas to Canada, tossed their manes in
the winds. The Indians captured them, learned to ride them, and

became the continent's horseback Indians—the best warriors, the most dreaded. In time, the cowboys and ranchmen would capture other wild ponies, break them to the saddle, and make them their own. When it came to endurance, the Spanish mustangs had no equals.

Another source of horses, in Texas, was the eastern United States—including horses that brought many a settler, maybe hauling his wagon.

Once the cattle had been gathered, in the first roundups, men —and boys—began to move them, in Texas and beyond.

James Alfred McFaddin, fifteen years old, in 1855 drove a herd of 400 cattle from Jefferson County to Refugio County, Texas. George F. Hindes, as a twelve-year-old cowboy, made a trip in the fall of 1856, he said. He took a small herd, from his father, in Caldwell County and drove it through San Antonio and out South Fulton Street.

James Washington Walker, fifteen, who later would be a cowboy, about 1856 took care of another kind of animal: camels. Walker was in charge of seventy-five camels, imported from Constantinople, Smyrna, and Tunis. The camels, together with Arab attendants, were kept at Camp Verde, two miles north of Bandera Pass. The hope was they could help the U.S. Army cross Western deserts, and might successfully carry messengers and freight to El Paso, on the Mexican border, and even further. The camels helped in laying a road to California, but in the United States they did not thrive. They ate little grass. They had to eat brush, and had trouble getting into the brush to get food. A cowboy who encountered the camels was Andrew D. Jones. He was with three or four horses when fourteen camels came along. They frightened the horses so much that, said Jones, "We did not see those horses again for some days." For years, other men—William B. Krempkau was one— were startled on Western plains when they came upon camels running wild. By day or by moonlight, the hump on the back of a wandering camel would begin a cowboy myth: that a headless rider (the hump) traveled the Southwest deserts.

In 1858, James McFaddin, then eighteen, drove again—as boss

of a herd of 600. He himself owned, at the time, about 50 cattle and 25 horses. McFaddin later would become one of the big cattlemen.

Texans were at first driving cattle to fill a special demand: for ox teams. (A bull calf, when castrated, is a steer—and in several years grows into an ox, and is likely to be quiet and tractable.)

One freight-hauling firm—Russell, Majors, and Waddell—in 1858 alone used 40,000 oxen. They hauled wagons of freight traveling west along the cross-continent trails. Texas longhorns by the thousand were bought for the great freight wagons that rolled across the land. Other oxen—other longhorns—hauled covered wagons and pioneers west.

Cattle from Texas were being driven—or had been driven—to Sedalia, Missouri; Baxter Springs, Kansas; Springfield, Missouri; St. Louis, Missouri; Chicago, Illinois—and one herd or several herds all the way (believe it or not) to New York City.

The discovery of gold in California in 1849 meant that the cattle-raising industry in California would disappear as men headed for the goldfields. This made California another market for Texas cattle.

In 1858 one man began to drive cattle out of Texas. His name was Oliver Loving, and that year he pointed his cattle north and traveled across the Indian Nations (Oklahoma), then through eastern Kansas, through northeastern Missouri, and into Illinois.

In 1859, Loving made a trip with cattle to Colorado. "He left the frontier," a friend and partner, Charles Goodnight, said later, "on the upper Brazos and took a northwest course until he struck the Arkansas River, somewhere about the mouth of the Walnut, and followed it to just about Pueblo [Colorado] where he wintered."

In 1859–60, Joseph H. Polley was a big operator in cattle in Guadalupe and Hidalgo counties, from San Antonio to the Rio Grande.

The Civil War began in 1861. Two ranchers named Allen and Paul were at that time among the large-scale cattle operators, on the prairies near Houston. In 1862, in central west Texas, near the Concho River, Rich Coffee established a ranch. Cattle drives supported both Union and Confederate armies. Jesse Chisholm, whose name would be given to the Chisholm Trail, pointed his cattle north and supplied some of Mr. Lincoln's armies. W. C.

McAdams in 1863 took a herd of cattle to Mexico to trade for sugar and other vitally needed goods for settlers in Texas. R. F. Tendersley ranched on the south Concho. G. W. De Long did likewise at Lipan Springs. In several counties west and north of Fort Worth, in the 1860s, George T. and W. D. Reynolds were ranching. Both would make many cattle drives to New Mexico and Colorado.

The Confederate government set up a slaughterhouse at Jefferson, Texas. Other packing businesses were growing up, a few in a place that would become a meat center, Fort Worth.

While men and boys were away from home in the Confederate army, women and children in Texas—with old men and very young boys—usually managed to brand most of the cattle each spring. Ten years old, J. W. Jackson, later a cowboy, was taking care of cattle that the able-bodied men had left behind. "That was when my hard work began," he said, "for I was expected to do the work of a man."

In 1865—after Lee's April 9 surrender at Appomattox—the last battle of the Civil War was fought in Texas. Texas had not gotten word that the War Between the States was over. A man in the scraggly frontier town of San Antonio, John Fitzhenry, said, "News traveled so slowly that it was forgotten before it got in or out of the state." The fight was in the southwesternmost corner of the state, at Palmito Hill, near Brownsville and Mexico. (Not far away, in May 1845, Gen. Zachary Taylor had defeated a Mexican army at the Battle of Palo Alto.)

A future cowman, Col. Albert G. Boyce, was at the last battle. Colonel Boyce in 1863 had been wounded at the Battle of Chickamauga in Georgia. When he recovered he went home to Texas—walking the entire distance. Colonel Boyce in 1867 started to drive Texas cattle to California, on a trip that was to last two years.

San Antonio's John Fitzhenry, who had arrived from Ireland in 1854, noticed that the Federal government, as the War Between the States wound up, was using a convenient local building as a storehouse. "Feed for the mules, oxen, and horses was piled to the ceiling," he said. The storehouse was a building that had been erected by the Spanish in 1714 when the Spanish Empire encircled the globe and extended into Texas and up to Kansas. Since 1836, however, the warehouse had been the shrine of Texas freedom. It was the Alamo.

Waco University (today Baylor) in 1865 took a giant step forward. It received Texas' first women students. It was to grant them a degree, Mistress of Arts.

For most of its history since the Spaniards arrived in the 1500s, and their longhorns spread across Texas, the state had had more cattle than people. After the Civil War, it is estimated, there were more than three million cattle in Texas.

Unlike the horses, which had left home and run wild all over the West, the longhorns during the Civil War for unknown reasons remained in the state of Texas. They did get into practically all of its 254 counties.

In the North people had flocked to the cities and factories and had to be fed. They were depending on poultry and pork. Cattle in the North sold at $6 at $11 a hundred pounds (and a longhorn might weigh 800 pounds or more). Accordingly, G. F. Swift and P. D. Armour and Armour's partner, John Plankington, established packing plants. The greatest, the Union Stockyards at Chicago, was finished in 1865, on Christmas Day.

Besides the factory workers and city dwellers, and the Texans themselves, there were other hungry mouths throughout the United States. There were immigrants from Europe arriving in the East. Out West, there were homesteaders flocking as far as the railroad tracks went, or traveling farther in covered wagons. There were soldiers in frontier forts who needed food. Indians in the Indian Nations and on reservations elsewhere needed food. The men building more new railroads needed food. And, throughout the South, where railroads had been destroyed during the war, people needed food.

The cattle could provide food for the nation. They also would help to furnish income for families in Texas, families that had almost none.

But the cattle had to be moved over great distances—at least to where they could meet the new railroads. In 1865 or '66 two brothers named Williams drove a small herd of east Texas steers to Vicksburg, Mississippi. In 1866, D. S. Combs drove from San

Marcos, Hays County, to New Iberia, Louisiana. On another trip, Combs varied the pattern; he took a herd of horses to Kansas and on to Waterloo, Iowa. Monroe Choate and B. A. Borroum, also in 1866, drove a cattle herd to Iowa to try to find a market; Jim Daugherty took his longhorns to Kansas and had to listen as the Jayhawkers talked over how to dispatch him.

Gradually, from small beginnings, out of necessity, the great cattle drives were getting under way.

8

Fathers and sons and brothers together fight Indians

IF TEXANS of the 1860s had to worry continually about disease, drought, a shortage of fuel, a shortage of water, about ticks on their cattle and ambushes by Kansas Jayhawkers, there was also another constant, nagging concern. Said a cowman, J. T. Hazelwood, about the time the cattle drives began: "The Indians, who were very numerous at this period, were making raids over the entire country on all 'light nights.' "

A light night was a night of the full moon.

The Texans had another phrase for such a night: "A light with a moon in it."

Only a matter of months before Jim Daugherty's 1866 drive to Kansas and his capture by Jayhawkers, there took place a battle with Indians that was heartbreaking. It was heartbreaking—and perfectly typical of what was happening all the time.

Even at that time, at the end of the Civil War, Colt six-shooters had not spread to nearly all settlers. On July 4, 1865, thirty-six Comanche Indians caught eleven Texans who did not have Colts. The results showed how devastatingly the Indians could defeat Americans armed only with single-shot cap-and-ball pistols and single-shot rifles.

45

None of the Indians were believed killed by the few rounds of firing the Texans could get off.

Eight of the eleven Texans were wounded or killed.

The battle took place southwest of San Antonio, near the mouth of the Leona River in Frio County. On the morning of July 4 Ed Burleson rode, alone, unarmed, and on a slow horse, a short distance from his ranch. Two Indians, one on foot, the other on horseback, attacked him and almost caught him. Burleson rode through a thicket to his ranch and got home safe. The story was told later by L. A. Franks of Pleasanton, Texas.

Eleven men set out from Burleson's ranch, where they had been celebrating the Fourth of July, to look for the two Indians.

They found them—not two, but thirty-six—sitting two on a horse. The Texans fired their single-shot guns and pistols. They were out of range. No harm was done.

The Indians mounted behind the others jumped to the ground and began to fire arrows at the settlers. Those remaining on horseback completely circled the settlers, discharging arrows meanwhile. As the Texans reloaded slowly, the Indians could fire ten or a dozen arrows for each shot a Texan could manage.

Dan Williams was hit, fell from his horse, and was surrounded by Indians. He handed his pistol to his brother, Frank saying: "Take this and do the best you can—I am killed—cannot live ten minutes. Save yourself."

Dan Williams was right. He was the first to die.

Frank Williams left Dan, then mounted, and barely got away. The Comanches raced after him, screaming.

Dean Oden was the next man to fall. His horse, wounded, began to pitch. He dismounted. He was wounded in the leg. He attempted to remount. Indians were all around him. He was wounded six times in the chest and back. L. A. Franks, nearby, saw Oden last: down on his knees, his horse gone.

Bud English was the next man killed. His father, Levi English, stayed with the dying boy till there was no hope, then got away amid the hand-to-hand fights going on between Indians and Texans.

The Texans finally were reduced to striking at the Red Men with unloaded pistols and guns.

An arrow badly wounded Levi English in the side.

An arrow hit G. W. Daugherty in the leg.

Ed Burleson was wounded in the leg.

A man named Aiken got it in his chest.

W. C. Bell was struck in one side.

The wounded and disheveled party got back to the ranch and told the news of their disaster. Those not wounded led other men out to recover the three bodies.

The bodies were badly mutilated.

Dan Williams' head was so nearly severed that they had to wrap a blanket tightly around him to keep his head and body together. Bud English had been killed by a wound in his chest. Oden and Williams, who were brothers-in-law, were buried in the same coffin.

The only three Texans neither wounded nor killed were L. A. Franks, Frank Williams, and John Berry.

9

A bullwhacker, thirty, improves a wagon

THE SAME year, 1866, when James Daugherty went to Kansas, Charles Goodnight and Oliver Loving tried another route for cattle: from west Texas through New Mexico to mining towns and army forts in Colorado. If, they figured, they could not sell their longhorns in Colorado, they could find empty ranges where they could graze and fatten.

Goodnight, thirty years old, had arrived in Texas in 1845, at nine years of age, from Illinois. His schooling had been farm labor, horseback riding, and driving wagons. In 1856, at twenty, he had become a cattle owner—of seventeen head.

During the four years of the just-concluded War Between the States, he had served with the Texas Rangers. Instead of fighting Northerners, he had fought Indians, bandits, and cattle thieves. By profession, Goodnight in 1866 was a driver of ox-drawn freight wagons. He had walked ahead of and led his plodding oxen out of a wide place among the wagon ruts that today is identified as Fort Worth. Bullwhacking was what people called Goodnight's job. It took little capital, and therefore was where Goodnight and many another young man began.

Oliver Loving, fifty-three, back in 1858 had pioneered in driving cattle from Texas to Kansas and Illinois, and in 1859 to Colorado. Loving's drive to Kansas and Illinois made him, Charles Goodnight said, "undoubtedly the first man who ever trailed cattle from northwest Texas." That is, from west and somewhat north of Fort Worth.

"In 1866," said Goodnight, "Oliver Loving joined me on the Upper Brazos."

Goodnight, an experienced scout of the west Texas country they would pass through, and Loving, one of the most experienced cattle drivers of the few there were, had one big problem: they were about to drive longhorns from the middle Concho River to the Horsehead Crossing of the Pecos River—ninety-six miles without water anywhere.

The Pecos is the principal tributary, in the United States, of the Rio Grande, the river that is the border—from El Paso to its mouth—between Texas and Mexico.

Water for men and horses could be carried in ox wagons—the kind Charles Goodnight drove. There never was a way to tote enough water for hundreds or thousands of steers; for them, you had to find a river or large creek.

For the ninety-six waterless miles to the Pecos River, Goodnight wanted a stronger, improved wagon—able to carry more kegs of water.

Goodnight therefore obtained the gear of a government wagon —the axles were of metal instead of wood. Moving parts of metal, as they rub against each other, require a coating of lubricant. Otherwise the parts grab or seize each other and stop moving. Goodnight's wagon carried lubrication for the axles: a can of tallow.

Goodnight hired a Parker County woodworker to rebuild the body of his wagon, out of the tough, seasoned yellowwood of the *bois d'arc* tree (also known as Osage orange).

The wagon, like the prairie schooners that were taking settlers west, was given a canvas top.

The canvas could be opened out and supported, tentlike, by poles. It provided a surprising amount of shade.

Besides the metal axles, and the *bois d'arc* body—both of which gave the wagon additional strength for kegs of water—and besides the spreading top, Charles Goodnight added a new wrinkle. This, at the rear of the wagon, was the chuck box.

"Chuck" was in Texas then a word for food. The chuck box, with shelves, drawers, and partitions, held small packages of food, ready for the cook to prepare a meal—beans, coffee, meat, sourdough for biscuits. The chuck box also held ready for use necessary cutlery and other utensils, and tin or iron dishes.

Larger—bulk—supplies of food were carried in the body of the wagon itself, along with the kegs of water and the cattle drivers' bedding (if any; sometimes they had none), extra clothing (if any), and personal belongings.

The lid or the back side or wall of the chuck box was hinged and had a leg that unfolded to support it. The lid or back side then opened downward to become a tabletop that the cook could work on.

Charles Goodnight, with his improvements, had devised a vehicle that would become famous on the Western frontier:

The chuckwagon.

It took some years, but the chuckwagon became standard equipment for men driving cattle.

Not only that, but, as the years went by, the chuck box would be taken out of many a wagon to make a cabinet and kitchen table —the first kitchen—for many a ranch or farm bride.

Ox-driver Goodnight used ten oxen, instead of the usual four, to haul his heavier, improved wagon.

On August 26, 1866, with the wagon and a large herd of 2,000 cattle, and with Oliver Loving, Goodnight set out for the Horsehead Crossing on the Pecos River, for New Mexico and for Colorado.

Also along with Goodnight were eighteen cowboys. One was a former slave, Bose Ikard. Another was the cross-eyed Nath Branner. With one of his crossed eyes, Branner said, he could watch the longhorns; while, with the other, he could watch for rattlesnakes.

"We struck southwest," Goodnight said, "until we reached the Pecos River." They went, he said, through "some of the most desolate country I ever explored." They reached Fort Sumner, in eastern New Mexico, and sold some of their steers. Goodnight put $12,000 in gold on a pack mule and went home to Texas. Loving went farther north. The reduced herd reached Denver, Colorado.

Because Goodnight had gone as far as Fort Sumner, the route to that point was named the Goodnight Trail. Because Loving had gone on to Denver, the route from Sumner to Denver was called the Loving Trail.

Loving sold his cattle to U.S. government people on army posts and Indian reservations.

The steers they sold in New Mexico actually started ranching in that state. And, later on, New Mexico ranching would provide cattle to be driven to Arizona, Nevada, and even California.

As Jim Daugherty in Kansas had been, Goodnight and Loving had been successful in finding customers for their cattle. They brought home cash to destitute Texas. Naturally they did not wait long to try again. The next year, 1867, they were to make a more eventful journey to Colorado over the same route, the route that was to become known as the Goodnight-Loving Trail.

10

A *herd crosses* the Pecos River country

I867. ALONG THE Trail: The Indians were using arrowheads that would break off and remain in wounds. Cowboy George Reynolds was struck in the back by an arrow; its head stayed imbedded in his back for fourteen years. Railroads were stretching out. The Kansas Pacific track was laid west as far as Abilene, Kansas. Kansas Pacific trains were held up for hours while buffalo crossed the line. The passenger cars had no springs. Their seats had no backs. Women came on west, sleeping on floors of the cars, as conductors stumbled into or stepped over them.

AROUND THE WORLD: The Russians sold Alaska to the United States, for two cents an acre, or a total of $7,200,000. The United States also acquired a tiny territory that would become famous in World War II: one-and-one-half-square-mile Midway Island in the Pacific Ocean. On May 21, 1867, a proclamation announced the establishment of the Dominion of Canada.

Late in June 1867 Charles Goodnight and Oliver Loving again set out for Colorado. A man called Bill Wilson was with them.

What happened to them has become a legend.

Goodnight and Loving and Wilson and a herd were in the

53

Concho and Colorado River country of central west Texas. They had met, and perhaps obtained cattle from, a man named Jesse Chisholm.

Early on their trip, Indians—Comanches—attacked at night and captured 160 of their cattle. In a second raid, the Comanches took 300 more. Then Loving rode ahead to bid on government contracts in New Mexico and Colorado.

Bill Wilson, "the clearest headed man in the outfit," Goodnight called him, went along with Loving.

Goodnight was thirty-one, and though twenty-three years younger than Loving, was, nevertheless, much more experienced in the central west Texas country, since he was a former scout and Texas Ranger. Goodnight knew that Loving and Wilson would be traveling through the Pecos River area.

Discovered in 1581 by Fray (Friar or Brother) Augustin Rodriguez, the Pecos River by the 1860s was regarded as a line between civilization and outlawry. West of the Pecos, any people a cowman might meet probably would be bandits or hostile Indians, Apaches or Comanches.

Goodnight tried to persuade Loving and Wilson to travel only by night.

He succeeded only partially. The first two nights they did. But the third day was "a fine morning." The two men rode by daylight. At two in the afternoon Wilson saw Comanches, fierce, warlike, the finest horsemen of all the Indians, among the most dreaded Indians on the Great Plains. The Comanches were heading, from the southwest, for Loving and Wilson.

There were five or six hundred Indians.

"The men left the trail," Goodnight later said, "and made for the Pecos River which was about four miles to the northwest and was the nearest place they could hope to find shelter."

They ran their horses.

A hundred and fifty feet from the Pecos, the bank dropped abruptly a hundred feet.

The men—still on horseback—scrambled down the bank and leaped off.

"They hitched their horses and crossed the river where they hid themselves among the sand dunes and brakes [thickets] of the river."

The Indians were right behind.

Some halted on the bluff.

One group captured the horses.

Other Comanches crossed the river. They swarmed into the brake of Spanish cane in which the men were hiding. The cane soon was full of Indians, who walked into, and were hidden by, the five- to six-foot tall cane. They did not dare advance on Loving and Wilson, still concealed, because they knew the men were armed.

Instead, an Indian asked the men, in Spanish, to come out for a consultation.

Wilson stepped out to talk to the Comanches.

At this point, the Indians fired on Loving, or at least his general vicinity. The shot went through Loving's holster, passed through his wrist, broke his arm, and wounded him in the side. "He came running back to me," Bill Wilson said later, "tossed his gun to me and said he was killed and for me to do the best I could. The Indians at this time made a desperate charge, and after I had emptied my five-shooting Yarger, I picked up Mr. Loving's gun and continued firing.

"There was some brush, only a few inches high, not very far from where I was, and the Indians would run to it, crawl on their bellies, and I could not see them.

"I managed to get Mr. Loving down to the river and concealed him in a sandy depression, where the smart weeds grew about two feet high." Wilson lay down beside Loving. "The Indians knew we were down there somewhere, and used all sorts of ruses to find our exact location. They would shoot their arrows up and came very near striking us.

"Finally an Indian with a long lance came crawling along parting the weeds with his lance as he came, and just about the time I had determined to pull the trigger, he scared up a big rattlesnake. The snake came out rattling, looking back at the Indian, and coiled up right near us.

"The Indian, who still had not seen us, evidently got scared of the rattlesnake and turned back."

The long summer afternoon dragged on.

Wilson and Loving lay there till night. Loving's broken arm and wound in the side caused him to run a high temperature. "I managed," Wilson said, "to bring up some water from the river in his boot, which seemed to relieve him somewhat."

The Comanches, right along, were howling.

"About midnight the moon went down, but the Indians were still around us. We could hear them on all sides.

"Mr. Loving begged me to leave him and make my escape, so I could tell his folks what had become of him. He said he felt sure he could not last until morning, and if I stayed there I would be killed."

Loving asked Wilson to return first to Goodnight and tell him what had happened. He asked Wilson to tell the Loving family that he would kill himself rather than be tortured to death by the Indians.

"But in case he survived," said Wilson, "and was able to stand them off we would find him two miles down the river."

The men exchanged weapons. Wilson left behind for Loving all the pistols both men had—five—plus his six-shooting rifle. Loving insisted Wilson take his Henry rifle with waterproof cartridges. "I could carry it through water and not dampen the powder," Wilson said. "I took his gun, and with a handclasp told him goodbye, and started to the river."

He had to cross it—to get on his way back to Goodnight. "How Wilson expected to cross the river," said Goodnight later, "I have never comprehended." For Bill Wilson, carrying a Henry rifle, crawling and swimming alone as he tried to get away from half a thousand Indians, without a horse, had a special handicap.

"He was," said Goodnight, "a one-armed man."

But Wilson could cross the river. It was only about four feet deep. Said he, "I had to pull off all of my clothes except my hat, shirt, and breeches [underwear]." He hid his boots and trousers underwater. He even discarded his knife, and hid it also beneath the surface.

He spotted a shoal in the river—the only shoal, Goodnight said, within a hundred miles.

There was an Indian at the shoal, Wilson saw, "sitting on his horse out in the river, with the water almost over the horse's back. He was sitting there splashing the water with his feet, just playing."

Three times Wilson tried to swim past the Indian.

In the process, Bill Wilson, one-armed, struggling to paddle through the sandy water, had to abandon his gun—that is, Oliver Loving's Henry rifle. Near the bank of the river, where the Indians would not find it, Wilson punched down the muzzle into the sand till the breech was underwater.

"I got under some smart weeds and drifted by until I got far enough below the Indian where I could get out." Then Wilson floated, as noiselessly as he could, for about seventy-five or one hundred yards downstream.

In addition to the Comanche at the shoal, there were others all around.

Wilson reached the bank. He crawled through a cane brake. "And," said Goodnight, "he started out to find me, barefooted and over ground that was covered with prickly pear, mesquite, and other thorny plants."

Wilson, with no horse, and no boots, had about one hundred miles of that cactus country to cover before he would reach Goodnight.

At first, he traveled by night—following Goodnight's original advice. Once out of the Indians' sight, he moved by day.

"I made a three days' march," Wilson recalled, "barefooted. Everything in that country had stickers in it."

Limping, he needed a crutch. "I picked up the small end of a tepee pole which I used for a walking stick."

He had not had a thing to eat.

The wolves followed him the last night of his journey—all night.

"I would give out, just like a horse, and lay down in the road and drop off to sleep and when I would awaken the wolves would be all around me, snapping and snarling.

"I would take up that stick, knock the wolves away, get started again and the wolves would follow behind. I kept that up until daylight, when the wolves quit me."

Wilson struggled across the plain around the Pecos River.

"About 12 o'clock on that last day," said Wilson, "I crossed a little mountain and knew the boys ought to be right in there somewhere with the cattle."

Wilson saw a cave with which he was familiar. It looked good to him. The cave ran back fifteen or twenty feet into the hill. He crept inside. Said he: "I could go no further."

That afternoon he came out of the cave. He looked around, and saw the herd, his brother, and Goodnight, riding up.

"His brother, who was 'pointing' the herd with me, and I saw him at the same time," Goodnight recalled.

"At sight both of us thought it was an Indian as we didn't sup-

pose that any white man could be in that part of the country. I
ordered Wilson to shape the herd for a fight, while I rode toward
the man to reconnoiter, believing the Indians to be hiding behind
the hills and planning to surprise us. I left the trail and jogged
toward the hills as though I did not suspect anything. I figured I
could run to the top of the hill to look things over before they would
have time to cut me off from the herd. When I came within a quarter of a mile of the cave Wilson . . . was between me and the de-
clining sun and since his underwear was saturated with red sedi-
ment from the river he made a queer looking object.''

But from some little distance Goodnight recognized the one-
armed Wilson. ''How I did it, under his changed appearance I do
not know. When I reached him I asked him many questions, too
many in fact, for he was so broken and starved and shocked by
knowing he was saved, I could get nothing satisfactory from him.

''I put him on the horse and took him to the herd at once. We
immediately wrapped his feet in wet blankets. They were swollen
out of all reason, and how he could walk on them is more than I can
comprehend. Since he had starved for three days and nights I could
give him nothing but gruel.''

After having rested, Wilson poured out his story to Goodnight:

''I think Mr. Loving has died from his wounds, he sent me to
deliver a message to you. It was to the effect that he had received a
mortal wound, but before he would allow the Indians to take him
and torture him he would kill himself, but in case he lived he would
go two miles down the river from where we were and there we
would find him.''

Said Goodnight, ''Now tell me where I may find this place.''

Wilson did. He told his full story. He said he could not swim
across the Pecos River, when he was first trying to get away, because his own splashing would have attracted the Indian splashing
the water beside the shoal.

Then Wilson told Goodnight how to find the things he had hidden underwater. ''He told me,'' said Goodnight, ''to go down
where the bank is perpendicular and the water appeared to be
swimming but was not. 'Your legs will find the rifle,' he said.''

Goodnight took twelve men and set out for the Pecos River.
In twenty-four hours on horseback they covered the cactus-car-

peted distance it had taken the barefoot Wilson three days to cross.

They sought Loving. They did not find him. They concluded he had been killed by the Comanches and his body thrown into the river.

Goodnight looked for Wilson's things. "I found every one," he said, "even to the pocket knife. His remarkable coolness in deliberately hiding these things, when the loss of a moment might mean his life, is to me the most wonderful occurrence I have ever known . . . [and] I have experienced many unusual phases of frontier life."

Goodnight and his men rode back to their cattle.

"About two weeks after this," said Bill Wilson, "we met a party coming from Fort Sumner [New Mexico] and they told us Loving was at Fort Sumner."

Goodnight and Wilson hurried there.

Loving had neither died from his wound nor been killed.

"The last night after I had left him," Wilson said, "he got into the river and drifted by the Indians as I had done, crawled out and lay in the weeds all the next day. The following night he made his way to the road where it struck the river, hoping to find somebody traveling that way. He remained there for five days, being without anything to eat for seven days.

"Finally some Mexicans came along and he hired them to take him to Fort Sumner." The wounded Loving paid the Mexicans $150 for a jolting 150-mile ride in their cart.

Loving's wounded arm was dangerously infected. Said Wilson, "I believe he would have fully recovered if the doctor at that point had been a competent surgeon. But that doctor had never amputated any limbs and did not want to undertake any such work."

"Such work"—an amputation—in the 1860s was performed by sawing off an arm or leg, tying up arteries, and cauterizing the wound with a red-hot branding iron. If no branding-iron was at hand, gunpowder was poured onto the wound and set afire.

After seeing Loving's arm, Goodnight sent to Santa Fe for a surgeon. Before the surgeon could get there, blood poisoning set in. Goodnight and Wilson persuaded the original doctor to cut off the arm.

"But too late," said Wilson. "Mortification went into the body and killed him. Thus ended the career of one of the best men I ever knew. Mr. Goodnight had the body of Mr. Loving prepared for the long journey . . . and carried it to Weatherford [near Fort Worth], Texas.''

When he told the story of their 1867 drive, Goodnight said: ''This is as I get it from memory. And I think I am correct, for . . . it is printed indelibly on my mind.''

Goodnight was telling his tale fifty years afterward. His account and that of Bill Wilson both appeared in *The Trail Drivers of Texas*.

The Goodnight-Loving cattle (those the Comanches had not stolen) reached Fort Sumner, 600 miles from their starting point.

The Goodnight-Loving Trail afterward was known for its hazards. One cowboy reached Fort Sumner with 170 sets of rattles from rattlesnakes he had killed on the way. Along the dry trail, a desert mineral, alkali, poisoned some of what water there was. Parched cowboys, instead of drinking, could only take off their clothes and roll around in it. Steers that drank alkali water would die. For years the signposts showing the trail were the bleached skeletons of the cattle along it.

Oliver Loving, though he died early during the cattle drives, is today memorialized by Loving, New Mexico; Loving, Young County, Texas; and Loving County in Texas. And the place on the Pecos River where Loving lay wounded is named Loving's Bend.

But perhaps the reward Loving himself would have cherished most came from his partner, Charles Goodnight. There were no profits from the drive in 1867. But Charles Goodnight maintained his partnership with Loving, exactly as though Loving were still alive, till there were profits—which Goodnight paid to Loving's family.

11

Two men sit on a pile of lumber

J. J. MEYERS in 1867 drove cattle north to Kansas.

Meyers, a small, quiet man from Lockhart, Texas, like Jim Daugherty in 1866 had no definite destination for his cattle, and he had to drive and look for a purchaser at the same time. He had driven a herd north the previous year, also on faith, and also looking for a buyer as he moved along. That was the herd that Dr. Hargus had caught up with at the Red River.

Meyers (in some accounts spelled Myers) as a young man had explored much of the western United States with John C. Frémont. He was a veteran of the United States' war in the 1840s with Mexico and he had been a white-haired colonel in the Texas cavalry during the War Between the States. He knew that farmers were settling in Kansas, and he knew—as J. M. Daugherty had painfully learned—that the farmers objected to Texas cattle because of tick fever. Meyers with his longhorns stayed west of the farmers and their settlements.

One day in June 1867 Colonel Meyers reached Dickinson County in the Abilene, Kansas, area. Here Meyers was introduced to a twenty-nine- or thirty-year-old cattle dealer from Springfield, in central Illinois, Joseph G. McCoy. McCoy previously had

61

bought some longhorns driven up from Texas. He had heard that there were immense numbers of longhorns in Texas. He knew people in the North needed food. He sensed an opportunity.

McCoy knew all about the troubles Jim Daugherty had had with the Kansans when he drove his cattle north—with no place to go. "A yelling, armed, organized mob," McCoy later called those Kansans.

When McCoy and Meyers met, McCoy—partly impressed by Meyers' frosty hair—steered him to a lumber pile and sat him down. There followed two hours of conversation.

McCoy had ridden the newly built Kansas Pacific Railroad. He had looked over the towns on the line, and he now told Meyers of a plan he had to construct a cattle depot on the railroad, well away from farmers, and from the depot to ship cattle in cattle cars to Kansas City.

The place McCoy had in mind for the depot was Abilene. In central Kansas, about 130 miles west of Kansas City, Abilene had been on the Overland stage route. The railroad had replaced the stagecoach. But nothing had replaced Abilene's principal business: to trap prairie dogs and sell them as curiosities to visitors. Thousands of prairie dogs teemed in their underground city of burrows in the earth at Abilene.

Abilene also had a few human inhabitants, one or two dozen. The records are not quite clear. They lived in fewer than a dozen low, small, usually dirt-roofed, log houses. They had one amenity, also in a log hut: a saloon.

There was grass for the cattle all around Abilene.

Would the trail drivers, McCoy asked Meyers, use Abilene as a destination—and as a shipping point?

Meyers thought they would.

Did they need a depot? McCoy asked.

Meyers said they did.

About the time McCoy and Meyers were talking, W. C. McAdams was driving cattle—with no certain destination. He had planned to go to Baxter Springs, Kansas, but instead had sold his herd at Fort Gibson, Indian Territory (today Oklahoma).

A definite goal—a sure place where cattle could be sold—was needed, and Colonel Meyers convinced McCoy that McCoy should make Abilene just that.

"There are moments in one's existence," McCoy said later, of his talk with Meyers, "when decision, or a purpose, is arrived at, shapes future actions and events—even the tenor of one's life and labor."

For $2,400, McCoy bought the entire town of Abilene, the dozen or so structures that made it up. It will not in the least surprise you to learn that later he became mayor.

McCoy at once set about building cattle pens at Abilene. He actually started building his yards on July 1, 1867—the first day of the next month after his talk with Colonel Meyers. Soon he had completed enclosures for 3,000 cattle. Every cattle town thereafter would have pens beside the tracks, as in the song "The Railroad Corral." McCoy installed large Fairbanks scales on which to weigh cattle, though most would be sold by head—that is, so much for each individual animal—not by weight. McCoy also constructed a three-story hotel, soon to become known as the Drovers' Cottage.

McCoy also sent a man named W. W. Suggs down to the south of Abilene to meet herds and guide them there. A cowboy originally from Bennington, Vermont, William E. Hawks, told what happened next: "The first herd to cross the Nation [Oklahoma] on that trail was Wheeler, Wilson & Hicks' herd of 2400 bound for California. This herd drove within thirty miles of Abilene and stopped and were later shipped from Abilene.

"The second herd to cross the Nation and drive direct to Abilene was owned by Mr. Thompson, who sold them in the Nation to Smith, McCord & Chandler." They also were shipped from Abilene.

The first trainload from Abilene—twenty carloads to Chicago —left on September 5, 1867.

Kansas farmers continued to hold a grudge against Texas cattle and tick (or Spanish) fever. McCoy used persuasion. He called a meeting of farmers. He invited some cattlemen, up from Texas, to attend the meeting. The cattlemen bought from the farmers—at somewhat above current prices—corn, oats, onions, potatoes, eggs, butter, and so on.

Said one farmer, "Gentlemen, if I can make any money out of this cattle trade, I am not afraid of 'Spanish fever'; but if I can't make any money out of this cattle trade, then I am d——d afraid of 'Spanish fever.' "

Opposition to the cattle drovers began to subside.

Altogether, in 1867, as many as 36,000 longhorns were shipped from Abilene.

That was only the beginning of the movement of cattle that grew out of the two-hour conversation on the lumber pile between Joseph McCoy and Col. J. J. Meyers.

For McCoy's pens made Abilene the focal point for shipping cattle, over the new Kansas Pacific Railroad, to the northeast United States. McCoy's pens would make Abilene the destination for herds coming up the trail, the first of the important cattle towns, the first of the towns that would make Kansas a center, about halfway between Texas and the North, for herds moving toward north, east, or west, to ranches in Northwestern states, even to as far away as California or as far north as Alberta, Canada.

As you might expect, because Texas had nothing but longhorns to sell, Colonel Meyers' four sons all became cattle drivers: George, who lived in Batesville, Texas; John G., who some of the time lived in New York City; S. E., San Antonio; and R. E. L. Meyers, Austin. He had a daughter, Mrs. John I. Peel, Lockhart. Colonel Meyers himself drove north four to sixteen thousand head of cattle each year, as many as three thousand in single herd. One of his early drivers, Dick Head, about eighteen, one night camped a herd of cattle where Wichita, Kansas, is today—amid hundreds of Indians.

Once Colonel Meyers had a destination and a selling point for his cattle, he was faithful to it. Year after year he headed for Abilene.

12

The trail
gets crowded

1868. ON THE Trail: Along with great drives of cattle from Texas, there was under way another mass migration, this one of people. The railroads brought out from the East, as far as their tracks were laid, thousands of men, women, and children. Many of the men would become farmers, and customers for cattle—but also would fence out longhorns from grazing on their land. Many a girl among them one day would marry a cowboy. In Hays, Kansas, there lived, with his wife and daughter, Arta, a former stagecoach and Pony Express driver, who had contracted to supply twelve buffaloes a day to workmen building the Union Pacific Railroad: William Frederick Cody, or Buffalo Bill. In Jasper, near Beaumont, Texas, an officer with flowing yellow hair had commanded post–Civil War troops: Gen. George A. Custer.

AROUND THE WORLD: Japan moved its capital from Kyoto, where it had been for a thousand years, to Tokyo. The average workman in an American city labored 65¼ hours a week. A newspaper, the *New York World*, began the publication of a yearly volume, "The World Almanac." In Albany, New York, John Wesley Hyatt started to use his new material, celluloid—the first plastic—to manufacture billiard balls. A holiday, May 30, was first observed as Memorial Day, remembering those who had fallen in the Civil War.

The Long Trail to Abilene became jammed with cattle the year after Joseph G. McCoy built his cattle pens there. 1868 was the first busy year on the rail line. Men in Texas, poor but hopeful, pushed one herd after another onto the trail.

Money was so nonexistent, in fact, that in Texas cattle and calves were currency. A cow and calf always were valued at $10. A man's bankroll might walk off into the wilds at any time.

George W. Steen borrowed $100, hired six cowboys, and headed a herd for Abilene. At his last stop in Texas, Gainesville, he had to talk storekeeper George Howell into providing groceries for the trip—entirely on credit. Howell had "only my word to pay," Steen said.

J. M. Hankins, seventeen, traded a five-year-old steer he had raised to go into a trail herd. "For which I received a pair of shoes, a straw hat and a linen coat, the value of all being about ten dollars, but I was fully rigged out for Sunday wear, and was satisfied with the deal."

E. P. Byler, an inexperienced cowboy, said he received $30 a month; a trail boss, $75. Byler and brother Jim drove 1,000 steers for Dan Pucket. "Strung out," said E.P., "it was over half a mile long."

W. F. Cude of San Antonio found grass for grazing all the way to the Kansas Pacific Railroad, nine miles west of Abilene. He ate buffalo calf (without liking it), burned buffalo chips (dry dung), and lost a horse to rattlesnake bite.

Col. A. R. (Shanghai) Pierce (sometimes printed as Pearce) bought cattle along the trail. He had a packhorse loaded with gold and silver. When he reached a camp, his money was dumped on the ground and stayed there till he inspected and counted the cattle. Then he paid off. Cattlemen, San Antonio's George W. Saunders remembered, "looked upon Pierce as a redeemer."

J. L. McCaleb of Carrizo Springs, Texas, went up the trail in 1868, that busy year. He was in front of the herd. "My place was always in front," he said. He didn't think much of the rear or tail of the herd, with its "lazy or sore-footed cattle."

He was so unfamiliar with money that he saw his first $5 bill on the trip.

"I saw a small piece of paper in a fence corner," he recalled, "and as the cattle seemed quiet, I got down and picked it up, simply because I was hungry for something to read, if not more than one or two words. We did not have papers forwarded to us while on the trail. Well, I read that it was good for $5.00. I had never seen one before, so after crossing our herd, and when we struck camp for dinner, I showed it to the boss. He said that it was sure enough good money, so I rolled it up, stuck it away down in the pocket of my leather leggins. Money was of no value on the trail, as there was no place to spend it, but I valued that $5.00 more than any $5.00 I have ever had since."

He bet the cook $5—against a two-year-old heifer—that, only one shot each, he could outshoot the cook.

The target was a bit of board with a soot mark on it, from the campfire. The two men were to shoot from forty-five feet away.

"I jerked my old cap and ball Navy out and just about one second before I pulled the trigger I saw the heads of six Indians just over a little rise in the ground coming toward the camp," McCaleb said. "This excited me so that I did not hit the spot, only about one-half of my bullet touched the board."

The cook, when he took his turn, was seeing the Indians plainly.

He missed the board completely. "So," said McCaleb, "six big Osage Indians saved me my valuable find—the five-dollar bill."

He was not to keep it forever.

Near Abilene, the cattle were bedded for the last time. McCaleb and another cowboy went into town. "As it had been a long time since we had seen a house or a woman, they were good to look at. I wore a black plush hat which had a row of small stars around the rim, with buck-skin strings to tie and hold on my head. We went into town, tied our ponies, and the first place we visited was a saloon and dance hall." The two cowboys had toddies. They separated.

McCaleb went on to other toddies and saloons. He was on his third of each when "a girl came up and put her little hands under my chin, and looked me square in the face and said, 'Oh you pretty Texas boy, give me a drink.'

"My, I was getting rich fast—a pretty girl and plenty of whisky. My old hat was now away back on my head."

He told the girl to relax while he entered the saloon's monte game. He ran his money up to $20, obtained another toddy, and went back to rejoin the girl. She was gone.

After that fourth toddy, he had had it. "It seemed to me that I did not care whether I broke [the old long-haired dealer] or not. I soon lost all I had won and my old original five."

McCaleb went back to Texas, where he fiddled, danced, and worked cattle for some years. "Wherever my horse, saddle, and hat were, I was there." When he went to a social event, he said, he "would civilize up a bit." That is, when he went to a dance he took off his spurs and tied a clean red handkerchief around his neck. He thought he was getting wilder "until I met a curly-headed girl from Atascosa County, fell in love, and married. It took her a long time to tame me. But she did," he recalled much later, "and for the last 15 or 20 years I do not have to be tied. Just drop the reins on the ground, I'll stay there."

13

A trail boss, twenty-two, completes a trip

MARK A. WITHERS, a cowboy from Missouri, was another who in 1868 drove his herd to Joseph G. McCoy's Abilene.

He had made his first trip on part of the trail in 1859—at age thirteen.

He was, in 1868, twenty-two years old.

He was the boss.

"I left Lockhart, Texas [southeast of Austin], April 1, 1868," he said, "with a herd of 600 big wild steers. The most of these belonged to my father, brothers, and myself. I bought some of them at $10.00 per head to be paid for when I returned from the drive." Lockhart was the home of Col. J. J. Meyers, who had persuaded McCoy to make Abilene a cattle town.

Withers made his drive with eight hands and a cook. "We crossed the Colorado River at Austin," he said, "the Brazos River at Waco, the Trinity River where Fort Worth now is. Only one or two stores were there then. We crossed the Red River where Denison now is."

Just before Wichita, Kansas, when Withers was watering his horse, seven Osage Indians surrounded him. "I thought," he remembered, "they were the largest ones I had ever seen." They took his tobacco and left. "It was a great relief to me," he said, "when I saw them whirl their horses and leave in as big a hurry as they came."

A few days afterward, when Withers and his men were barbecuing a steer, thirty Osage Indians raced on horseback to their camp. Each said "How." They placed their guns around a tree, and they gulped down barbecued meat. They asked for another steer, were given one, butchered it, and began to eat it. "While they were thus engaged," said Withers, "we moved the herd away as quickly as possible."

Not everyone on the trail to Abilene escaped trouble as fortunately as did Withers. Between Wichita and Abilene, Withers said, "we found the skull of a man with a bullet hole in his forehead. Whose skull it was we never knew."

Their trip in one way was easy: "We found plenty of grass and water. The cattle arrived in Abilene in fine condition." They were "rolling fat" when the end of the trail, for Withers, was reached. Not one of the cattle had been lost on the trip—a remarkable thing on one of the earliest drives to Kansas.

The end of the trail for Withers was twelve miles north of Abilene. Here four men were discharged. The other four were to range-herd the cattle till autumn.

At Abilene, which they reached about July 1, after three months on the way up, the men found a railroad track, three saloons, a store, two hotels—and Joseph McCoy's pens for the cattle. That was the entire town. Longhorns were being shipped on the Kansas Pacific Railroad to Kansas City for slaughtering.

Withers' cowboys learned that one of the two hotels in Abilene, the Drovers' Cottage, had been taken charge of by Mrs. Lou Gore. Mrs. Gore for many years would feed, shelter, and even nurse the men in from the trail till she became to them a ministering angel, a Florence Nightingale. Years afterward, the president of the Old Trail Drivers Association, George W. Saunders, would make her daughter, Margaret Gore, an honorary member for life in tribute to her mother.

Withers found the McCoys' firm in Abilene, and to the McCoys he sold his cattle at a price that made the drive worthwhile. They had cost $8 to $10 apiece in Texas; $4 apiece to walk to

Kansas. Now they were sold to W. K. McCoy & Bros. of Champaign, Illinois, for $28 apiece. "I received," Withers recalled, "$1,000 in cash and the remainder in drafts on Donald Lawson & Co. of New York City, signed by W. K. McCoy & Bros."

In addition to the meat-packing plants at Kansas City, there were others at St. Louis and Chicago. The packers in these towns had to be sold on the idea of buying cattle in Abilene. Joseph G. McCoy hired Withers for a publicity stunt to advertise Abilene. Withers, an expert with his lasso, was sent to the Fossil Creek siding of the Kansas Pacific Railroad to rope buffalo. So were three other cowboy rope artists—Billy Campbell, Tom Johnson, and Jake Carroll.

The men arrived near Fossil Creek—and rode out to where the buffalo roamed.

They chased what they thought was one.

It was a man on a horse—perhaps an Indian—hunting buffalo.

They chased what they thought was another.

It was a white man driving a milk cow.

He thought Withers and his companions were Indians, so he ran for his life.

He said that an Indian on a white horse had attempted to spear him.

Cowboy Tom Johnson, who was riding the white horse, never had gotten closer to the fleeing farmer than 400 yards.

Withers and the other three buffalo hunters got the man's story when they reached a dugout where he and other terrified people had taken refuge. These people, when they saw who Withers and his companions were, came out of the dugout and talked.

Finally, Withers and the three other cowboys succeeded in driving six buffaloes to within several hundred yards of the railroad. Two were roped. One by Withers and Billy Campbell. This one kept charging first, one and then the other. Finally, its legs were roped and the buffalo lay on the ground.

Then a block and tackle lifted the buffalo into a cattle car. His head was tied, his feet untied.

Withers and his men captured twenty-four buffaloes. Some died fighting capture. Only twelve were loaded into stock cars for St. Louis and Chicago.

Signs advertising Abilene as a cattle center were put on the sides of the stock cars.

Withers rode along. When the train stopped, he roped the buffalo to show the public how it was done.

Illinois cattlemen then were taken on a tour to Abilene where they saw herds of the longhorns that had come up the trail from Texas. They bought some. Northern men from then on accepted Texas cattle. Chicago and St. Louis grew as meat-packing centers. And Abilene grew as a cattle market.

While Withers was occupied with his buffalo and his publicity for Abilene, some of the boys who had originally driven longhorns up the trail with him were on their way home again.

They went through Arkansas. Here they loaded their wagons —they had bought new wagons—with fresh apples. A fresh apple then was a luxury often as scarce as, and comparable to, the one fresh orange that a Texas child might see once a year at Christmas.

"After reaching Texas they placed an apple on a twig on the front end of the wagon and began to peddle them," Withers later recalled.

"They received a fine price for those that they did not eat or give away to the girls along the road."

Withers himself took a different route home. "I went from Abilene, Kansas, to St. Louis, Missouri, and took the last steamer down the Mississippi River which would reach New Orleans before Christmas. It took eleven days to make the trip, for the boat stopped at every landing and added chickens, turkeys, ducks, etc., to her cargo. There was a dance on deck each night except Sunday night.

"I came from New Orleans to Galveston, Texas, by steamer; from Galveston to Columbus by train, and from Columbus to Lockhart by stage, and arrived at home on Christmas day, 1868." A few scattered lengths of railroad track then were being laid in Texas itself: the stretch from Galveston to Columbus was one.

Gone since April 1, Withers had been almost a full nine months away from home. A young man whose name is not to be found in any history books I ever have read, Mark A. Withers, the adopted Texan from Missouri, nevertheless earned a footnote in history. Not for his buffalo roping and publicity. But because of his cattle drive to Abilene. The grass and water he found along the way, and the successful sale of his cattle to the McCoys at Abilene, would be among the things that would assure that he would be followed by thousands of other trail drivers and that his longhorns would be followed by millions of others.

14

A man who didn't drive the trail

THE TRAIL to Abilene in 1868 was being given a name, the Chisholm Trail, which was probably a mistake.

The name was for Jesse Chisholm, born in Tennessee in 1805, the son of a Scottish father and a Cherokee Indian mother.

The family in 1815 had traveled with the Cherokees to the then-wilderness of Arkansas. The boy grew up at Fort Gibson, an army post in today's Oklahoma. Fort Gibson was a busy place: Indians brought furs and hides to sell. Pioneers stopped as they sought homesteads. Explorers, businessmen, officers, and soldiers came and went. Here Jesse Chisholm knew Sam Houston.

From 1832 onward, Jesse Chisholm was out on one trail or another—or finding trails when somebody needed one. In 1832, he found a 147-mile-long route for the Choctaw Indians. In 1836 he led some adventurers toward a supposed Arkansas gold mine—one of many gold mines rumored to exist ever since the time, three hundred years earlier, of the Spaniard, Coronado. In 1849–50, Chisholm led Comanche Indians to a trading post at Holdenville, Oklahoma—then the white man's farthest-west outpost. By 1853 Chisholm was selling cattle. During the Civil War, he drove cattle to supply the Union army. This took him through Oklahoma to many army posts in Kansas.

75

At the end of the Civil War, Charles Goodnight said, Jesse Chisholm drove two herds of cattle—fewer than a thousand head—to Little Rock, Arkansas. Goodnight said that Chisholm used what was called the U.S. road all the way to Little Rock.

In 1865, on the north fork of the Canadian River, at Council Grove, Chisholm established a trading post—Council Grove would become famous as an Indian meeting place. In 1866, according to Goodnight, Chisholm drove 600 steers from the west Texas, Colorado and Concho River country to the Pecos River. Chisholm wintered at Bosque Grande on the Pecos, and sold his cattle to government contractors. Then Chisholm returned to his Colorado-and-Concho-country ranch.

Later, I imagine on his own 1866 trip, Goodnight himself drove Chisholm cattle to Colorado. In February 1867 Chisholm met Bill Wilson and Goodnight in the Pecos River country. It may have been cattle delivered by Chisholm that Goodnight, Oliver Loving, and the one-armed Bill Wilson were driving in 1867, when Loving lost his life on what became the Goodnight-Loving Trail.

In 1867, Chisholm was asked to find a trail to move Wichita Indians. He did; the place the Indians left became known as Wichita, Kansas.

Chisholm, working out the route as he traveled, headed a long team of ox wagons. Ahead of the wagons he drove a hundred mustangs. He drove the horses back and forth, at four river crossings, to pack down quicksands.

The trail, between the Arkansas and Red rivers, was used later by soldiers, Indians, and others.

After 1867, as the cattle drives proceeded, many of the longhorns that went north from Texas to Kansas followed deep ruts once made by Chisholm's wagons or used parts of old military trails that Chisholm had followed. Many longhorns trod part of the Arkansas River routes that Chisholm had used.

Therefore, many a cowboy who came north was following what he knew as, and called, the Chisholm Trail. The name became established. It has hung on to this day. The belief grew that the route was named for Jesse Chisholm, because supposedly he had driven the first herd up from Texas to Abilene.

The Chisholm Trail, so-called, was used from 1867 to 1882, or for fifteen of the twenty important years of the cattle drives, to reach Abilene, Ellsworth, and other shipping points in Kansas.

The name was even given to that part of the trail that reached southward all the way to southwest Texas, below San Antonio, that region near the Gulf Coast and the Mexican border where the longhorns by the thousands ran wild and that was, consequently, the starting point for many a cattle drive.

The fact is that Chisholm drove no herd to Abilene. He did not open a new trail at all. He never asserted that he had.

So in the sense of a trail established by Jesse Chisholm, the Chisholm Trail never existed. "I see no sense," said Charles Goodnight later, "in naming a trail for a man who never used it."

The Chisholm Trail, however, did exist in name for many a cowboy. That was what they called the route they followed.

To confuse the situation even further, there was another man in the cattle business whose name was John Chisum or Chissum. Chisum's cattle had one of the most distinctive of brands: the long rail (a long bar on a cow's side) and jinglebob (a slit in each ear so part of the ear flopped down). Chisum's cattle were driven north by Charles Goodnight to Dodge City, Kansas. Goodnight's route became known as the Chisum Trail.

Some people in Paris, Texas, the boyhood home of John Chisum, have insisted that both the Chisum and Chisholm trails owe their names to John.

In 1868, Jesse Chisholm engaged in what was for him a new activity: the production of salt. On a trip to his trading post at Council Grove, he stayed for a night at Chief Left Hand Spring. This was near what today is Greenfield, Oklahoma. He died, apparently from food poisoning, that night.

His grave was unmarked until 1933. Then, in an Indian burying ground, what was believed to be his grave was located. Students of Greenfield High School erected a marker. Chisholm, wherever he might have been living at any particular time, had been known for his hospitality. The marker read:

JESSE CHISHOLM
Born 1805
Died March 4, 1868
No one left his home
cold or hungry

Chisholm's travels actually had taken him over only about two hundred miles of the trail from Texas to Abilene; he by no means had covered all of what came to be called by thousands of cowboys —and probably will forever be called by others—the Chisholm Trail.

There is no reason to suppose that Jesse Chisholm ever knew or even suspected that one day a trail would acquire his name. Men were just beginning to call it that when he died.

15

"A thousand steers swimming . . ."

I869. ALONG THE Trail: Thousands and thousands of years when the horse was man's principal long-distance overland transportation were coming to an end. On May 10, a golden spike was hammered into a railroad roadbed at Promontory Point, Utah. Laid along old stagecoach and Pony Express routes, the first track to cross the continent was completed. The track joined the Central Pacific and the Union Pacific. People could ride on steam-driven wheels (turned by wood or coal) all the way to California. . . . In Wyoming, a new law was passed. It was the first in the United States to give votes to women, plus the privilege of holding public office.

AROUND THE WORLD: At New Brunswick, New Jersey, on the afternoon of November 6, about ninety spectators watched two groups of young men, some of them with mustaches, pummel each other. They were from two colleges, Rutgers and Princeton, and what they were doing was playing the first varsity football game. Princetonians yelled "Siss, boom, ah"—the Civil War yell of New York's Seventh Regiment. Rutgers men sang "Oh! Susanna" and "Wait for the Wagon." Thus college yells and music at football

games began. . . . Also beginning was a long scientific campaign by
medical science against bloodsucking insects—a campaign that
would help end Texas fever in cattle. The start came when a man
called Raimbert showed that the bacteria of anthrax, a sudden,
almost always fatal disease of cattle, horses, sheep, goats, hogs,
sometimes dogs, many wild animals, and a disease that can attack
men, could be carried by flies. Robert Koch in 1876 and Louis
Pasteur would observe and confirm the existence of the anthrax
bacteria.

Cattle bought in Texas for $12 a head in 1869 sold at Abilene
for $30. Therefore, more and more cowmen jammed the Abilene
trail, and drove cattle elsewhere as well. It was a year of problems
and adventures on the cattle routes.

Bill Greathouse, trail boss, C. A. Mitchell, and Lump Mooney
took a thousand cattle from Gonzales, Texas, to Kansas. They all
contracted cholera. Indians nursed them. Mooney and Greathouse
died in Kansas, but Mitchell got well and made it back to Gonzales.

J. M. Cowley, twenty-two, of Fentress, Texas (he had been
born in Alabama, May 29, 1847) started in the spring for Abilene
along with J. H. Smith, George Eustace, Bill Hardeman, S. W.
Eads, Count Rountree, and 1,500 cattle. They met almost constant
rain and flooded creeks and rivers. At one flooded river, Cowley
saw a man he did not know trying to cross on a bobtailed horse.
The horse sank. Cowley threw a rope to the man. He missed it and
was drowned. The body was found three days afterward.

Westerners were learning to promise to do something only
with a qualification: "God willing and the creek don't rise."

W. F. Cude of San Antonio—whose mother in 1836 had been
within earshot of the Battle of San Jacinto—drove a herd to
Shreveport, Louisiana. The buffalo flies were so bad, he said, "we
never went any more to Shreveport." He explained: "Sometimes
we would get farms to put the cattle in at night and the farms were
stocked with cockleburrs and the cattle's tails would get full of
burrs, and when the buffalo flies would get after them they would
lose their tails fighting flies. Their tails would become entangled in
small pine trees and there they would stand and pull and bellow
until they got loose. You could hear them bawl a mile. Some of the

cattle would run off and lay down, crazed with misery, and it was hard to drive them back to the herd."

Damon Slater of Llano, Texas, was trail boss of a herd that went from Texas to California. One of his cowboys was James Washington (Jim) Walker, who had herded camels during the Civil War. In New Mexico they saw the first white woman since they had left Llano. "She seemed perfectly happy," said W. G. Ozment, "with her husband in these wilds." The herd went through Tucson, Arizona, then through ten or fifteen miles of Mexico, across today's Imperial Valley, California, and on to the Pacific coast. At one point, Jim Walker and several of Damon Slater's hands encountered a cowman, Crockett Riley, driving another herd, just as Riley was surrounded by eighty Pima Indians. Walker set some kind of a distance record for marksmanship: he killed the chief's horse—at 500 yards. The Slater herd was delivered twenty-five or thirty miles from Los Angeles in the spring, a year after it had started out.

Col. D. H. Snyder, who already had driven to New Mexico and Colorado, following Charles Goodnight and Oliver Loving, in 1869 drove to Abilene. J. W. Snyder was with him. Indians drove off 140 of their cattle. Thereafter, the Snyders would change their destination: they would go to Schuyler, Nebraska, in 1870—seventy miles west of Omaha, on the newly built, continent-crossing Union Pacific Railroad. They would go to Cheyenne, Wyoming, in 1878, and would make Cheyenne their destination until 1885, their last drive. For the Snyders, as for Damon Slater driving to California, the cattle trail was beginning to stretch farther and farther till it eventually would run the entire south-to-north length of the United States, and reach to Calgary, Alberta, Canada.

L. D. Taylor of San Antonio was twenty when he was with a herd that walked north to Abilene on what he called the Chisholm Trail. In the spring of 1869, his two brothers, Dan and George, rounded up a thousand longhorns, four to twelve years old, and headed for Kansas. "I had never been out of our home neighborhood before," he said, telling his story in *The Trail Drivers of Texas*, "so I went along to get some experience on the trail."

The herd was rounded up in Gonzales County near the town of

Waelder (southeast of Austin and Lockhart). At Waco, the Brazos River was level with its banks. The cattle swam it. "It was a wonderful sight," L. D. Taylor said, "to see a thousand steers swimming all at one time. All one could see was the tips of their horns and the ends of their noses as they went through the water."

In the Indian Nations the Taylors had trouble: "The first night there we rounded up the herd, but next morning they were gone, for they had been stampeded by Indians shooting arrows into them, and it required several days to get them all together again. The Indians resorted to that kind of a trick to get pay for helping to get the cattle back again." Taylor called the territory from here on "a wild, unsettled, hostile country.

"After a few days' travel we struck the Chisholm Trail, the only thoroughfare from Texas through the Indian Territory to Kansas, and about this time two other herds fell in with us, and, not knowing the country we were going through, the three outfits agreed to stick together, stay and die with each other if necessary."

One day the cattle stampeded. Taylor at the time was in the chuckwagon. "I just kept right on traveling," he recalled. When he halted the wagon for the night, no cattle and no other cowboys were anywhere in sight. The young Taylor was all by himself in Indian Territory—the cowboys called it No Man's Land—and, besides, he was among Indians who had already stampeded the cattle. It was not a comforting situation.

His brother George found him. George reached the wagon about suppertime. George told L.D. that the herds and other wagons were ten miles behind. "He gave me his pistol and went back to the herd," said L.D., "and I stayed there alone that night.

"The next day the herd overtook me, and I felt somewhat relieved."

Another stampede (the Texans pronounced it "stompede") took place during the night. "I was awakened by the shaking of the earth and an awful noise, and found the whole herd coming down upon us in a furious run. I was bunking with Monte Harrell, and when I jumped up Harrell tried to hold me, but I jerked loose and ran around to the other side of the wagon. I soon had Mr. Harrell for company. I think every beef must have jumped over the wagon tongue, at least it seemed to me that every steer was jumping it."

Some time afterward, and after traveling about three hundred miles without seeing anyone or knowing their exact location, the three Taylors and the men with them looked ahead and saw "something that looked like a ridge of timber." It was about four hundred Comanche Indians, heading toward them.

"They were on the warpath and going to battle another tribe. When they came up to our herd, they began killing our beeves without asking permission or paying any attention to us. Some of the boys of our herd went out to meet them. They killed 25 of our beeves and skinned them right there, eating the flesh raw and with blood running down their faces, reminding me of a lot of hungry dogs."

Then the Comanches showed the skill that made them a threat on the Great Plains:

"Here I witnessed some of the finest horsemanship I ever saw. The young warriors on bareback ponies would ride all over the horses' backs, off on one side, standing up, lying down, going at full speed and shooting arrows clear through the beeves.

"We were powerless to help ourselves, for we were greatly outnumbered.

"Every time we would try to start the herd the Indians would surround the herd and hold it. Finally they permitted us to move on, and we were not slow in moving, either. I felt greatly relieved.

"These Indians had 'talked peace' with Uncle Sam, that is all that saved us.

"We heard a few days afterwards that they had engaged in battle with their foes after leaving us, and had been severely whipped, losing about half of their warriors."

The day after leaving the Comanches, the Taylors met Col. John D. Miles, an Indian agent who had been appointed by President Ulysses S. Grant. Colonel Miles, L. D. Taylor said, "was traveling alone in a hack on his way to some fort, and to me he looked very lonely in that wild and woolly country."

The men and the herd crossed the Arkansas River. "There were a few houses on the Kansas side, and we began to rejoice that we were once more getting within the boundaries of civilization." They found a store and "plenty of booze," and some of the boys got 'full.' "After leaving that wayside oasis we did not see another house until we were within ten miles of Abilene."

Then came a storm. Monte Harrell predicted a "regular Kansas twister." "We had prepared for it," said L. D. Taylor, "by driving a long stake pin into the ground, to which I chained the wagon, and making everything as safe as possible. At midnight the storm was on, and within a moment everything was gone except the wagon and myself. The cattle stampeded, horses got loose, and oxen and all went with the herd.

"The storm soon spent its fury and our men managed to hold the cattle until daylight and got them all back the next morning and we resumed our drive to Abilene, reaching there in a few days. . . . Here we tarried to graze and fatten our cattle for market."

One day at Abilene one of what L. D. Taylor called "desperate characters" pulled a gun on the bartender in a saloon. Then several "bad men" began to shoot up Abilene. "I was not feeling well, so I went over to the hotel to rest, and in a short time the boys of our outfit missed me and instituted a search, finding me at the hotel under a bed."

Earlier, Taylor had been awed by "1000 steers swimming" the Brazos River. Once he had been alone with his chuckwagon in No Man's Land—Indian Territory. Now he would have another adventure.

He became a passenger on a railroad train.

The men, as they started back to Texas, went by train to Junction City, Kansas. "It was the first train I ever rode on, and I thought the thing was running too fast, but a brakeman told me it was behind time and was trying to make up the schedule."

At Junction City, they left the train and were joined by several other men who wanted to travel to Texas, elected a boss, bought new horses, and started south on horseback.

The men reached Fort Gibson, on the Arkansas. Here high water compelled them to stay a week. With no cattle to herd, "the boys chipped in and bought a lot of whiskey at this place, paying twelve dollars a gallon for it." An old Indian brought a horse and outfit into camp; L. D. Taylor bought horse and outfit, paying $75. "So I left the bunch and pulled out alone through Indian country. I reached Red River safely and made it through to my home without mishap, reaching there with only 75 cents in my pocket."

16

A steamboat man locates a ranch

OFFICIALLY REGISTERED in Nueces County, Texas, in 1869 was a new brand that would become known as the Running W. It was a wavy letter. Mexicans called it *viborita*, or little snake.

It was the brand of the King ranch.

Richard King had been born in Orange County, New York, on July 10, 1825. He had reached Texas when he was twenty-two. With other men, he operated twenty-six steamboats on the Rio Grande: steamboats that were, before the railroads, the only mechanized transportation in the Southwest, and, indeed, in the United States. A total of 4,000 early steamboats on U.S. rivers helped settle and populate the nation along with the covered wagons.

Captain King in 1852 left a steamboat at the mouth of the Rio Grande, the border between Mexico and Texas, and rode on horseback across 165 miles of chaparral-cock and rattlesnake country of southwest Texas. He saw lots of game, including wild turkeys and deer, and probably saw wild longhorns and ponies. He might have seen another animal the Spaniards had brought for food and set loose: wild hogs, or razorbacks.

He reached a new town on the Gulf of Mexico, Corpus Christi, around which he thought there might be good ranching land. The next year, 1855, he acquired what was called the Rincón de Santa Gertrudis, a land grant spreading over a vast area along the Gulf.

Captain King bought cattle. At first he ranched longhorns, and, before the trail to Kansas was available, he shipped hides and tallow to market by sea.

Longhorn meat could be improved. It was tough; it had few choice cuts. King bought, in Kentucky, Durham or Shorthorn cattle. He and others bred Durham or Shorthorn bulls with Longhorn cows, and a fine, squarely built steer resulted—with shorter horns than those of the longhorns, and better beef. Thus Captain King had begun to seek better breeds of cattle—to improve his herd by crossbreeding—as far back as the time when the first longhorns were walking north.

One of the men from whom Richard King purchased cattle was William Mann. Mann's brand was a wriggly Running M. Captain King may have turned over the M into a W to make his own brand, the Running W.

King also bought sheep in the north.

From 1852 to 1868, Captain King and Capt. Mifflin Kenedy were partners in owning the Santa Gertrudis Ranch, the old land grant. In 1868 the men broke up the partnership. Captain Kenedy bought from Charles Stillman the Laurels or (in Spanish) Laureles Ranch, containing 121 leagues of land, 10,000 cattle, and many horses and sheep. King continued to own the Santa Gertrudis Ranch.

So many outlaws and thieves were operating in Texas in those post–Civil War years that Captain King sought a way to protect his cattle. He decided to fence them in, and in 1868 he did so. Captain Kenedy also enclosed 132,000 acres of the Laureles. These two men were the first in Texas to fence in large amounts of the until then wide-open land. The lack of fences throughout the West had made the cattle drives possible. Thus 1868, the first year the trail to Abilene was busy with cattle, was also the first year when fences began to bar the way. The days of the open range began to end right here, right at the very beginning of the cattle drives.

Richard King had married Henrietta M. Chamberlain of Brownsville, Texas. The 1860s were a time when the rights of women, as we know them today, had not been established. Yet in those days when women were not granted the same rights as men,

Richard King pioneered as he had at improving cattle and fencing in his land: he left his wife as his sole heir, and his executor without bond.

Richard King owned altogether 100,000 cattle, 20,000 sheep, and 10,000 horses. When King died, he owned 500,000 acres of land. His son-in-law, R. J. Kleberg, increased the King ranch to more than 950,000 acres. People said the ranch house's front door was 100 miles from the front gate.

Captain Mifflin Kenedy in 1874 crossed Brahma cattle with his herds.

The Brahmas and their resulting mixed breeds were not only better beef cattle, but they also had a characteristic invaluable in Texas in those days: in a land full of cattle ticks, they were immune to tick fever.

In 1912, hard at improving the breed, the King Ranch crossed Brahma cattle (which come from India, and are also called zebu cattle) with English shorthorns. The Brahmas are able to resist disease and heat. The president of the King Ranch, Robert J. Kleberg, Jr., sought an animal able to turn south Texas grass into excellent beef. A dark red bull named Monkey resulted from the efforts. In the fourth-quarter 1972 magazine *Exxon USA*, Bern Keating told what happened next.

"Monkey was one of those genetic wonders all breeders hope for, a pre-potent sire able to stamp his fatherhood on generations of progeny. He became the founding sire of the Santa Gertrudis herd. In 1940, the Department of Agriculture recognized the Santa Gertrudis as a distinct breed, the only one ever developed in the western hemisphere and the first new breed of cattle developed anywhere in perhaps two centuries. So powerful is the Santa Gertrudis heritage that introduction of a single bull into a herd of common cows produces a pure Santa Gertrudis herd within four generations, if all cows are bred back to a purebred sire. The breed now flourishes in 49 states and many foreign countries."

Today the ranch produces gas and oil as well as cattle. On it live wild deer and wild turkeys, javelinas (small wild hogs—not the same as the razorbacks), and the West's pronghorn antelope. In addition, the ranch experiments with imported wild animals: the nilgai antelope from India, North Africa's Barbary sheep, Sardinia's mouflon sheep, Europe's red deer, India's axis deer, Africa's eland antelope (the size of a Santa Gertrudis bull), and Africa's impala. Not all of these have been successfully transplanted, but most have thrived.

Today on Texas 141, west of Kingsville, you can visit and drive through some of the over-a-million-acre King Ranch. You can see its wild animals from over the globe. You can see its stable of thoroughbred and quarter horses. You can also see, right here in their home where the first one of all was born, Santa Gertrudis cattle.

17

At home, things were difficult

THE ONLY thread was that made at home.

To sew you must have thread.

To weave cloth you must have thread.

When you have to make your thread, you really have to begin at the beginning.

I suppose it is impossible in the late 1970s to understand just how difficult and how primitive conditions were in the land where the trail began, Texas, just a little more than a hundred years ago.

The men who rode the cattle trail remembered the conditions of their times in their book, *The Trail Drivers of Texas*.

FOOD: W. M. Shannon was five years old when, in 1861, the Civil War began. "We lived on milk and butter, and wild game was plentiful," he said. "Prairie chickens, wild turkeys, and deer could easily be obtained." Both Shannon and A. E. Scheske of Gonzales hunted wild hogs (peccaries) or javelinas. There were coons, possums, and squirrels, and, in rivers, bass, catfish, and perch. If a man shot a rabbit, he could count on rabbit stew for breakfast. Although some people did not like them, the small, gray, white-tailed cottontail rabbits were good to eat to many others.

Near Castroville, citizens found a ready-made source of food: rattlesnake meat.

"But breadstuff," said Shannon, "was scarce. Sometimes we had biscuits on Sunday morning." Said W. T. (Bill) Brite of Leming, Texas: "Flour bread was unknown to me until about 1867, and the first biscuits I ever saw I thought were about the prettiest things in the world."

Said Jesse M. Kilgore, whose father had come to Texas in 1850: "I know I was a good-sized boy before we had any flour. My father owned the first cooking stove and buggy on the Cibolo. Our few neighbors came over to see our stove, and, of course, pronounced it a fake, but it was not long until the old skillet was cast aside and stoves were plentiful."

"For coffee," Shannon remembered, "we often used parched okra or canned corn." Other substitutes for coffee (which reached $1 a pound): parched meal bran and sweet potato peelings.

"We had plenty to eat," Joe Chapman recollected, "although we had to take our grain 50 miles to a mill to have it ground. We had no money, but did not need much, for we could not buy such things as coffee, sugar, soap, matches, pins, or anything to wear, and we were compelled to spin and weave all of the cloth that made our clothing. Rye, corn, wheat, okra seed, and roasted acorns were used as a substitute for coffee."

A cowboy, Joseph Cotulla, who had been born in Grosslelitch, a town sometimes in Poland (as it was when he was born), sometimes in Germany, described a meal in 1862, when he was eighteen. With Ben and John Slaughter, Lee Harris, two brothers named Forest, and a man named Moody, he was on his way to Mexico. The group stopped one night and had dinner with John Burleson. Said Cotulla: "The dinner was fine, the menu consisting of cornbread and clabber, and we enjoyed it immensely, for we were all very hungry and could have eaten the skillet the bread was cooked in." Cotulla in 1868 drove a herd to Abilene, which he called "a log cabin and three houses on Smoky River." He located in Nueces County, Texas, in 1868, and—with additional trips up to the railhead in 1873 and 1874—lived in Nueces over fifty years. The town of Cotulla, Texas, was named after the cowboy from Poland.

At home, gardens became common; food grown at home included lettuces, tomatoes (including little yellow ones), onions, carrots, radishes, corn, potatoes, black-eyed peas, cucumbers, okra, beets, cabbages, squash, and cauliflower. Grapes came from vines with branches so thick children swang from them.

People went to some lengths to get salt. John Craig, father of cowboy Hiram Craig, once hauled it home (to Sandtown, Washington County, Texas) from the King Ranch. The salt was loose in his wagon bed.

Matches at first did not exist, any more than did thread. Flint was used to strike a spark to light a fire. A stump in a field might be left burning to provide at any time a shovelful of coals.

One source of food, turkeys, also provided something else: you could pull feathers out of their backs and from the feathers make writing pens.

For those with no or little money—practically everybody— longhorns provided a food bargain. Beef, even if you bought it instead of raising or hunting your own, cost only four or five cents a pound.

And in the land where Joe Chapman said "we had no money," there was one advantage in hunting, growing, or scrounging your own food: "No weekly bills."

CLOTHING: Cowboy Hiram G. Craig remembered that his mother, Mrs. John Craig—Caroline—spun the thread that during the Civil War made the family's clothes. Hiram helped her. "I also peeled the blackjack bark and gathered the wild indigo to dye the cloth that made our clothes," he said.

Cowman C. H. Rust of San Angelo, Texas, remembered that a boy went around all summer in only a shirt. It was likely to be the only garment he had.

"My father killed many deer and dressed their hides," J. T. Hazelwood recalled, "and my mother made clothing of these for the boys and I remember very distinctly the 'coon-skin' caps and the 'home-made' shoes which were made for the children of our family, and which we were glad to get and took great pride in wearing." Hazelwood, who was reminiscing in 1916, said the boys had deerskin britches, buffalo coats, and buffalo shirts.

Said Henry Fest, a cowboy whose folks were from Alsace, France: People "burned their own lime, dressed the hides, tanned them with liveoak and mesquite bark; while the mother made the shoes for the family and for the neighborhood, made hats of coon skins, and still found time to spin the wool clipped from our flocks, which was woven into cloth on the neighborhood loom. The cloth was dyed with a weed called 'indigo' that grew in the creek nearby and my mother made it into clothes for herself and children.''

Both buffaloes and longhorns were processed for hides and tallow and this led to the establishment of processing plants that furthered the cattle business.

Eventually, cowboy boots were made in Texas. For years, and perhaps still, they were exported as genuine Texas cowboy boots. The cattle drivers and cowboys, meanwhile, obtained their boots from Boston and St. Louis.

SHELTER: In the 1860s, said J. T. Hazelwood, ''we lived in picket houses, covered with sod and dirt and the flooring was buffalo hides.''

In Texas' Red River country—in Montague, Cooke, Wise and Denton counties—said Joe Chapman, who was there, houses mostly were of logs, some with the bark still on. Cracks were ''clinked'' with sticks and mud. Floors were dirt. There was a big, wide chimney. ''Sometimes a family would get 'tony' and hew logs on one side and make a puncheon floor for their home and thus get into the 'upper class.' '' Families lived in their log houses only in summer; in the winter, the Indians chased them back into forts.

If a woman dropped and lost on that dirt floor what probably was her only good needle, it could take hours or days to find it. But the needle had to be found; there was no other, and without it the making of clothes would stop.

There were of course no indoor bathrooms, no toilets—water closets they were beginning to be called—not even wooden out-houses in most places. When you had to go, you went behind a bush or on the open prairie. Or you might enter a small grove or island of post-oak trees (east Texas) or live-oak trees (west Texas). These trees—they often had gray Spanish moss hanging from them —provided a little wood in a land without fuel, and some privacy where there was very little.

As has been the case with other advances in human customs, the first one-hole or two-hole privies or outhouses were ridiculed. In some towns the first citizens to erect them actually were accused of *indecency*. They filled a need, though, and they gradually caught on. But not at once. One town contained a dozen or so. During one holiday season, as a prank, all of them were taken and lined up around the public square.

TOWNS: Both counties and towns were rudimentary.

In many a county, the only town was the county-seat village. It might not be impressive. Frederick Law Olmsted rode through a county-seat town, he said, "without noticing it." It had consisted of six buildings.

Cowman Luther A. Lawhon recalled that the county seat eventually had "a rock or timber court house, which was rarely of two stories, and nearby, as an adjunct, a one-cell rock or lumber jail." Around the public square there would be a store (dry goods and grocers) and a saloon. A two-story hotel might be the most imposing building. Houses were around the center of the village or close by. A school and a simple church were within walking distance. The church might be used by many denominations. Frederick Law Olmsted asked what denomination a church was, and received the answer: "Oh, none in particular. They let anybody preach that comes along."

Around the village, grass and bluebonnets (in Texas they turn landscapes blue) and other wild flowers covered prairie, hill, and valley.

Everywhere around the village you could see cattle and horses grazing—except when, as the longhorns kept right on doing, they wandered away. When some calves belonging to Sam Maverick did wander off, young cattle (yearlings or two-year-olds) that strayed came to be called "mavericks." And one Englishman in Texas, Bill Hughes, complained of the vast area over which he had to look for his work oxen: "Just fancy," he wrote home, "having to hunt one's cattle for miles and miles around!"

SOCIAL LIFE: One of the scarcest things in Texas in the trail days was a chance for a woman to talk to someone—anyone at all. To have any kind of companionship, she often had to walk or ride, two on the back of a mule or horse, to whatever town she could reach—tiny though the town might be. In Fredericksburg, a town established in 1846–47, men had built Sunday houses—small, low houses that were used only over weekends for families that came in from the country.

From miles around people came to attend a religious revival or camp meeting. Families came in ox wagons. In the wagons they brought food, cooking utensils, bedding, children, and themselves. At the meeting site, the men put up small brush shanties. If they had the lumber, they might build a shed, covered with brush, for the audience.

Horses neighed, children cried, and people visited and talked. Everyone ate, and everyone drank from the same tin cup. Finally a horn would sound. Dogs or children, if possible, were quieted. People sat on boards or on the ground. The camp meeting began.

Usually at first the preacher called for a hymn. In time, he would warn the congregation about the wrath to come. Besides social life, better behavior—on the part of at least some—was fostered by the camp meeting.

LAW ENFORCEMENT: A policeman who was there summed up the situation. John Fitzhenry, born in Ireland in 1844, arrived in San Antonio in 1864. He was to be a policeman there for fifty years, from 1871 to 1921. "A cow town of 8,000 souls," he said San Antonio was when he arrived. "It was so wild in those days we couldn't wear uniforms. The six-day policeman wore the clothes of a civilian. If we had worn uniforms of the law there would have been a shooting as soon as we came in sight. A policeman didn't make an arrest, either, as he does today. None of the boys in those days would have stood while a warrant was being read to him. We had to throw them down and tie them and then read the warrants for their arrest." San Antonio, he said, was a rendezvous for bandits; farther west, there were Indians with only scouts and soldiers among them. The only railroad lines in Texas, he said. were short ones from Bryan to the coast and from Victoria to Port Lavaca. In his long career in the San Antonio police, Fitzhenry never shot a man nor was he himself shot.

TRANSPORTATION: The land where the trail began was to revolutionize transportation. When the longhorns were being rounded up and fed into the trail to Abilene, there was a sign of things to come. Not far from where Beaumont is today, in east Texas, and where some longhorns for the trail were captured, there was a place called Sour Lake where there was "a fountain of lemonade." The queer-tasting water, which people drank for their health, had in it natural gas. Petroleum seeped up in nearby bogs. A pond, Sour Lake also contained on its banks and bottom sulfur which would be a key element in the age of chemistry.

Sour Lake was also an indication of the Texas oil that one day would provide fuel and lubrication to make possible automobiles and airplanes and make more efficient ships and locomotives, and of the oil and gas that would provide fuel for cooking, the heating of homes, office buildings, and factories, and power for electric generators.

But all that, in the late 1860s, was far ahead. At that time, trains went out to west Texas (El Paso), New Mexico (Santa Fe), and California. These were wagon trains—not railroad trains. At two to six miles an hour, they took a month to make a round trip between Austin and Houston.

Along with a train of wagons to California, there might be driven several hundred cattle.

Wheels—the ox wagons had solid ones—were sawed by hand from sweet-gum logs. Hiram Craig remembered that his father John's wagon once broke an axle—out back of beyond. John with only an axe chopped down a hickory tree and hewed out an axle. He rode horseback till he found a settler and borrowed an auger to bore the necessary holes in the axle. He completely repaired the wagon, out there in the wilderness, and made the wagon so strong and satisfactory that he could drive it to where he could load it with cotton, take the cotton to its destination, and then return home.

Like wagon wheels and thread, farm implements—including plows—were made by hand. "During the early days in Texas," said cowman W. F. Cude, "there were no farming implements. Plow lines were cut out of rawhide. Horse collars were made from shucks."

At the time when Texas was an independent country, a farmer, Daniel Hartzo, put down a few lines that showed how many things a man had to make himself. From his diary:

November 22, 1841, I maid [made] a wheel. . . .
November 29 . . . maid a coffin. . . .

December 1 . . . maid a reel . . .
January 8, 1842 . . . hude [hewed] puncheons.
February 3, grained deer skins . . .
April 7, maid a chern [churn].
July 25, maid a pr. [pair] of shoes.

Roads—or trails—where trees existed were indicated by marked trees. Where there were no trees, a trail might be marked by a single plow furrow in the ground, or it might be only a general direction to travel.

A road was considered finished, and ready for use, if stumps in it were no more than a foot high.

In rainy weather, mud bogged down wagons, carts, stagecoaches, horses, mules and oxen—even the fourteen oxen that hauled a large, loaded freight wagon. Often men had to walk and lead their animals. Even stagecoach passengers had to walk.

Other road barriers were the thickets and quicksands beside unbridged rivers. It took fair weather to enable a coach to cover five to eight miles an hour, and reach California from Texas in a month.

In an unexplored land of long distances and almost unmarked trails, transportation was usually four-footed, and often was a horse. A horse meant life and no horse meant death. Not everyone was as lucky, when a horse was desperately needed, as one woman whose cattle drifted away. She was desperate for something to ride. She roped a wild-looking mustang on the prairie, vaulted onto it, and rode bareback after the cattle far away over the wide land.

Horses were so vital that the mounted Plains Indians stole them with such frequency that Texas farmers had to use oxen to draw wagons or plows. Others besides Indians yielded to the temptation to steal horses. And to take a man's horse was to put him afoot in a land where water holes or rivers were tens of miles apart. And it was to put him afoot in a land of horseback Indians who could cut him down easily.

Something had to be done. Horse thieves were hanged. Said Hiram Craig, "A strong dose of hemp would always tend to kind of 'deaden' the desire to steal."

When a horse thief was caught, he might be placed on a horse, the loop of the rope put around his neck, and the horse driven from under him. Courtesy was extended to the guest of honor at such a necktie party. A condemned man was allowed a few last words. One horse thief regretted that, for his hanging, he was forced to "sit on this sorry old hoss, instead of that fine critter I stole."

18

Men on horseback ride a long way

AT FIRST the longhorns selected for the journey north were the biggest and oldest steers, five to seven years old. That is, those ready for the meat market. All ages of cattle were at times taken up the trail, including cows and one- and two-year-olds to be fattened on grass on ranches up north.

The trail animals had to be gathered from those a cowman owned, or from the wild. A roundup, lasting several days to several weeks, gathered the cattle an owner would send. To make up a herd for the trail, cattle of other owners were likely to be added. They would have different brands from the cattle of the original owner, who himself might use several different brands. Therefore, all the animals in a trail herd would be "road-branded": They would be run through a chute, and lightly branded, on side hip or shoulder, with a slash or bar.

Every longhorn was as different in personality from all other longhorns as it was different in color or in its horns. "After a herd is thrown on the trail," said San Antonio's John G. Jacobs, "cattle of different temperament take their different places in the herd while traveling—they, like men, have their individuality."

One animal, either a steer or a cow, would take the lead and would lead the herd the entire way. "Others follow and keep their places. Then comes the middle and principal part of the herd, and what is called the drags, and they are drags from the day they leave the ranch to the end of the drive: When watering and grazing they mix and mingle but when thrown back on the trail each division finds its respective place." Each animal had its own position in the herd and stayed there all the way.

The lead animal meant a greal deal—how much Col. D. H. Snyder had learned. Driving cattle to the southern states east of Texas, during the War Between the States, he had to get them across the widest river of the cattle trails, the Mississippi.

His lead steers plunged right in.

The others followed.

The cattle were captured anywhere in Texas. From hundreds of starting points, from hundreds of remote locations, men fed cattle into the great drives north.

In the cactus and mesquite and yucca and sagebrush chaparral (thick brush) and roadrunner country south and west of San Antonio, between that frontier town and the subtropical hot-and-humid Gulf of Mexico coast—here, halfway between the equator and the Arctic Circle—and at hundreds of other starting points, the longhorns were rounded up.

S. B. Brite of Pleasanton, Texas, was one cowboy who started in the cactus-covered country south and west of San Antonio. What happened to him happened to others. He was dumped by his horse in the middle of cactus—prickly pear. "When the boys pulled me out of that bush they found that my jacket was nailed to my back as securely as if the job had been done with six-penny nails."

From as far southwest as the streets of Laredo, the cowboy and his cows plodded not only through cactus but through dozens of fragrant and colorful tropical plants: the palmettos with their fan-shaped leaves, date palms, huisache, mulberry, pomegranate, daisies, bluebonnets, and where people had flower gardens, ligustrum, oleanders, bougainvilleas, roses, and geraniums.

Through the thinly populated length of Texas the cattle walked, ten to fifteen miles a day, along what became the most heavily pounded trail in history.

"From the Rio Grande," which is the border between Texas

and Mexico," said cowman John G. Jacobs, "to the Red River, which is the north line of Texas, going over the cattle trail is a distance of about 600 miles, as it took cattle leaving the southern part of the states from six weeks to two months to cross the northern border of Texas."

Texas at its longest extends 801 miles from south to north, 773 miles east to west. The cattle plodded diagonally across a state that occupies one-twelfth of the entire area of the forty-eight continental United States. They crossed a state larger in area than the combined areas of Illinois plus Ohio plus Pennsylvania plus New Jersey plus New York plus New England. The cattle walked from a desertlike land of palms and cactuses and catclaws and century plants that bloom every twenty years on past cypresses and oaks and pines and pecan trees that, in groves, often indicated a river. They walked from the Rio Grande—today its valley is full of oranges, grapefruit, limes, and lemons—on through north Texas where the winters are as cold as they are in central Illinois and where twelve-inch-deep snowfalls are not uncommon. Said a verse by an unknown traveler:

> The sun has riz, the sun has set,
> But here we is, in Texas yet.

A cattle herd, grazing as it moved northward slowly at one to two miles an hour, would eat the grass over a wide band. A new trail therefore was not a single narrow path. It was nothing like a footpath, a sidewalk, a narrow city street, or even a railroad right-of-way. It was a wide swath. Cattle trails, some of them, might be narrow, fifty to one hundred yards wide. But where a herd grazed leisurely, or where it reached a river and spread out to drink, a trail might spread from one mile to two miles wide.

A man who started out with cattle in the early days of the trail, and who stayed with it for fifty years, George Saunders, explained the route—or log, as it was called—of the trail. He said the trail began at the Rio Grande, in Texas' Cameron County. That's at the very southern tip of Texas, on the Gulf of Mexico, snuggling up against Mexico. In Cameron County are Brownsville and Port Isabel. They compete with Key West, Florida, for the title of most southern point of the United States. Cowmen of the 1860s found a hotel near Brownsville: a ship that had been driven by a storm onto the beach.

In the 1860s, counties—not towns—were the organized units. They were what the trail drivers referred to, rather than the few tiny towns or cities that existed.

After leaving Cameron County, said Saunders, the trail ran through Williamson County, then Hidalgo County (today the town of Edinburg is in it), Brooks (Falfurrias is in it), Jim Wells (Alice is in it), and Live Oak County, where the herds crossed the Nueces River.

A branch of the trail ran parallel to the one through Hidalgo, Brooks, Jim Wells, and Live Oak counties. On this branch the cattle might instead walk through Kenedy County, Kleberg County (home of Kingsville and the King Ranch), Nueces County, and San Patricio County. Kenedy and Kleberg are south of the city of Corpus Christi, between Brownsville and Corpus. Nueces County contains Corpus. San Patricio is just to the north.

In these counties, near or on the shore of the Gulf of Mexico, the cowboy's eyes and nose found subtropical plants, crepe (or crape) myrtle, oleanders, poinsettias, hibiscus, hydrangeas, jasmines, azaleas, banana trees.

Offshore of these counties, between Brownsville and Corpus Christi, lies 113-mile-long Padre Island, largest of today's U.S. National Seashores, with its fine white sands for swimmers, its surf, and occasional relics (pieces of eight) from Spanish treasure ships from the era when the Spanish were introducing longhorns and horses into Texas. Padre Island was named after Padre (Father) Nicholas Belli, who reached it in 1800, at the height of the Spanish Empire, about twenty years before Mexico (including Texas) revolted and won freedom from Spain.

The trail, Saunders said, next ran through Bee County (Beeville), Goliad, Karnes (home of Karnes City), Wilson, Gonzales, and Guadalupe (both slightly west of San Antonio).

On the trail went to Caldwell (the county contains Lockhart, where dozens of herds to be driven up the trail originated), Hays, Travis (Austin, where many herds crossed the Colorado River), Williamson (which contains Georgetown), Bell, Falls, Bosque, McLennan (Waco and the Brazos River to cross), Hill (Hillsboro), Johnson (Cleburne), Tarrant (home of Forth Worth, a city built by the cattlemen that years ago nicknamed itself "where the west begins"). Fort Worth at the time was described by C. H. Rust: "Just a little burg on the bluff where the panther lay down and died."

Next came Denton County (Denton) or Wise County (Bridgeport), Cooke (Gainesville) or Montague (Bowie, the name of Robert Bowie, likely inventor of the Bowie knife, and his brother Jim, killed at the Alamo). In either Cooke or Montague County, the cattle reached the Red River, the northern border of Texas. The Red River was the Rio Rojo of the Spaniards. It was the farthest south of all the principal tributaries of the Mississippi. This was a river that, after coursing through a canyon in the Texas Panhandle, next ran through rich prairies in a red clay soil that gave it its name. It eventually carries fallen trees and debris through a land of bayous and swamps in Louisiana and reaches the Atchafalaya River and the Mississippi River near the border of the state of Mississippi.

Cooke and Montague counties are just west of today's Lake Texoma, on the Red River (today—but not in cattle-trail days—one of the United States' largest man-made lakes, with a shoreline fifty miles long). Not far away, at Denison, Texas, in the last days of the cattle trail after 1890, a barefoot boy toddled through his first years. Although most of the herds were then being driven to the westward, the lad must have seen some of the longhorns and their drivers. The small boy was Dwight David Eisenhower.

Altogether, the cattle walked through thirty-one counties to reach Texas' northern border.

In the 1870s, George Saunders said, farmers settling in Texas caused the trail in Texas to be moved farther west. It then ran through Wilson County, Bexar (San Antonio), Kendall, Kerr (Kerrville), Kimble, Menard, Concho, McCulloch (where the Colorado River was reached and crossed), Coleman, Callahan, Shackelford, Throckmorton, Baylor, and Wilbarger counties to a crossing on the Red River where a man named Doan built a trading post, Doan's Store.

Still later, the longhorns coming up from the southern part of Texas quit the original trail in San Patricio County (near Corpus Christi) and went through the counties of Live Oak, McMullen, La Salle (named after the French explorer who had landed in Texas in 1685—with cattle), Dimmit, Zavala, Uvalde, Edwards, then to

Kimble where they joined the western trail described in the previous paragraph to the Red River and Doan's Store.

The store was near where the Red River ceases to be the Texas-Oklahoma boundary and enters the Panhandle of Texas, at a place called Doan's Crossing.

C. F. Doan had established a home there, plus a store to outfit cowmen for going up the trail. He had pens for the cattle. He had furnaces so the cattle might be road-branded.

His first home, Doan said, "was made of pickets with a dirt roof and floor of the same material." The original furniture was made with an axe and a saw. "The first winter we had no door but a buffalo robe did service against the northers."

Doan's family sat around a huge fireplace, along with cowboys, Indians, and buffalo hunters. "The warmest spot," said Doan, "was the one reserved for the baby and (holding the baby) proved to be a much coveted job."

Doan's Store—at first it was the other end of his home—was the last chance for outfits to stock up for the trail. The store sold cartridges, Stetson hats, Winchesters, canned goods, sow bosom, bacon and flour in carload (or chuckwagon) lots. It got its food supplies from nearby Texas towns, Denison, Sherman, Gainesville, and Wichita Falls.

An adobe store and later a frame store were built. Log cabins were added as homes. Doan's Crossing grew in size.

At a blacksmith shop near Doan's Store, the horses were shod for the trail. The cattle required no iron-or-steel horseshoes; their strong, tough hoofs could take the beating of the trail. The blacksmith might possess other skills. He might cure a horse's lameness, or treat equine diseases, in those days before veterinarians.

After a post office was established, Doan was the first postmaster. Said he: "The last mail for the trail drivers before a herd started to Kansas was delivered here. Many a sweetheart down the trail remembered her letter bearing the postmark of Doan's, and many a cowboy asked self-consciously if there was any mail for him while his face turned a beet red when a dainty missive was handed him."

"Some herds," said Saunders, "left the main trail in Wilson County, passed through Bexar County, via San Antonio, to get supplies, then through Comal County, intersecting the main trail in

Hays or Caldwell Counties. All of these trails zigzagged and touched lots of adjoining counties not mentioned in my log."

He explained: "Herds starting from ranches in all parts of the state would intersect the nearest of these northern trails, coming in from both sides and I doubt if there is a county in the state that did not have a herd traverse some part of it during trail days"

Many a herd from many parts of Texas entered the Indian Territory, from Montague County, by the Red River Crossing. This was near today's Fleetwood, Oklahoma, about seven miles downstream from today's Terral, Oklahoma; almost due east of Wichita Falls, Texas; and not far from Lake Texoma and Dwight Eisenhower's earliest home.

Once across the Red River, the cowmen and cattle went up the trail through the Indian Territory—Oklahoma today. Oklahoma still contains more Indians than any other state.

Across the Red River, the cowboy might at first cross the Choctaw Nation and then the six-million-acre Cherokee Nation. Or, to the east, he might go through the Chickasaw Nation, or the Sac and Fox Agency.

Next, farther north, were the Kiowas, aggressive but not overly troublesome. Then came the Osages, tall and powerful, of Sioux stock. "Like the other Plains Indians," writes Edward Everett Dale, "they owned many horses, hunted buffalo, and lived in round tepees of buffalo skin. Then came the Cheyennes and the Arapahoes, of Algonquin stock, both horse Indians, counting their wealth in many ponies."

The Osages and the Indians of Algonquin background could be called buffalo Indians, so dependent were they on the buffalo. Their tepees were only among the things they obtained from buffaloes. They lived on buffaloes for food and clothing (robes and moccasins). From buffalo horns they made spoons, cups, and ladles. Buffalo bones became needles. Buffalo sinews became thread.

Near the Cimarron River, northern Oklahoma–southern Kansas, the cowboy was in the country of the Comanches, the warlike riders who, further west, had attacked Oliver Loving and Bill Wilson in 1867. This desolate part of the Nations had, along with Comanches, cattle- and horse-thieves. The cowboy called it by the name he sometimes used for all the Indian Territory, No Man's Land.

In Oklahoma there were no counties organized as there were in Texas. The cowboys remembered the route by the rivers they had to cross.

"From Red River to Abilene, Kansas," said George Saunders, "as I remember the streams were:

"The Big and Little Washita.

"Turkey Creek.

"South and North Canadian [Oklahoma City is on the north branch of the Canadian].

"Cimarron."

In northernmost Indian Territory, near the southern Kansas border, there was a neutral strip—a twenty-mile-wide band of land. The Indians might harass the herds across Indian Territory, across the neutral strip, across the Cimarron River, all the way to Abilene, Kansas, two or three months after the start of a drive.

In Kansas, as in Indian Territory, streams were the signposts. According to Saunders, they were:

"Pond Creek.

"Salt fork of the Arkansas.

"North fork of the Arkansas at Wichita, Kansas."

From there the trail went through Newton.

"The next stream was the Smoky River, on which was located Abilene, Kansas, the great cattle market at that time."

Caldwell, in Sumner County, Kansas, was, cowman C. S. Broadbent said, "one of the chief herd rendezvous after running the gauntlet of the Indian Territory." From Caldwell, the trail led north through Sumner County to Wichita, Newton, and Abilene—the route George Saunders outlined.

It was a slow walk for the cattle all the way. "The average drive in a day," said C. H. Rust, "was eight to ten or twelve miles and the time on the trail was from sixty to ninety days from points in Texas to Abilene or Newton or Ellsworth in Kansas."

At any one of these towns, or others, the end of a drive might be reached: at the farthest-west tip of the track of one of the then-building brand-new U.S. railroads. The trains, from the start, hauled cattle to slaughterhouses and to Eastern markets to feed the crowded northeast United States. Their small, clumsy, crude, puffing locomotives, aside from riverboats driven by steam, were the first mechanical transportation the cowman—or for that matter, any Americans—ever saw.

Almost the whole midcontinent was covered with grass—grass in the springtime knee-high or higher, the height of a man, the height of a man on horseback. A "sea of grass," it would be called later by novelist Conrad Richter—rich, edible grass that, besides the buffalo, fed hordes of pronghorn antelopes, jackrabbits, and prairie dogs. The jackrabbits and prairie dogs, says Edward Everett Dale, sometimes "ate more herbage than did the larger animals." There were, in Texas alone, 550 different grasses of a total of 1,100 to 1,200 in the United States. The grass kept cattle—and horses—well fed up the trail, and made other food unnecessary. This vast pasture land, sometimes sprinkled with wild flowers—sunflowers, white and yellow daisies, Indian paintbrush, verbenas, phlox, 4,000 different flowers in Texas, others to the north—reached to the Rocky Mountains in the west, and to Canada in the north. In the springtime, there were the bluebonnets of Texas; March is their big month. They had a very special origin. The legend is that a little girl, hoping that a long drought would end, and wishing that her brothers and sisters and parents would be helped, and perhaps would not go hungry, sacrificed her doll. She burned the doll, probably her only toy, her only possession. Next day, the color of the doll's bonnet—blue—covered the ground. One version is that the youngster was an Indian girl and the doll's bonnet (or dress) was of bluejay feathers.

The whole area, Texas to Canada, to the Rockies, was unfenced; open, open range; nothing stopped the longhorns. "There were," said cowman E. P. Byler, "no fences—the range was open from the Gulf of Mexico to North Dakota, as far as I went."

The sea of grass would mean that the trail throughout its history would keep growing longer. When cowmen had learned that young cattle could fatten on the grass of northwestern states, the steers were driven on past Kansas. Ranches were established. Farther and farther the longhorns walked on their capable, long legs: to Colorado, Nebraska, Wyoming, the Dakotas. "Some of the herds," said John Jacobs, "were headed for Montana and often snow would be flying by the time they reached their destination."

On to the Bow River, Alberta, Canada—in the range around Calgary, between Winnipeg and Vancouver, near the foothills of the Rocky Mountains—went the cattle. Here, nine months or more from home in Texas, in the frigid northern winter, a cowboy might shiver in his homemade cotton shirt and trousers or under his cotton blankets. Here the cattle, in more winters than one, starved and froze amid the winds and cold and the piling, drifting snow of the blizzards of the North.

But more of the cattle would survive the winter and would grow fatter on the grass that grew wild all the way to Canada.

All the way the longhorns walked. Other superior cattle would replace the longhorn, but none would have its long legs and strong hoofs, and no other ever would be trailed to any extent. Said W. E. Cureton, who came out of the Ozark mountains of Arkansas to be in cattle raising over sixty years: "I honor the old longhorn; he was able to furnish his own transportation to all the markets before the advent of the railroads."

For days or weeks the men on horseback with the cattle would see no sign of human habitation; the men rode through a woman-less land where, if a woman ever was observed, the event would be remembered in full detail, told over and over at a dozen campfires, and handed down by word of mouth, and sometimes in writing to become a legend of the trail.

All the way to its northernmost points, inside Canada, the trail always was short of women. The cattle country was a "he country in pants." The absence of women made the cattle drives and the trail seem even longer than they were. The trail, from Texas into Canada, took from spring to the next winter to cover, on horse-back, over a route up to 2,000 miles long, the first 600 of them through Texas. The rest ran through the Indian Nations, and un-settled parts of Kansas and other states or territories. At all times, and at most all places, the trail lay through wild, rugged country, and was beset by Indians, rustlers, and bad weather—lightning, thunder, the worst hailstorms in North America, pelting rains that flooded the rivers and made crossing them hazardous (the same rains that grew the grass the longhorns and horses ate all the way up the trail). For the slow, weary route with all these troubles, and almost no women, the cowboy had a short and simple name. I have never seen the name on a map, but the cowboy often used it in talking. The name told how he felt about the trail and what it meant to him.

He called it the Long Trail.

19

The men on the trail were boys

LIKE NINETEEN-YEAR-OLD Jim Daugherty, he was in his teens or early twenties, usually, the cowman who drove the cattle north, and who came up with the name for the route he followed, the Long Trail.

At seventeen, Hiram Craig was on the trail to start 1,500 to 2,000 steers north toward Kansas. He had tried before. At age fourteen, already blind in one eye from meningitis, he had run away from home to become a cowboy. His brother had caught him and brought him home.

From the beginning, the cattle driver had a name for himself, too, one that would stick.

The cowboy.

"The cowboys, or cow-punchers, sometimes called waddies," said one of them, George W. Saunders of San Antonio, "were men who did all kinds of ranch and trail work with cattle."

Other names, more or less synonymous, by which a cowboy might call himself: a cowman, a hand, a cowhand, a cow driver, a cow herder, a screw, a buckaroo, and a trail driver or drover.

A tenderfoot cowboy might be called an Arbuckle. There were trading stamps in those days—Arbuckle stamps—and a tenderfoot cowboy could supposedly be bought for the trading stamps that people received as premiums.

One reason why the cowboys were so young was that the boy in Texas of a hundred years ago wanted to go up the trail—just as other lads have wanted to be Pony Express riders (many of them, incidentally, afterward became cowboys), soldiers, sailors, aviators, firemen, astronauts. Said J. R. Humphries of Yoakum, Texas: ". . . the great ruling ambition was to become a cowboy." Said Charlie Barsley: "The dream of my life was to go up the trail, and the dream of my life was realized in 1883 [he was sixteen] when I went with John and Bill Blocker. Louis Deets was foreman."

"I worked as a cowboy," said Claude Hudspeth of El Paso, Texas, "from the time I could sit in the saddle and whirl a lasso."

Branch Isbell was twelve, in Sumter County, Alabama, when Confederate soldiers in 1863 drove a herd of 200 Texas cattle through. For the next eight years he wanted to become a cowboy, and, in 1871, at age twenty, he would make his first drive up the Long Trail.

When L. B. Anderson was small his family had arrived in Texas from Mississippi in a mule-drawn buggy. His mother had made him wear a sunbonnet against the sun on his neck like a burning iron. He kept throwing it off. She cut out two holes in the sunbonnet, pulled his hair through, and tied it. Anderson said he made his entrance into Texas "looking like a girl but feeling every inch a man."

At twenty, Anderson in 1869 delivered oxen to Eugene Millett, and his brothers, Alonzo and Hie.

"I told my father," said Anderson, "I wanted to go with the herd. He very reluctantly gave his consent."

Anderson's dad gave him a $10 gold piece for the trip. His mother sewed it into his trousers. Anderson went up the trail with the oxen and cattle. He returned home—his family was living at Seguin, Texas—with the $10 gold piece and gave it back to his father.

Young Anderson had known what he wanted when he went up the trail. "I drove every trail," he said, "from the Gulf of Mexico to the Dakotas and Montana. . . . The places I most often delivered cattle to were Baxter Springs, Great Bend, Newton, Abilene, Ellsworth and Dodge City, Kansas; Ogallala and Red Cloud Agency,

Nebraska; Fort Petterman, Wyoming; and Dan Holden's ranch in Colorado on Chug River."

He said: "I went twice as a hand . . . sixteen times as boss of the herd." Anderson kept going up the trail till 1887, near the end of the great days of cattle driving.

When a farm lad, W. B. Hardeman was heading for church one Sunday. He ran into Tom Baylor. Baylor previously had written and asked young Hardeman if he wanted to go up the trail. "Are you going?" Baylor asked the boy. The answer: "Yes." Said Tom Baylor that Sunday morning: "Well, you have no time to go to church." He took Hardeman to the chuck wagon and remuda, six miles away.

That was how W. B. Hardeman came to start up the Long Trail dressed as few cowboys, before or after him: in a white shirt, collar, and tie. Later he commented: "You can imagine how green I was."

Partly because he was so young, the cowboy needed his sleep. Lack of rest was named as the greatest difficulty of the Long Trail by many a cowboy. On his first trip up the trail W. B. Hardeman learned what lack of sleep was. "I was just a farmer boy," he said. "I was always left to hold the cattle." One day, when the cattle were chomping green, ten-inch grass, he got off his horse, sat in the shade, and went to sleep. "The first thing I knew Tom Baylor was waking me." Hardeman's conscience troubled him; "I have gone to sleep on guard. I had just as well put my hand in Colonel Ellison's pocket and take his money." He never got off his horse again —when on duty. "Though I have seen the time when I would have given five dollars for one-half-hour's sleep. I would even put tobacco in my eyes to keep awake."

One cowboy, Joe Buckner, became so tired he was heard to say: "I am going to Greenland where the nights are six months long, and I ain't a-going to get up until ten o'clock the next day."

The owner of the herd was the big boss. The head of the men on a drive was the boss or trail boss or boss of the herd. His No. 1 helper was the right-hand man, or the straw boss, or the top screw, or top waddy.

The cowboy might be one of the two men riding, on each side, near the front of the herd. "At the point" was the most responsible position, guiding the herd. Or he might be one of two swing men, at either side a third of a mile back, where the herd would bend as it turned. Some way behind them were two more men on the left and right flank. Or—often the youngest or newest hand, perhaps an Arbuckle—he might be at the rear of the herd, choking in the dust of anywhere from 100 to 3,000 cattle, eating dirt for three or four months or longer all the way to Kansas or wherever, forever rounding up the dregs, the sore-backs, the lame cattle. Even the boy, often fourteen to sixteen years old, in charge of the outfit's horses (four to ten for each rider) was called a cowboy.

Whenever he rode on the cattle drives, the cowboy at first did not know where he was going. He had a rough idea: north. He improvised a sort of compass—or at least a signpost—from his chuckwagon. That useful vehicle, drawn by four oxen or four mules, had spread in popularity ever since Charles Goodnight had invented it in west Texas.

In the mapless, roadless, largely railroadless, often unexplored middle of the North American continent, the cowboy after dark would point the tongue of the chuckwagon at Polaris, the north star, the sailors' star that hardly changes position. At daybreak, the cowboy would move out the herd in the direction the wagon tongue pointed. The wagon tongue saved him on mornings that were cloudy or overcast.

He hitched his wagon to a star.

The cowboy was tough and muscular. He survived and thrived in the harsh, sunbaked, sometimes treeless land he found in Texas. He was lean and wiry, smaller and lighter than many other men. A heavy man was hard on a horse.

He could cope; he could take care of himself. He could wash his clothes, his bed blankets, his saddle blankets. He could chop wood (where he could find it) or collect dry dung (cattle or buffalo) for a fire and then if necessary cook his own meals. Besides driving a herd on the Long Trail, he could brand, build a corral, round up cattle from a wide territory, and, by a rope attached to his saddle horn, he could pull a mired steer from the mud.

He could pour tobacco onto a piece of rice paper lying flat on his thigh and roll a cigarette—when he was on the back of a moving, sometimes violently moving, horse.

In the early days of driving cattle, his clothes consisted of one pair of pants, several shirts, maybe a vest whose pockets held his tobacco and perhaps a gun, and as an overcoat, raincoat, and blanket, a Confederate army coat or cape.

He wore a black or brown low-crowned hat—the Stetson. The son of a Philadelphia hatter, John B. Stetson in the 1860s had gone out west to try to cure his tuberculosis. He got cold, and he came up with a rabbit-skin felt hat that protected a man's head against cold—and also against hail, rain, wind, and sun. A cord under the chin or across the back of the neck held it on. The Texas Rangers were among the first to wear the Stetson. The cowboy adopted it.

He used it to carry water for his horse, to give himself a drink, to fan a campfire into a blaze, to beat out a prairie fire, as a pillow, for signaling, and as a sunshade. He paid two to six months' wages for a fine, soft, smooth, felt Stetson. Once he had it, he ate with it on, and he danced with his girl with it on. He creased it according to where he came from: Montana peak, Texas peak, etc.

John B. Stetson died, at seventy-six, in 1906. His factory at Philadelphia had made as many as four million Stetsons a year.

If he had a yellow slicker, the cowboy laid it down when he had to sleep on wet ground. He rolled up in it his eating utensils and other possessions. He waved it in the face of lead cattle in a stampede. He might even wear it himself, but probably he would first get soaked by rain. He put it on, said a cowman, when he was "darn sure the rain's plumb wet and is going to hang on for a few hours."

Loosely around his neck, knotted, the cowboy wore a large cotton or, preferably, silk handkerchief, never white (white would be seen by Indians for a long distance), but blue or black or (usually) red: a bandana. If he were at the rear of a herd, he tied it around his cheeks, mouth, and nose, exactly like a holdup man, to keep out the dust. In the winter, it was some protection against sleet, snow, and wind. It was a face towel, a blindfold for horse or calf, a bind to tie a calf's feet together, and a potholder to hold a smoking-hot branding iron. The cowboy strained muddy water through his bandana (or bandanna). He dried dishes with it.

He even sometimes used it as a handkerchief to wipe off his sweat.

That single pair of pants was all cowboy Jim Dobie had on the trail. One morning, L. S. Boatright remembered, a pitching bronco hung Dobie's pants onto the pommel of the saddle. They became rags. Said Boatright: "I gave him a pair to relieve his distress."

The cowboy's pants and shirts were of a long-wearing material, denim. Denim had a history almost as long as that of the longhorns themselves. Way back in the 1500s, a blue cotton cloth had been made in Nîmes, France, and called *serge de Nîmes*. It was tough; in 1492, Columbus may have used it as sails on his ship, the *Santa Maria*. About that time men in Dhunga, India—India was reached by European sailors soon after Columbus' first trip—were making denim into work pants, or dungarees. England imported the cloth, also about the same time, and shortened its name to denim. A German immigrant to the United States, Levi Strauss, brought denim to America, and tried in 1849 to sell it to California gold miners—for tents. Instead, they put it into pants. Levi's and denim became the work clothes of the West, and its jeans. The word "jeans" is from the port of Genoa, *Gênes* in French, where Columbus had come from.

Americans throughout their history have had fine tools—the frontiersman's axe, for instance. The tools of the cowboy—like his longhorns—were largely from Mexico. They were splendid for their purposes—again like his longhorns. The saddle had a horn, or pommel, that stuck up in the front of the saddle and therefore in front of the cowboy, and he used it to hang his rope, also called his twine, his lariat, or his lasso. The rope, thirty to forty feet long, was of rawhide (Mexican) or hemp (American).

The saddle had a cinch—a leather belt around the horse. A cowboy tightened the cinch as you tighten your belt.

The horse's reins usually were not joined or tied together behind the horse's neck; thus there was no loop to catch on a bush or branch or entangle the cowboy. When a cowboy dropped his reins onto the ground, a well-trained horse would stand still—and not wander.

Chaps, full-length leather leg coverings, were worn over trousers to prevent scratches from scrub, cactus, or the thorny chaparral.

A cowboy usually rode with his foot back all the way to the high heels of his boots in his stirrups—stirrups of wood or metal, most often of wood bent to shape and bolted at the top. High-heeled boots and Spanish steel spurs he had from the start. To mount, the cowboy put his left foot into the stirrup on his horse's left side, and swung himself up. The Plains Indian mounted from his horse's right.

By today's standards, the cowboy had little education. "My education," said Claude Hudspeth, "consists of three months in a log cabin on the banks of the Medina, where I thoroughly mastered the contents of Webster's Blue-back speller and reader combined. This constitutes the curriculum and extent of my literary studies."

Said J. B. Pumphrey of Taylor, Texas: "The Blue-back Speller and Dog-wood Switch were considered the principal necessities for [a] boy's education."

The cowboy read—at least many cowboys did. The covers were worn off and the pages were thumbed into tatters on any printed material that was found in the land of the Long Trail: Shakespeare, *Paradise Lost,* Dante's *Divine Comedy,* collections of poetry, Horatio Alger, Jules Verne, or the love stories of the day.

The cowboys themselves left a thick book (well over 1,000 pages) of their memoirs, *The Trail Drivers of Texas.* No other migration, not that of the covered wagons west, nor that of John Smith's first colonists in Virginia, nor that of the Pilgrims, left anything like this book. It is the main source of information on the cowboy—the cowboy's horse's mouth. I have again and again used it for information. I quote, whenever I can, from the book, because in it the cowboys tell their own story in their own words.

Like Branch Isbell and L. B. Anderson, the cowboy was generally a new arrival into Texas. He has been called a Texan, by later generations, and this in his outlook the cowboy certainly was. That outlook was shaped by vast distances (one cowboy said you had to look twice to take them in). By blazing blue skies (over a hundred years ago, Mrs. Vielé called them "calm, blue sunlit heavens"; today novelist A. B. Guthrie, Jr., calls them "the big sky"). By blue northers (cold spells of winter). By the orange or pink or flashing-red sunsets that gave the Southwest the name Sunset Land. And the cowboy's outlook was shaped because he was under a Texas moon, a moon full, round, and beautiful, a moon that rose at night among big and bright stars. A moon that shed a mysterious glow, almost like daylight, a glow that regularly set off raids by Indians. The cowboy, however, arrived in Texas from all over North America—and from all over the world.

E. C. Abbott, a cowboy who was nicknamed Teddy Blue, said: "I was born at Cranwich Hall, Cranwich, County of Norfolk, England." He was "the poorest, sickliest kid you ever saw." At ten, Teddy made a trip up the trail from Texas to Nebraska with a herd belonging to his father. A doctor told him to remain "in the open air." He did—all his life, on the trail. "If I hadn't have been a cowpuncher," he said, "I never could have growed up."

Capt. William Carroll McAdams, who had made very early drives up the trail, came from Tennessee. His father, Douglas, from Scotland, had built the first macadamized road in the United States. That was a road covered with small stones bound together with tar or something else—the predecessor of paving.

George May was born in Scotland. F. Cornelius explained: "I was born in Horsfeld, Germany, on the 2nd day of December, 1850." He came by sailing ship to New Orleans. The parents of Henry Fest, who first went up the trail at age fifteen, were from Alsace, France; they took three months to cross the ocean and get to Indianola, Texas.

England, Ireland, Wales, Belgium, Holland, Sweden, Norway, and the Austro-Hungarian empire furnished cowboys for the Long Trail. There were Africans, Canadians, Mexicans. There were Russians, Poles, Bohemians, Danes, Dutchmen, and Spaniards.

Cowboys from within the United States came from Nebraska, Ohio, Massachusetts, Illinois (Charles Goodnight), Michigan, New York. G. W. Mills, on the trail at seventeen, was born in Kentucky. "I first saw the light of day in Jackson Parish, Louisiana," said James Marion Garner; he was driving cattle at eighteen. George F. Hindes, who had first driven cattle at age twelve, was from Alabama. G. O. Burrows, who went up the trail eighteen times, was born in a log cabin in Mississippi.

The young cowboy from Texas was from almost anywhere.

20

The trail to Wichita, Wyoming, Utah, Idaho

1870. ALONG THE Long Trail: This year a village of twenty families and a blacksmith shop sent forth its first trainload of cattle —Fort Worth. Open grass in Texas started to disappear, and a boom began that would increase the number of farms (which would reduce even more the grass available to cattle) from 61,125 in 1870 to 174,184 in 1880. Ranches (which eventually would be fenced in and would reduce open grazing) were established in Texas by M. B. Pulliam, Phil C. Lee, J. Willis Johnson, J. E. Henderson, R. W. Murchison, W. B. Worsham, John Glenn Halsell, D. W. Gardner, D. W. and J. W. Godwin. One man explained about grazing land: "We didn't buy from nobody. It was outside country and we just took it."

On January 6, 1870, with cattle moving up the Long Trail past Waco, a ferry across the Brazos River was replaced by a single-span suspension bridge. Designed by Thomas Griffing, it was at the time the longest in the United States—a contribution to big-bridge building and to man's present transportation system. Its wire cables had been manufactured by John Augustus Roebling of New York, sent by ship to Galveston, then hauled by oxen to Waco. Across the Waco bridge marched longhorn herds and ox-drawn wagons, sometimes in long trains, piled with cotton, wheat, and other freight.

AROUND THE UNITED STATES: William A. Bullock was finding a way to print both sides of a roll of paper at once—newspaper printing. Henry R. Heyl projected an early type of motion pictures. Bret Harte wrote *The Heathen Chinee* and *The Luck of Roaring Camp*. A new American writer was climbing: Samuel Langhorne Clemens (Mark Twain). Robert E. Lee died. A steamboat named for him defeated the *Natchez*, by over three hours, in a race from New Orleans up the Mississippi River to St. Louis. The *Robert E. Lee* took three days, eighteen hours, fourteen minutes. Over a million dollars had been bet on the outcome.

It was a year full of buffaloes, Indians, and new destinations for the longhorns.

W. R. Massengale saw so many buffaloes he couldn't count them.

"Once, just as we were getting our herd on the trail, a little after sunrise," said Massengale, "a man from the herd just ahead of us loped back and told us that the buffaloes were coming, so we held our herd up. I went to the top of a little hill and I saw a black string. It looked as though it was coming straight to our herd. I went back and we rounded up our cattle so we could hold them if the buffaloes did strike them but they passed just ahead of us. Our cattle got a little nervous, but we held them all right. It took the buffaloes two hours to pass us. Sometimes they would be one behind the other, and then they would come in bunches of 300 or 400. I don't know how many to guess there was, but I think there must have been at least fifty thousand. Another time a bunch of about 300 ran through our herd while they were grazing."

William Baxter Slaughter of San Antonio, with 180 steers, came upon Indians where Kingfisher, Oklahoma, is today. "It was a city of tepees made out of buffalo hides," he said. The Indians demanded cattle, "so I cut out three large steers that had sore feet, caused by wet weather. They had these steers killed in less time than I can say it and took the hides off . . . and ate it raw while it was warm. But I could not understand why they wanted beef while there were thousands of buffalo in sight.''

E. P. Byler had grown more prosperous. He had started at $30 a month in 1868. Now (1870) he was up to $75 a month. He drove the trail, again with his brother Jim. On one flooded river, the men put a wagon sheet around the wagon bed, thereby turned it into a boat, and could get their things across in it. ''On the banks of the North Canadian,'' E.P. said, ''we found a newly made grave with a headboard bearing the inscription, 'Killed by Indians.' I do not know who the unfortunate victim could have been, but these graves were not uncommon.'' The Bylers delivered their cattle at Wichita, Kansas, then becoming a shipping point.

C. H. Rust of San Angelo, driving cattle to the Nations, ran into forty Comanches. Years later he still was puzzling over the fact that every one of them had a parasol.

Pleasant Burnell Butler saw a little more to Fort Worth than those twenty families and a blacksmith shop. Fort Worth, he said, also had ''a livery stable, a court house and a store operated by Daggett & Hatcher, supply merchants, on the public square, through which we swung our great herd of cattle.''

H. D. Gruene, nineteen, of Goodwin, Texas, was paid $30 a month to drive to Abilene. Then he was asked to drive the cattle on to Cheyenne, Wyoming, and later to Bear River, 110 miles above Salt Lake City, Utah. Gruene went along—after he had had his salary doubled to $60 a month, and it was agreed that he would not have to work at the tail end of the herd. At Salt Lake City, ''we bought some new clothes and had a general 'cleaning-up,' for we were pretty well inhabited by body lice, the greatest pest encountered on the trail.''

Marcus L. Dalton in 1870 did not get home at all. On November 4, driving a wagon, and carrying the proceeds from a cattle drive, he had arrived six miles north of today's Mineral Wells, Texas, and only twenty miles east of his home on the Brazos River.

Indians attacked. They took what they could carry, but overlooked $11,000 in an iron-bound leather trunk and $4,000 in Dalton's shoes. They killed Dalton and two other men.

On a drive to Colorado, L. B. Anderson's herd was attacked by Sioux Indians.

He had been the boy whose mother made him wear a sunbonnet as he traveled into Texas. Hunts for wild longhorns, and those early roundups, had been his first experience with cattle. At twenty, he had delivered oxen. He was the one who, in 1869, had gone up the trail with the $10 gold piece—and returned home with it.

Now, in 1870, the Sioux made off with all the provisions and most of the horses. For 200 miles, Anderson and his men, with their few remaining horses, hunted antelope and buffalo and lived on their meat.

In 1870, Dick Withers' brother, Mark A. Withers, plus J. W. (Bill) Montgomery, George Hill, and Dick himself, headed for Abilene with what, all the way, was called "the big herd"—3,500 cattle. At Abilene, Bill Montgomery sold his longhorns to be delivered beyond the Snake River in Idaho. Dick Withers went along to help Montgomery drive them.

Dick Withers wrote down his route. "From Abilene to the Big Blue River, from there to the South Platte below South Platte City, going up that stream to Julesburg." They crossed the South Platte, and had the oxen re-shod at Cheyenne—"the gravel had worn their hoofs to the quick." Up the North Platte they traveled to Fort Petterman. Then "we went up the North Platte and struck across to Sweetwater, following the old California immigrant trail, going by the Enchanted Rock and Devil's Gate."

Then the cook broke one of the ox yokes. Dick Withers had to hack out a new yoke with a dull axe—after he first had had to cut down with the same dull axe a small cottonwood tree. The yoke needed six holes in it, and these Dick Withers had to burn out. "It took me all evening and night to burn the holes in the yoke." Then on to the Rocky Mountains and across a forty-mile stretch of them. A snowstorm killed twenty-five horses. Back at Fort Petterman, Dick Withers had traded for sixteen fat steers. These the men began killing. Nature provided refrigeration. "The meat would freeze in just a little while, so we lived on nothing but beef for over a month. We had no flour, salt, or coffee, and nowhere to purchase these things. Only a few trappers and miners were in the country, and they did not have enough to supply us." The horses gave out; the men had to work on foot. They bought mules; the mules tired in an hour on the steep slopes of the mountains. Cattle got away from the herd. The drive reached Salt Valley, acquired more horses, and had to send back men to try to find the strayed cattle. Dick Withers, working with one other man and a pack mule, himself found fifty of the missing steers. One morning, in the snow less than thirty feet from where he slept, he found the tracks of a grizzly bear. He thought the bear had failed to smell the camp.

On Snake River, Dick Withers rejoined the herd. It went on to the Idaho destination with no other incident. Already, in 1870, the Long Trail stretched from the Gulf of Mexico to Wyoming, Utah—and to Idaho. Only Canada, which the trail would reach, was farther north.

21

*A day
on the trail*

FOR THE cook, the day began earliest—an hour before dawn. He would get up, then would call the horse wrangler or remuda man—generally a youngster ambitious to become a cowboy. The boy would get together the horses and bring them to camp.

The cook would make coffee (a life-giving drink to the sleepy men in the morning) in a big tin pot with a wide base so that it could not easily be knocked over. The coffee was boiled in the pot. There was almost never such a thing as sugar or milk to go in it. It was served scalding hot.

The cook mixed up a batch of sourdough biscuits, and started them baking in one or two big Dutch ovens. Steak, often from a steer that had been slaughtered on the trail (if possible not one of the owner's), or bacon was put into a great long-handled skillet to fry.

The cook set out syrup and dried fruit.

The cook's uniform was likely to be a well-worn flour sack. His credentials for the job were likely to be that he was an overage cowboy—or too stove in to continue to ride. He was called dough-roller, hash-slinger, grub-wrangler, biscuit-shooter, dinero, or cooky. Behind his back, he was called the old lady or old woman.

He nevertheless had one special privilege: He was allowed to be cantankerous. A cowboy had to be polite to him. "Only a fool argues with a cowman, a mule, or a cook." "Crossin' a cook is as risky as braidin' a mare's tail."

The cook might do additional jobs. He might keep the harness in repair, hold stakes for bets, pull teeth, cut hair, sew on buttons, or act as a veterinarian for the horses or as a doctor for the men. His medicine chest in the chuck box in the chuck wagon might include a laxative, quinine (for malaria), liniment and whisky for snake bite (the only whisky allowed on the trail).

To drink on the trail was, in fact, so dangerous that the cowboys themselves enforced a rule against it. Once when a trail boss persisted in drinking, his cowboys, near Monument Rock, pitched his tent over a bed of sleeping skunks and tied the front of the tent together. The drinking man was discomfited.

If the cowboys, upon being waked, were already mostly dressed—as they would be if they feared a stampede—they had to put on only boots and belts. After a warm night, with little fear of a stampede, when they would have stripped to their underwear, they first put on pants and shirt. Then a cowboy would wash his face in cold water—he called this "bathing out his countenance"—and he would drag a pocket comb through his hair. He then picked up his tin cup, plate, and spoon, and his wooden or bone-handled knife and fork, and went and got a breakfast as big as the piles of flapjacks a lumberjack in the north woods could consume. Including the coffee. There is no record that a cowboy ever refused a cup of coffee, no matter how long it had been boiled, and no matter what that did to the taste of the coffee.

During breakfast, the horses would be held in an improvised rope corral, the ropes running from the chuck wagon into the hands of a couple of cowboys. A cowboy rode, in succession, for a day or a day and a half, all but one of the six to ten horses he had along with him on the trail. The exception was his night-herding horse.

Each cowboy picked out the horse he wanted to use. They mounted, drove off and relieved the men on duty—usually two night-riders, riding in opposite directions around the herd, so as to meet each other when they completed the circle.

By now the cattle were up and grazing. They grazed a little while. They then were drifted off slowly toward the north. By about nine in the morning they had eaten enough, and had strung themselves out into a moving column a mile or a mile and one-half long. The horses trailed along beside the cattle. Or went ahead of them.

The cook washed the dishes, loaded the bedrolls and camp equipment into the chuck wagon, and hitched the oxen or mules or horses that would haul it. Four horses or mules or oxen were the usual number, instead of the ten oxen that wagon-driver Charles Goodnight in 1866 had used on his original chuck wagon on the trail through west Texas and New Mexico to Colorado. The chuck wagon started with a month's supplies. It had a hammock underneath it. This was called a cooney or caboose, and contained fuel for the cook's fires. The fuel often was dried cow or buffalo dung, which the cowboys called prairie coal, plus kindling or wood (if there was any). Also hanging beneath the wagon were buckets. Barrels of water in the chuck wagon were so arranged that a faucet in the side of the wagon would let a man get a drink.

In a box in front of the wagon—the "jewelry chest"—there were tools: a hammer, axe, hatchet, horseshoeing equipment, branding irons, ammunition, strips of rawhide (untanned leather) for repairs, and—in case a grave had to be dug—a spade. The jewelry box might contain also hobbles—which were loops of leather to tie a horse's forefeet together and thus keep it from moving far.

A scout, often the trail boss, or boss of the herd, went out ahead, sometimes a full day ahead, to find the way—and water. The scout looked, explained cowman W. F. Cude, for stands of trees: "When we came in sight of timber we knew there would be water."

The water had to be drinkable by men, horses, and cattle. It did not have to be a pleasure to drink it. The water might contain the carcass of a steer. The water might be full of sand. It might taste of sheep. It might be—as one cowboy described it—"muddy as pea-soup." It might be warm, and there would be no way to cool it; in this case, the cowboy "drank his cold water hot."

While the herd was still grazing, the cook pulled out past it and headed for the spot near water that the scout had designated, usually five to seven miles away.

The cook halted, prepared dinner (lunch), and at about twelve the cowboys arrived ready to eat it, and then to rest. They called this "making our nooning." Afterward, the cook again washed up, packed up, and drove to the next near-water spot the scout had picked, where he fixed supper. He might put on beef and beans to boil. At this point, he might have a couple of hours to himself before the herd caught up. He might take a nap. Or he might try to vary the menu for the trail drivers: he sometimes fished, using a willow or a dogwood pole he had just cut. He sometimes picked wild dewberries or blackberries or hunted quail or other birds. There were plenty of water birds—if they were not flying too high or if it was not the wrong season for them. The Canada goose, with its clarion call, in its V-shaped flocks, the snow goose, the white-footed goose, mergansers, canvasbacks, green-wing and blue-wing teals, pintails, wood ducks, American widgeons, baldpates, red-heads, and mallards.

Perhaps most of all, from Texas on north, the cook and the cowboys hunted the wild turkey, the largest American game bird— up to four feet long, up to thirty pounds in weight, or about twice the size of any Thanksgiving turkey you are likely to sit down to. Said John B. Conner, a cowboy from Yoakum, Texas: "We often captured wild turkey gobblers which had strayed out from the rivers to the level prairie. When we jumped them they would fly for a mile or two, then we would run them down." A wary bird, the wild turkey was hunted so much that it was keeping out of sight in the swampy bottomlands before the cowboys stopped driving cattle up the Long Trail.

Pedro Niño is said to have obtained some wild turkeys (then unknown to European man) in 1500; he got them in Venezuela and took them to Spain. Hernando Cortez, the Spaniard who in 1519 had conquered Mexico and had introduced horses there, obtained wild turkeys in Mexico and took them to Spain. Eventually, the turkey spread throughout Europe; the Pilgrims knew about it, and brought it to North America, and so it became a Thanksgiving dish.

The cattle caught up with the wagon while the sun was an hour or so high. The cattle were allowed to drink, with two or three riders to guard them, while the other men ate supper: sourdough biscuits, beans and beef or whatever the cook had shot, caught, or gathered; dried apples, peaches, apricots, or rice, canned corn, or tomatoes. Sometimes there was cake, pie, or doughnuts. Sometimes slumgullion—a bread pudding of cold biscuits, sugar, and raisins.

Afterward, on fresh horses, the cowboys who had eaten relieved the others so that they might eat. About sundown, the cattle were moved on to a fairly level space that would be their bed ground. Then, ideally, the cattle, tired and full of water and grass, chewed their cuds and lay down to rest. (In the wild, longhorns moved and grazed at night; on the trail, like domestic cattle, they grazed by day and needed about eight hours to do it.)

Sometimes the cattle fidgeted.

"When the cattle are restless on the bedding ground," said John Jacobs, "the boys on night herd hum a low, soft lullaby (like a mother to her child). It has a quieting effect and often saves trouble."

The singing, Frank M. King said, in the stillness of many a night let the cattle know someone was looking after them.

The cattle were quieted and trouble was saved by "Bury Me Not on the Lone Prairie" (Mark Withers' favorite for putting cattle to sleep), "The Dying Cowboy," "Get Along Little Dogies," "Barbara Allen," "Green Grow the Lilacs" (from the Mexican war), "When You and I Were Young, Maggie," "The Days of Forty-Nine" (from the California gold rush), "Sweet Betsy from Pike."

Some cowboys played the violin, banjo, guitar, or harmonica (mouth organ) as they rode horseback around the cattle. Lake Porter of Falfurrias, Texas, did: "Often I have taken my fiddle on herd at night when on the trail and while one of my companions would lead my horse around the herd, I agitated the catguts, reeling off such old time selections as 'Black Jack Grove,' 'Dinah Had a Wooden Leg,' 'Shake That Wooden Leg, Dolly Oh,' 'Give the Fiddler a Drum,' 'Arkansas Traveler,' and 'The Unfortunate Pup' . . . those old long-horned Texas steers actually enjoyed that old-time music."

The cowboys sang about their horses: "The Horse Wrangler,"

"The Zebra Dun," "The Wild Bronc Peeler," and what became the last waltz at a cowboy dance, "Good-by Old Paint" ("I'm a-leavin' Cheyenne"). About a mythical wild white stallion of the Great Plains, the cowboys sang "The White Steed of the Prairies."

One ballad told the story of Sam Bass, from Indiana, who had driven cattle (unfortunately, somebody else's cattle) up the trail. He owned a winning racehorse—a little sorrel called the Denton mare (for Denton, Texas). He at first robbed stage coaches near Deadwood, South Dakota, than as railroad trains became more common, took to robbing them with alarming frequency, not to say regularity. In 1878 at Round Rock, Texas, he was shot and killed. Bass had generally shared his loot, and he had become a north Texas folk hero. When he died, his Bowie knife went to a Texas Ranger, his compass to another. Countless north Texans claim to have his guns. His bullets and cartridge belt went to the University of Texas library.

Cowboy Charles Siringo said the song about Sam Bass quieted the longhorns during thunderstorms.

There was a song about another outlaw, Jesse James, from Missouri. (One tale says he paid off a $1,400 mortgage for a widow.) Another song was about Mustang Gray, who had fought at the Battle of San Jacinto and in the Mexican war, and told of his exploits: after a buffalo hunt, on foot, he lassoed a wild mustang and got home.

There was a ballad about Quantrill, the guerrilla in the War Between the States, who as a cowboy had gone up the trail in 1866 with Dr. J. W. Hargus. It called him a "lion heart" and a "bold-hearted boy."

The cowboy heard, as did practically everyone in the United States, the songs of a Northerner, the ninth child in a Pittsburgh family, who captured much of the feeling of the South. This was Stephen Collins Foster, whose first published song, "Open Thy Lattice, Love," appeared in 1844 during the time when Texas was an independent nation. His songs were spread down the Mississippi on steamboats and across the nation by singing families and covered-wagon travelers. The country worked and played to the rhythms of "Oh! Susanna" (the theme of the California forty-niners), "Camptown Races," "Massa's in the Cold, Cold Ground," and others. Foster died in 1864. One tune of his, "Old

Uncle Ned,'' was to be taken over by the cowboy, who added endless verses to come up with ''The Old Chisholm Trail'' (''Whoopee-ti-yi-yo-git along little dogies'').

Joe McCoy, the man who had made Abilene a shipping point, said he would sit on the fence of a corral and sing to the cattle to keep them quiet when trains passed by.

Besides singing to their herds, the cowboys sang to each other. At night they kept track of each other this way. Their songs also might warn away cattle rustlers. They also sang when visiting another's camp. If one liked a song he hadn't heard before, he asked the man who sang it to write down the words. Some cowboys with good voices and memories became entertainers, who were welcomed anywhere. They were the wandering minstrels of the cattle country, as they sang: ''Thou wilt come no more, gentle Annie,'' ''Close the brown eyes gently, beautiful Mabel Clare,'' ''I'll sell my horse and I'll sell my saddle and I'll bid farewell to the longhorn cattle.'' Of the Red River valley: ''From this valley they say you are going.'' And about a life to come: ''I wondered if ever a cowboy would get to the sweet bye and bye.''

There were on the trail three night shifts. Each normally was handled by two cowboys. The first lasted till 11 P.M. Watches and clocks being scarce, the time was told by the moon or by the Great Dipper circling the North Star. On rainy or cloudy nights, a cowboy's hunch was pretty reliable. At the end of a shift, one cowboy rode in and woke up the next guard. The next two men stood guard till 2 A.M.—this was the middle shift and generally considered the least desirable. At about midnight, the cattle would get up, walk about a bit, and stretch. The middle shift riders would halt any tendency to keep walking. Then the cattle would lie down and rest till about dawn. At 2 A.M. the last night riders took over the herd till daylight. The other cowboys, sleeping, then would be awakened by the cook's call to breakfast.

With eight or nine riders to one herd, and only three shifts of two men each needed, this meant that each night (unless a stampede kept all hands in the saddles all night) two or three cowboys were able to sleep the night through—to get the rest boys and young men so sorely need. The idea was for every cowboy to get a complete night's sleep once or twice a week.

The cowboys on duty at night were riding their night-herding horses.

These were the best horses of all, and used for no other purpose. Bill Jackman listed the characteristics a night horse needed: "Perfectly gentle, easily handled, clean footed, of good sight, and to have all qualities of a first-class horse."

Said Hiram Craig, the cowboy who had watched his mother spin thread and had helped her make clothes: "This night herding is nice and novel in fair weather, and on a nice moonlit night; but when it comes to one of those dark nights of thunder, lightning, and the rain pouring down on you, your life is in the hands of God and your faithful night horse. There is to my mind no nobler animal in God's creation than a faithful horse. We would always pick out the cleanest-footed, best-sighted horses for this work. All horses can see in the night, and better than a man, but there are some horses that can see better than others."

The grass of the Great Plains was the short mesquite or buffalo grass; the tall bluestem; and sage or bunch grass in the low sand hills along the rivers. The grass usually was high enough—it had "risen enough" to feed cattle and horses abundantly by early April, when, accordingly, many a drive began. The grass often was fine in Texas and even better in Indian Territory (Oklahoma). On it, "cattle and horses began to fatten," said W. C. Fielder, after a herd had crossed Red River into Indian Territory. "You could see their hides moving away from their bones."

In locations, generally in Oklahoma, where the grass was high, rank, and luxuriant, the cattle might be held ten days or so to rest, graze, and fatten up. If weather was good, and Indians and rustlers were not around, and it took only two cowboys at a time to guard the cattle, the cowboys's life would for a few days become one to envy. He could gather wild fruit, or pecans, or rest, or play cards, or fish, or hunt. Meanwhile, the cook, with more time to spare, varied and improved his menu: it might include barbecued ribs, dumplings, roasts, fish or deer (whatever the cowboys caught), or wild greens. Someone might even find a wild turkey's nest; there might be eggs. Some might find a bee tree; that meant honey.

As the cattle drives progressed, the herds were driven farther and farther to the west—in order to avoid the new settlements of farmers and troubles like Jim Daugherty's in 1866 with the Kansas Jayhawkers. Once near a Kansas town selected as the goal of the herd, the boss rode in and made arrangements to sell or ship the cattle. The cattle, guarded by the cowboys, stayed a few miles outside. Then the cattle might be shipped by rail for immediate slaughter and U.S. meat markets.

As the years went by, cattlemen learned that many of the grasses on the Long Trail were immune to drought and actually dried to a hay right where they grew in a hot Western summer. And they remained sweet and nourishing through the winter.

This made it possible for the longhorns, which needed nothing to eat but the wild grass, to survive winters in the North. Cattle could be bred in Texas, held there for a year or two, then fed and fattened in the North, and sent to market. Cattle for the Northern ranches and ranges were two years old or younger instead of the seven-year-olds ready for market. The cattle on the trail became much younger.

To reach Northern ranches was another reason the trail moved west; it went through Colorado and avoided Oklahoma and Kansas. ("All a-long, a-long, a-long, the Colorado Trail.") The same cowboys might drive the cattle from the Gulf of Mexico coast all the way. It was a long drive, perhaps nine months, from Texas through Colorado to Montana or the Dakotas or Wyoming. And any cowboy who made it, even once, had earned his spurs. From then on, he automatically qualified as a top hand.

22

All sorts of things kept happening

1871–75. ON THE Long Trail: Immigrants from Russia were bringing to the midcontinent several species of weeds, known in Russia as thistle or pigweed, that break off near the ground, roll before the wind, and scatter their seeds: the tumbleweed. . . . In Idaho-Montana-Wyoming, where hot water spurts up in geysers, and where what the Indians called the River of the Yellow Stone cuts a gorge, the United States opened "a public pleasuring ground": Yellowstone National Park, the nation's first. . . . Only a few machines, sawmills, flour mills, cotton gins, steamboats, and locomotives operated in Texas; otherwise muscles of men or animals did every bit of the work. . . . A packing house in Denison, Texas, may have been, in 1873, the first in the United States to apply refrigeration to meat packing. . . . Two men were showing that once the West had had bigger animals than the six-foot-high, nine-foot-long buffalo: dinosaurs. Othniel Charles Marsh of Yale and Edward D. Cope were digging up the bones. . . . The Black Hills, South Dakota, in 1875 were opened to gold seekers; soldiers under Gen. George Custer had found gold there. . . . New ranches in Texas were those of Dan and his son W. T. Waggoner, E. F. and W. B. Ikard, Joe B. and J. A. Matthews, A. B. (Sug) Robertson, and Winfield Scott.

Meanwhile, AROUND THE WORLD: In unexplored central Africa (today's Tanzania), Henry M. Stanley found the long missing Dr. Livingstone. . . . The heart of Chicago burned when a cow—according to one story—upset a lantern in a barn belonging to a Mrs. O'Leary. . . . The name of a current technological and mechanical marvel had been picked up as a trade name that was selling a brand of playing cards: Bicycle. . . . For the first time, cities were being lighted at night. A new source of energy made it possible: gas. . . . Oil, by 1873, was replacing tallow as a lubricant in machines and in locomotives and railroad-car wheels; the new lubricant would make machines infinitely more practical. Kerosene was replacing candles and whale oil as a household light. . . . At least fifty-one men had invented impractical typewriters; in 1875 Christopher L. Sholes built the first satisfactory one. . . . The first U.S. postal card was issued. . . . A new horse race, the Derby, was held at a place in Kentucky called Churchill Downs. . . . Three Frenchmen in a balloon reached a record altitude of 28,000 feet (over five miles); two of them died from exposure or from lack of oxygen; but one, Gaston Tissandier, survived.

Ben Drake of San Antonio, on the trail in 1871, was sixteen. He was equipped with new $14 boots, bell spurs, a Colt cap-and-ball six-shooter, a rim-fire Winchester, and $12 leather leggings (chaps). "This was the first time in my life that I had been rigged out," he said, "and you bet I was proud."

He saw his first Indians in the Territory. "Then I wished I was home with my mother."

B. A. Borroum of Del Rio, Texas, ran into buffalo north of Red River station: ". . . countless in numbers; in fact, the whole face of the earth seemed to be literally covered with them, all going in the same direction." He had to halt his cattle till they passed. "Buffalo, horses, elk, deer, antelope, wolves, and some cattle were all mixed together, and it took several hours for them to pass, with our assistance, so that we could proceed on our journey.

"I think there were more buffalo in that herd than I ever saw of any living thing, unless it was an army of grasshoppers in Kansas in July, 1874." That was a locust plague that wiped out plants and crops in much of the Midwest.

An Indian chief, Yellow Bear, begged bread (in 1871) from L. B. Anderson's outfit. When he was turned down, Yellow Bear stamped his foot in the dough the cook was working up to make the next bread.

John S. Kritzer, a cowboy from Independence, Missouri, was captured, near the Cimarron River, by Osage Indians, each with his face painted red on one side, black on the other side. After about an hour, Kritzer pointed to a cloud of dust—an approaching herd of cattle driven by Jim Scobey. The Osages turned Kritzer loose.

L. B. Anderson in 1871 drove to Newton, Kansas, "about the time the railroad reached there."

Something new was occurring: The Kansas Pacific railroad used some of the first refrigerator cars that, for T. L. Rankin and others, took dressed beef to market.

During the Civil War, Arnold W. Capt had been a lad called on to round up cattle. "When the men and boys were nearly all in the army, cattle on the range plentiful and very wild, it was mine to ride the range alone, everybody's roustabout," he said. People rounded up any cows at all, he said, penned them, and milked them. A calf was given the brand of its mother.

One hot July day, to keep cool, Capt and a number of cowboys along with him and a herd stripped to undershirts and shorts and left their clothes in the chuck wagon. The wagon went on ahead. A camp-meeting crowd of young women passed the herd—on both sides of it. "Some of the boys," said Capt, "went off at a tangent east to see how the range looked, others went west in search of water to fill their canteens, a few thoughtfuls dropped to the rear to push up the drags."

By August 1 the cattle were grazing on the plains of Kansas. The herd went to Abilene, then on to the Platte.

In a poker game, S. B. Burnett drew four sixes, and with them won a ranch. When, in Denton County, Burnett started to ranch, he bought a small herd and used, as a brand, *6666*.

D. S. Combs and Dock Day took a herd from San Marcos, Texas, to Red Cloud, Nebraska. They decided to keep the cattle through the winter in Nebraska. "This was my first bad setback," said Combs, "for the winter was the worst I ever saw or heard of; the country froze over early in November and never thawed till spring. Our cattle literally starved to death, snow covered the grass and the water froze so they could not drink. I left in the spring a busted and disgusted cowman.

"I have never been back to that particular country and have tried all these years to forget it, but the memories of that dreadful experience will forever remain with me."

Branch Isbell in 1873 contracted to buy "104 head of big steers" from one of the Bylers. Byler did not require a note as security. Isbell joined his cattle to a herd driven by J. P. Cox and A. B. (Arch) Lockhart. The drive was completed without one of Byler-Isbell steers being lost. "In September," said Isbell, "I sold them to J. B. Hunter & Company for $20 per head. They paid me $580 and were to pay $1500 in a few days. Before the time expired the memorable 'Black Friday' fell on Wall Street and Hunter & Company's failure lost me my $1500. I returned to Texas owing Mr. Byler the original cost of the steers, $1248. I worked for him and others, paying a little at a time on my debt, until it was finally paid in full."

George Webb Slaughter, who in 1836 had been a messenger to the besieged Alamo, and who had married his Sallie after the Battle of San Jacinto, was presented by her with a son, John, on December 14, 1848. At seventeen, John was on the trail. One day at dawn, an Indian leaped up, right at John's feet, and put a bullet through his right chest. Six weeks later, John was in the saddle again, driving cattle. Indians attacked, and a herd boss named Adams and the cowboy with him were missing. John Slaughter took charge of the herd and directed a search, the cowboys setting out two by two. After three days, beneath a swarm of vultures, the bodies were found. The chest of one man had been cut out and his heart laid on his stomach. The other man had had his sexual organs cut off and stuck in his mouth. The bodies were rolled in blankets and buried under the bank of a creek.

Once, after fifteen Comanches attacked Slaughter and his party, the men were left with one horse apiece—to handle two thousand cattle. They reached Abilene, and sold the herd there. When they reached Abilene, they were on foot.

James Marion Garner of Texarkana drove up the trail in 1873 "440 head of my own horses and mares." As ranches were established in the North, there would be more and more demand for horses, and more and more would be sent up the trail. Another market for them was opening up in Northern cities: to pull horse-cars.

It is hard in the 1970s to imagine how completely without machinery of any kind Americans (and all men) were just 100 years ago. The single railroad line that linked the East and West Coast of the nation had been finished in 1869, but few persons in the Southwest ever had seen a locomotive.

A story from Atascosa County, Texas, south of San Antonio, about 1873, shows one way people reacted to their first look at machinery—in this case, at clocks. "One day," Jasper (Bob) Lauderdale, who was from Missouri and was then nineteen, said, "a Mr. Isabell came traveling through the country trading eight-day clocks for cattle, giving one clock for four cows and calves, and as no one had a clock, it did not take Isabell long to gather a herd. One of the settlers with whom he traded took his clock home and, after winding it, set it on the mantle, and when the family gathered round after supper, the clock struck eight. It scared the family so that they scattered, thinking it was something super-natural, and it took the old man until nearly midnight to get them together and in the house."

The Civil War caretaker of the Federal government's camels, James A. McFaddin, had become a cattleman, and, by 1874, prosperous. He handled not only his own money, but that of others. He filled every safe in Refugio, Texas, with silver, and his own safe and two nail kegs at home. He often had to leave his wife at home alone. Not a cent ever was stolen.

As a boy, Hiram Craig had seen his mother spin thread. He had helped her make clothes. He had plowed with a wooden plow.

He told how his father had repaired by hand a broken-down wagon—out in the wilderness. As a child, he had survived meningitis, when many of his playmates died. At seventeen he had become a cowboy, and by 1874 he was making money. He turned it over to his wife. She would put it into her stocking, which he called a woman's money purse. She called her stocking the First National Bank.

One south Texas cowman decided to bury his money in the ground. One night he did, beneath a fence post, which he replaced. Later, he needed the money. He had to dig up half his fence posts to find it.

In 1874, Sol West, a veteran of three trips up the trail, bossed a herd. He is said to have been the youngest man ever to have been a trail boss. I do not know how old he was, perhaps seventeen or eighteen. None of his hands was over twenty. They left Lavaca County early, on February 27. A blizzard hit. "The cattle at once turned their heads to the south and began to drift with the wind," he said. His men had matches, "but our hands were so numb that we could not strike one, even if we could have gotten the box out of our pockets." Next morning, the two men who had been taking care of the remuda—the sixty-five horses the cowboys were not riding when the blizzard struck—told Sol West that all the horses had frozen to death. "My horse was the last to go down," said West. He and his cowboys now were on foot. They traded with Indians and settlers for a few horses, and reached Ellsworth, Kansas—the first herd to do so that spring. Ellsworth businessmen gave young West, accordingly, a new suit, hat, and boots. Back in Texas, the profits of his drive were figured: $1.50. He received half: $.75.

One night near Dodge City, Kansas, cattle in a herd attended by J. M. Hankins stampeded. When the herd was quiet again, the cowboys saw a light and heard a voice, right out of the ground, or so it seemed. The stampeding steers had run over the roof of a dugout, and crushed it in. Its owner, a farmer, was calling. One steer had gone through the roof, tumbled through, and disturbed the man's slumber.

Robbers in Omaha, Nebraska, attacked a man who had driven cattle north to Kansas in 1867, and was largely responsible for the trail to Abilene, none other than Col. J. J. Meyers. Meyers had just delivered a herd of cattle to Utah. The robbers chloroformed him. When he returned home, he died from the effects of the chloroform, in December 1874.

Some new hands in 1875 were for the first time starting up the trail. E. C. Abbott (Teddy Blue), at fourteen, was one of them. He overheard Al Harmon, a trail boss for John T. Lytle, say: "In a year or two Teddy will be a real cowboy." Teddy Blue remembered: "And I growed three inches and gained ten pounds that night."

23

"I was barely 17 years old"

GEORGE W. SAUNDERS of San Antonio had two brothers, Mat and Jack. They had taken a herd to Baxter Springs in 1870. George was thrilled by their stories of stampedes, buffalo chases, and cowboys and Indians. He wanted to go up the trail, and in 1871 he got his chance. Said he: "I was barely 17 years old, and felt that I was able to take care of myself on a long trip as well as any man."

Saunders' trail boss was Jim Byler. Saunders, Byler, a chuckwagon, and a handful of other cowboys went to the Mays pasture on the Cibolo near Stockdale, Wilson County, Texas. They made their first contact with the herd they would walk up the Long Trail: a thousand steers. "Mr. Byler," said Saunders, "pointed the herd north."

In Indian Territory, many Indians came up to them. By now they had a usual greeting: "How, John?" Said Saunders: "Byler got by these Indians without any trouble. One day the Plains were covered with buffaloes."

Byler, Saunders, and the herd headed for Abilene. They had lots of company besides Indians and buffaloes.

"Imagine," said Saunders, "all the ranchmen in south, east, and middle Texas at work at the first sign of spring, gathering and delivering trail herds." That was the way it was from April 1 to May 15, 1871.

On a single day, April 6, the *Abilene Chronicle* figured that 90,000 cattle were pounding their hoofs en route to Abilene. On May 15, there were estimated to be 30,000 cattle right around the town. Along with them were 5,000 cowboys.

Said Kansas' *Saline County Journal* of July 20, 1871 (Saline County was about the last stop before Abilene): "The entire county, east, west, and south of Salina down to the Arkansas River and Wichita is now filled with Texas cattle. There are not only cattle 'on a thousand hills' but a thousand cattle on one hill and every hill."

Altogether, Abilene attracted 600,000 cattle in 1871. It was the busiest year the town ever would have.

There already were signs of changes to come. Near Abilene, George Saunders said, the prairies "were nearly taken up by grangers [farmers], who lived in dugouts, a square hole in the ground, or on the side of a bluff, with timbers placed across and covered with dirt. Each granger had taken up 160 acres of land, part of which was cultivated. They had no fences, so to mark the boundaries of their homestead, they would plow a furrow around it."

The farmers asked trail bosses to bed cattle on their land. There was no fuel—no trees except a few cottonwoods—and the farmers needed something besides buffalo chips to burn in their fires—cattle chips. "One evening," said Saunders, "I noticed several men and women in buggies and buckboards going to different herds and begging each boss to bed his herd on their respective lands." The farmers figured that a thousand cattle would leave enough chips on the ground in one night to give them five hundred pounds of fuel in a few days.

Said a trail boss, Levi Anderson: "Down in Texas, if you gave a man dry dung he would fight you, but here in Kansas they will fight you for the dry dung."

Twenty miles from Abilene, on Holland Creek, the herd halted and selling began.

One thing that happened when cattle were sold near Abilene would impress Saunders to the end of his days. The buyers brought their money, in gold and silver, in sacks on the backs of packhorses. At meeting places with cattle owners, they dumped the moneybags onto the prairie. The bags remained there several days without molestation—and without a guard of any kind. When the deal for the cattle was completed, said Saunders, "the sacks were opened, the money dumped out on a blanket in camp, and counted out to each man who had participated in the trades."

Saunders went into Abilene to help load the cattle onto trains. Pushed by Joseph McCoy and others, it had grown into a full-fledged cattle town. McCoy's hotel, the Drovers' Cottage, managed by J. W. and Louisa Gore of St. Louis, had been enlarged into a 100-room hotel with a new laundry and a barn for a hundred horses and fifty carriages. A two-story hotel, the Gulf House, had opened. In the hope of influencing the behavior of guests, hotels of the time added signs, "Gents requested not to spit on the walls." Or requested "to keep their boots off the bed clothes." A cowboy, if any, who asked for a napkin might be told a hotel provided napkins "only for ladies."

The cattle pens by the tracks at Abilene had been enlarged to cover many acres. Abilene had H. H. Hazlett's drovers' outfitting store and a dry goods and clothing store run by a Russian, Jake Karatofsky.

On A Street, there were four saloons in a row. Three sets of double-glass doors made the entrance to the Alamo Saloon, where City Marshal Wild Bill Hickok held forth. A district of thirty one-story wooden houses provided feminine company for the cowboys. These were moved by Mayor Joseph McCoy to a location called "McCoy's Addition" or the "Devil's Half-Acre."

Twenty-five years afterward, George Saunders again would pass through the same part of Kansas, even through the herding ground where farmers had begged for cattle manure: "I was astonished to see the changes that had taken place. Pretty farms and new dwellings covered the whole region, and there were fine herds of good cattle, horses, sheep, mules and hogs everywhere, and the whole country looked prosperous."

Jim Byler, the trail boss who had taken along George Saunders, also had his brother E. P. Byler on the 1871 drive. "On this trip," said E.P., "we saw plenty of buffalo and antelopes, and the country was full of wolves." Jim turned back—along with Saunders—after reaching Kansas.

For E.P., the Long Trail stretched longer.

"I went north with the cattle a thousand miles," he recalled, "passing through Nebraska, crossed the Platte River, and struck the Missouri River which was a mile wide, and steamboats were on it. The stream was so wide the cattle could not see the landing on the other side, and we worked nine days trying to get them across. . . . Three hundred head of cattle refused to swim the river and we sold them on this side to the government. . . .

"We went on up through North Dakota to a point near the line of Canada where we delivered the cattle, and then started back home."

E. P. Byler stopped off at Wichita, Kansas, because he got a job as boss of Read & O'Connor cattle till November. He then returned to Texas. "For nine months," he said, "I had not slept in a house."

When trail boss Jim Byler originally had agreed to take the seventeen-year-old George Saunders, Byler had remarked, "His age is all right, if he has staying qualities, but most kids are short on sleep."

Saunders himself later recounted a story about how short on sleep a cowboy might be. The story became a legend of the Long Trail. Saunders said it happened to another cowboy, Jack Potter.

Potter said (according to Saunders) that in Kansas he got lost and asked a granger for shelter till morning. The farmer lived in a dugout, one room, fifteen feet square, with a bed, table, four chairs, a stove, the farmer, his wife, and two small boys.

It was crowded.

Potter saw no place for him to sleep.

The boys meanwhile fell asleep on the bed.

At her bedtime, the mother picked up the boys, still asleep, and sat them over in a corner, leaning them against the wall. She told Jack Potter he could have the bed; she and her husband went up a ladder. Potter turned in, and slept soundly all night.

But when he woke up the next morning, Potter found the farmer and his wife in the bed.

He himself was in the corner with the two small boys.

When, on that trip north, George Saunders and the herd reached the Washita River, it was flooding. A rope had to be carried across the 100-yard-wide flood to haul a raft across. One cowboy after another tried and failed. "I was the fifth one to try," said Saunders. He bit on the rope, held it in his teeth. "I made it across, by grasping an overhanging willow limb and pulled myself ashore with the rope still in my mouth . . . there was a cowboy yell of approval from the other side.

"I felt very proud of myself, and think I added several inches to my stature right there, for I was only 17 years old, and had succeeded in an undertaking in which four stalwart men had failed, but I am willing to confess I could not have gone ten feet further in my exhausted condition."

Saunders, with his morale high, in Kansas decided to dress up for the girls back home. He bought shop-made boots and two new suits. One suit was "a changeable velvet affair that I had paid fifty dollars for" (in Kansas). "I carried these clothes in a pair of saddle bags all the way home." He was determined to "cut a shine." When he reached home he received a surprise. He could have bought his new clothes cheaper—right there, in a local store.

24

A woman travels the Long Trail

W. F. BURKS, in the spring of 1871, rounded up a thousand of his cattle and started north with ten cowboys, most of them Mexicans, and cooks. A day later, he sent back Marcus Banks to ask his wife, Amanda Burks, to come up the trail with the herd. Mrs. Amanda Burks became one of the first women to ride north with the longhorns.

She set out after them in "my little buggy drawn by two good brown ponies." After she caught the cattle, all the rest of the way, she did not need to hold the reins. The ponies followed the slow-moving cattle (ten miles a day), and Mrs. Burks could nap in the carriage.

That was the easy part. There were difficulties, both for the herd and for Amanda.

They came to thick trees. The cattle had to be driven through without a pause. If a halt was made, some of the cattle would be lost in the woods.

They ran into lightning and thunder. Said Mrs. Burks: "The lightning seemed to settle on the ground and creep along like something alive."

They ran into a hailstorm. Mr. Burks drove the buggy into

the woods so Amanda would be better protected. To take care of the cattle, he had to leave her alone. The horses sought better shelter and worked their way to one side of the buggy. She thought they would run away. She came out of the buggy into the storm and tied the horses. "I got back to the buggy and sat there cold and wet and hungry and all alone in the dark. Homesick! That is the only time of all the months of my trip that I wished I was back on the old Ranch at Banquette" (near the King Ranch, and near Corpus Christi on the Gulf Coast).

She heard wagon wheels. But saw nothing. It was the chuckwagon moving ahead. But the cook and the chuckwagon became lost in the woods, and Mr. Burks had to chase them and bring them back.

Mrs. Burks was alone in the woods in the hailstorm till I A.M., when her husband came for her. The hail had made big blood blisters on his hands. One of the cowboys said, "The beat of the hail on my head made me crazy. I would have run, but didn't know which way to go."

Mrs. Burks found few people living along the trail, but in Ellis County (south of Dallas) "we saw an old woman sitting in the doorway of a small house stringing beans." Said she, "I'm the first woman that made a track in Dallas County (Dallas), and I would be back in Tennessee now, only I would have to go through Arkansas to get there. I guess I'll stay right here."

At Fort Worth, there were fifteen herds waiting to cross the flooding Trinity River.

They ran into blistering heat. A cloth was hung inside the buggy top to reduce the heat on Mrs. Burks.

They ran into rustlers, who threw rocks at the longhorns. "I called on them," said Amanda, "to stop, and said they would stampede the cattle. The answer: "That's what we're trying to do." Some of the cowboys rode up and drove away the rustlers.

They moved through Indian country, where all the men and Mr. Burks had to guard the herd, and Amanda again was alone. The Indians (they thought) stampeded the cattle. "Nothing but exhaustion would check it" (the stampede). It took about a week to gather all the cattle back.

One night a burning candle set fire to some small articles of Mrs. Burks', "including my comb." Another time a prairie fire moved down upon them; the Burks and their cowboys and their cattle fled to a part of the plain already burned. Two days after that, Amanda struck a match to light a fire to cook on. That started a prairie fire. Before it was through, it had swept ahead fifty miles. Investigators came to seek the person responsible. When they learned it was a woman, they said nothing except that one man said that he was glad he hadn't struck the match.

One night in the rain, Mrs. Burks' tent collapsed on top of her. She was unharmed.

Near Newton, Kansas, they ran into snow and cold. In the first snowstorm, nine horses died. "Many of the young cattle lost their horns from the cold. Blocks of ice had to be chopped out of the streams in order that the cattle could drink."

At last Mrs. Burks got to a hotel at Ellsmore. But here she was burned out by yet another fire.

Mr. Burks decided to sell his cattle and return to Texas. Said Amanda, "He met with no discouragement . . . from me."

The Burks went home by train from St. Louis to New Orleans, and by ship from New Orleans to Indianola, Texas.

She never did look back on her trip up the cattle trail as a hardship. She was in better health when she arrived home than when she had departed, nine months earlier.

Don't think, she told her listeners to her tales of the trail, that "the journey was one of trials and hardships. These incidents served to break the monotony of smoothness on such a trip.

"For what woman, youthful and full of spirit and the love of living, needs sympathy because of availing herself of the opportunity of being with her husband while at his chosen work in the great out-of-door world!"

Another woman of the land of the Long Trail was Mrs. Mary Kate Cruze. As a girl, she had been Mary Kate Cox, born in Baton Rouge, Louisiana. Her stepfather, Albert Heaton, ran a shop to make casks and barrels. Nine men worked for him. Yellow fever—one of the terrible diseases in the subtropical South— struck Heaton's shop. It killed eight of the nine men working for Heaton. He never could go back into the shop after that.

Both Mr. and Mrs. Heaton themselves contracted yellow fever, but none of their children did. Heaton rode horseback into

Texas, bought land near Austin from a man named Rufus Cannon, and wrote to Mary Kate's mother of the trees, flowers, grass, and a spring at the edge of their lot. Mary Kate's mother, at twenty-seven, with four children, traveled on the sailing ship *Charles Morgan* from New Orleans to Galveston, by stagecoach to Austin, and by an ox-drawn covered wagon twenty-five miles to what was called Cannonville, but never did grow into a town.

A preacher came to Cannonville's three houses every Sunday, or to some other house in the area. People walked miles to attend. "If too far to walk," said Mary Kate, "Father hitched Lion and Berry to the ox-wagon and took us in style." Some families even were hauled by oxen over rough ground as they sat on slides, something like sledges.

"Mother had a hand loom and spinning wheel made, on which she spun and wove most of our clothing," Mary Kate recalled. "I felt dressed up in my homespun dress and Father's home-made shoes. We knitted our stockings and gloves and braided our hats of wheat-straw or corn husks."

Mary Kate was married on July 24, 1865, to Joseph S. Cruze. In three days he was to be twenty; she was to be sixteen on her next birthday. Yet, she said, "we felt full grown and far from children."

Joseph at first hauled lumber for a sawmill. The mill broke down. Mary Kate and Joseph both became ill with chills and fever. They moved to the mountains—"in a little vacant shanty that someone had built near a spring." It had neither chimney nor floor. It was clinked with mud. When it rained, the mud fell on the bride and bridegroom. But, said Mary Kate, "Mr. Cruze soon built a chimney and floored the house and we lived there for four years and were happy as larks."

Joseph took part in cow hunts, after the wild cattle. "I have baked a thousand biscuits for his trips," said Mary Kate. "The time he spent on the trail seemed very long to me, as I stayed at home, took care of the babies and the place." One day Joseph Cruze's pack turned under his old packhorse. This made the horse uncomfortable; the horse ran away, kicking the pack to pieces. It "scattered the biscuits for a mile," Mary Kate said.

In 1866, Joseph Cruze established the Cruze Ranch. In 1870

and 1871, he drove cattle over what he called "the old Chisholm Trail." For the Cruzes things looked up. "Mr. Cruze drove his own cattle and made wages besides, which was more money than we ever had before."

Prosperity had caught up with them. And what they bought shows what prosperity was like, just over one hundred years ago: a Wheeler & Wilcox sewing machine, some moss agate jewelry, a side saddle, bridle, blanket, riding skirt, a pony for Mary Kate, and two wagons.

After the four years in their first home, that vacant shanty clinked with mud, and about fifty more years on the Cruze Ranch, which was in Hays County, Joseph and Mary Kate Cruze decided to take it easier. They took two daughters and one grandson and moved into town, San Antonio. When they left the ranch, it was 1917.

Cowboy E. P. Byler was lucky with his girl in 1872. He had been, in 1871, nine months without sleeping in a house. He duplicated that experience in 1872. But, he said, "I got back in time to be married to Miss Fannie M. Crossley, on Christmas Day, 1872."

Cowboy Branch Isbell had been the twelve-year-old who, in Alabama, had admired Confederate cattle drivers and wanted to be like them. At twenty, he had gone along with the Burks, when Amanda went up the trail. It was his first cattle drive, and he was a tenderfoot. Just before the trip he had got lost on the prairie. Thinking did not seem to help, so he sat down and started playing mumble peg. John Burks, Amanda's brother-in-law, came along and led him back to safety.

The following year, 1872, Branch Isbell went to a dance near San Patricio. He probably square-danced to tunes like "The Old Gray Horse Come Tearing through the Wilderness," "Cackling Hens," "Hogs in the Cornfield," "Black Jack Grove," "Old Dan Tucker," and "Cotton Eyed Joe." He had met, a few times, a girl named Lizzie Hinnant. She was sixteen. Branch Isbell asked her for a dance. She said "No." "I thanked her," said Isbell, "and told her that since there remained in the sea as good fish as had ever been caught, I'd cast my line in another place. Instead of wilting, as I thought she would, she came back with this: 'Certainly there are, but unfortunately for you they have quit biting at toads.' " Added Isbell: "Since then I have known that the 'Yellow Rose of Texas' grows on a thorny bush."

The Yellow Roses also were strong and healthy. The girls, far fewer in number than the cowboys, would dance almost every set—till the dawn came—then ride horseback fifteen or thirty miles home.

On the morning after the dance, Isbell himself was not idle. He returned to camp about daylight. That day, Sunday, "a blessed spring Sabbath," he called it, he and his outfit branded more than three hundred calves.

25

Men, women, and horses keep trying

WHEN SHE married and went out to a ranch, Mrs. Mont Woodward never in her life had cooked a meal. She was on the ranch as long as eighteen months without seeing another woman. Yet she learned by herself; she became a competent and respected cook and homemaker.

More than once, from the door of the ranch, she saw Indians stealing horses. When Indians attacked, in 1873, Mrs. Woodward —the former Helena Thomas of Austin—was asked to hide in the brush with her children. She hid them, then picked up a gun and went out to face the Indians. She was told: "Go back to those children." She replied: "No, I will not. I will stay here with you and fight for those children."

Helena Thomas—and Amanda Burks and Mary Kate Cruze and many another woman of the Southwest frontier—had this in common: They got into unexpected situations, sometimes odd or dangerous. So did the cowboy himself. Both the cowboy and his woman tried to cope. Sometimes they succeeded. Sometimes they failed. But they tried.

By 1870–75, the cowboy had learned often he had to face up to sudden, unusual or frightening situations.

"I was 17 years old," said J. C. Thompson of Devine, Texas, of his first joining a drive to Kansas, "but was not a novice in the business by any means as I had been gathering, roping, and branding mavericks all my life."

One day, when Thompson and his brother caught a maverick, they had to mark it—but they lacked a knife to nick its ears as a brand or mark. Unable to cut the young cow's ears, the boys bit into them—one boy to each ear. "It took some chewing," said J. C. Thompson, "but we did a fairly good job of it."

A man who during the War Between the States had trailed cattle across the Mississippi River to the Confederate states, Col. D. H. Snyder, in 1868, had driven cattle through New Mexico to Colorado, following Oliver Loving and Charles Goodnight. When Snyder started, a whole herd owned by Jesse Chisholm had just been captured by Indians in New Mexico across the border from Texas. Snyder made it through New Mexico and to Colorado, and on the way learned something new for cowmen.

Previously it had been customary, especially when driving cattle across plains where water was scarce, to kill at once any newborn calves. This was hard on cows and their calves, and hard on the tender hearts of many a cowboy. The reason for it had been that it was thought the calves could not stand the tortures of thirst. But Colonel Snyder allowed the calves to traipse along. They arrived at the end of the drive in as good condition as any of the other cattle. Snyder's men always let the calves follow along after that. Some trail drivers let the calves ride in wagons.

Rain for days on end, and flooding, raging rivers to cross, gave many a cowboy a chance to cope. "The elements didn't let up in their tear-shedding job," cowboy W. C. Fielder said of a storm in Indian Territory. "It thundered and lightninged so it was hard to tell whether it was thundering at the lightning or lightning at the thunder."

The trail would be a mud bog. Fires could not be lit, and raw, half-cooked, or cold food would be served for days to the cowboys, hollow-legged at best. At night, a cowboy would have to wrap a tarpaulin around his bedroll (two or three blankets). At a river in flood, he would have to cut cottonwood logs and lash them to each side of the wagon to get it across. He had to get the cattle over. They might follow a lead steer. They might follow a man on horseback.

They might not.

They did not for W. E. Cureton, born in Arkansas, the man who said he honored the longhorn because it "furnished its own transportation." His herd, when it reached the Red River "full of muddy water," refused to cross. The sun was in their faces. At twenty-one years of age—he was to be a cowman sixty years—Cureton decided to wait till afternoon to try to drive the cattle across. It worked. "By the time," he said, "the drags got near the river the leaders were climbing the east bank."

Another time at the rampaging Red River, the cattle in midstream began swimming in a circle, a mill. The trail boss called for his son, a cowboy named W. B. Foster. Foster tried.

"I stripped to my underclothes," he remembered, "mounted Jack Moore [his horse] and went to them. I got off the horse and right on to the cattle. They were so jumped together that it was like walking on a raft of logs. When I finally got to the only real big steer in the bunch I mounted him and he pulled for the other side."

The other cattle followed the big steer.

When the big steer was approaching the bank, Foster drifted downstream to his horse, then rode to the far bank with the cattle. Until evening, no other cowboys were able to cross the tumultuous Red River.

So—in his underclothes, with no hat, and no food—Foster by himself had to hold the herd together, all day, till sundown.

Another cowboy rode a mule to point the herd across the Red. The waves were so high he was swept off. He grabbed the tail of a big steer. He hung on. The steer crossed the river and pulled the cowboy up the bank.

Deep water could drown horses or mules or cattle or cowboys who could not swim. A cowboy's rope could tangle him and pull him to death by drowning. Crossing a rushing river, a cowboy wanted the most faithful and most experienced and coolest cowhand on the other side of the herd from him—a man who, in every sense, could cope. He wanted, in a new phrase the cowboy gave the English language, "a good man to ride the river with."

Like a flooding river, a stampede tested the cowboy's ability to cope. When the cattle ran, fast and furious and out of control, it was so dangerous that it was avoided at all cost. The start of a drive was a crucial time. Foremen, getting the cattle "road broke," did one of two things: (1) They pushed the herd so hard it would get tired and lie down at night and rest. They walked the cattle twenty or thirty miles a day, twice as far as they would later. (2) They took it easy, traveled slowly, let the longhorns get used to the trail. In either case, the object was to stop a stampede before it started—because, as John Jacobs pointed out, stampeding was apt to be habit-forming. In either case, it wasn't easy for a cowboy to learn his job. "I've learned how to drive wild cattle, which is something," Tim Hughes said. "The first time I tried I could do nothing whatever with them, and had to go back for help."

Almost anything could start a stampede. A saddle might rattle. A cowboy might get off his horse too fast. Sometimes, when the cattle were lying down contentedly at night, and the night riders were moving slowly around them, either dozing or singing, nothing at all would be seen to happen—and the cattle would suddenly run, with crashing horns and thundering hoofs, out of control.

Said Charles Goodnight, who knew: "The heat developed in a large drove of cattle during a stampede was surprising, and the odor given off by the clashing horns and hoofs was nearly over-powering. Sometimes in cool weather it was uncomfortably warm on the leeward side of a moving herd. . . . Animal heat seems to attract electricity, especially when the cattle are wet, and after a storm I have seen the faces of men riding with a herd scorched as if some furnace blast had blazed against them."

Once the cattle were running, the cowboys had to spend time trying to turn it into a mill, a circle. In the river, a man kept the cattle out of a mill (if he could); in a stampede, he tried to force the longhorns into one. Then a cowboy would spend hours trying to keep the herd together. Often, the cattle scattered and it took days to get the cattle back, if it could be done at all.

Most women rode sidesaddle, in long woolen skirts. The wind could balloon out a skirt. This often started a stampede. One woman impressed L. B. Anderson. She looked back. The cattle were gaining on her. She forgot her modesty and swung herself astride of the horse and pulled off. "She outdistanced everything in that herd and rode safely away."

W. B. Foster and his horse Jack Moore—the pair that had got Foster's father's cattle across the flooding Red River—also coped in the case of a stampede. "At Hillsboro," said Foster, "the cattle stampeded around a school house." Most of the children were safe inside, but one little girl, with a red shawl, was still on her way to school. The wind blew the shawl, and that did it. The cattle ran. "I was behind the herd and saw what was exciting the cattle, so I got all there was out of Jack Moore and picked her up just in time."

Teddy Blue's cattle stampeded in a country full of cactus. "The country south of San Antonio," he explained, "is brush country, south Texas brush, mesquite and cactus and thorn and I don't know what else, but I know everything that grows has thorns on it except the willows, and some of them are an inch long."

He was asleep beneath his slicker one night when someone yelled, "They're running!"

"I grabbed my hat and jumped for my horse, forgetting to put on my chaps, and I spent half the night chasing the cattle through that thorny brush. When daylight came and we got them all together we hadn't lost a head. But I was a bloody sight. I had a big hole in my forehead, and my face was all over blood, my hands was cut to pieces—because I'd left my gloves in my chaps pocket— and my knees was worst of all. I was picking thorns out of them all the way to Kansas."

Near San Antonio, C. W. Ackermann, eighteen, was starting for Kansas with a herd. The first night, a rainy one, the cattle stampeded eighteen times. One of his cowboys—none was over twenty-two—was run into by the stampeding cattle. His horse was crippled. He himself was carried on the backs of the cattle for about a mile, but escaped with only bruises.

Ackermann on one trip encountered an Irishman who had invented an antistampede device: a cattle pen on rollers. When steers inside the pen stampeded, Ackermann said, they took the pen right along with them. Running cattle frequently moved it as much as fifty yards, he said.

Richard (Dick) Withers, during a stampede, fell off his horse. He had the presence of mind to lie still on the ground. It saved his life. The steers ran around him.

John Pat Bryan of Skidmore, Texas, managed to stay with the herd during a stampede, the only cowboy who did. But he got lost. "When the sun came up it rose in the west for two mornings before it rose in the east with me."

Not every cowboy was successful in coping with a stampede. R. J. Jennings of San Antonio never knew what hit him. The herd started to run at suppertime; it was a black night. "I straddled my horse and went down the hill in front of the frightened cattle. That was the last I remembered until about midnight.
"The boys missed me, and supposed I was somewhere with a bunch of cattle, but finally they discovered me sitting on my horse in the middle of the herd." A cowboy named Sam Oden found Jennings. Dazed, he had to be helped back to camp. He had been injured so that he could not lie down to sleep. "For two weeks afterward I could sleep only when I was leaning against the end gate of the wagon." He suffered from his injury for years. But he was lucky, too: "I do not know how I came to be on my horse when they found me."

One night the cowboys milled cattle to hold them during a storm. Next morning a cowboy was missing. His body was found, among the prairie-dog holes, next to the body of his horse. Both were pounded flat into the ground. Only the handle of his Colt revolver retained something of its original shape. To save his parents' feelings, the men with him wrote his folks in Henrietta, Texas, that he had been struck by lightning.

If the cowboy was capable—and most were—he received a lot of help from his horse.

When a cowboy joined an outfit, the boss told him what horses he was to ride—and nothing else about them. It was a compliment to let a man himself learn about his horses. From the first day, the cowboy himself would saddle them and take care of them. Except in a crisis, he would not lend a horse to anyone else. If the boss noticed an abused horse, his rider was likely to be fired. If the boss took a cowboy's favorite horse away from him, a cowboy might as well quit before he was discharged.

A cowboy of Big Wells, Texas, B. Vesper, had been born in Germany in 1845. In the 1870s, in his twenties, he was a greenhorn on the Long Trail, one of the men driving 700 cattle from Fort Worth to Abilene. After a stampede, he got lost. His horse wanted to travel in the opposite direction from the way he thought camp was. "I told the old horse if he knew more about its location than I did to go ahead. And right there I learned that a good cow horse knew more than a green Dutchman, for in just a little while he took me right into camp."

In 1872, M. A. Withers of Lockhart, who had lassoed buffalo to advertise Abilene, Kansas, was near Hays City, Kansas, when his cattle stampeded. "I saw by a flash of lightning that I was on the edge of a big bluff of the river. There was nothing left for me to do but jump." He spurred his horse; the horse jumped; horse and rider landed in three or four feet of river water. "Neither my horse nor I was hurt, although some of the steers were killed and many crippled."

A cowboy, when he could afford to buy and keep his own mount, would do so. One of a cowboy's favorite mounts was likely to be a cutting horse—a horse that could move into a herd of cattle and cut out a cow or steer that the cowboy wanted to separate. A quarter horse made a fine cutting horse. So did an Arabian, from the same line of horses Columbus had brought. So did the Morgan horse, which came from Vermont in the 1800s.

A cutting horse could be shown, by a flick of the rope, a cow the cowboy wanted cut out. Then the horse went into the herd and worried the cow, wheeled and turned it, till it came out of the herd.

This intelligence of the cutting horse the cowboy called "cow sense."

Buck Gravis said his cutting pony, a dun, was so smart all he had to do was to read a list of desired brands to the pony.

Comrade Briscoe said his pony would pick the Briscoe cattle out from among the O'Connor cattle. Briscoe said his cattle, just as soon as they saw the pony, Gotch, "would detach themselves."

Hiram Craig at a C. C. Slaughter roundup watched open-mouthed as two horses, with no riders aboard them, cut out steers. The horses that did it were a black, Old Popsy, and a slim bay, S.B. "Each horse," Craig said, "brought out the right cow without a miss. This was just great work for a dumb animal."

One day a wild little bay horse got Teddy Blue into trouble. It bucked while Blue was attempting to ride him. Off went Blue's six-shooter. Off went his Winchester rifle. Off went Blue. As he flew through the air and hit the ground, the ligaments of one of Blue's arms were painfully torn—he blamed later rheumatism on the incident. Nevertheless, Blue liked the little bay so much he made Billy, as he named him, his top horse for twenty-six years.

26

The cowboy obtains a better Colt

AT FIRST the war with Mexico, and then the War Between the States, had meant that Colt pistols were manufactured in large numbers. Their use spread. An Army revolver, the Colt model of 1873, became the cowboy's gun. It was called the Single-Action Army Revolver, and also the Frontier Model, and the Peace-Maker.

Texans named it the six-shooter.

The most popular models, the Colt .44 or .45 caliber, weighed 2¼ pounds and had 8-inch-long barrels.

Colt eventually chambered his revolver so that it would take the same ammunition as that used in a Winchester rifle. A cowboy then had to carry only one type of ammunition for both.

Colts became so common that people said a cowboy might take cold "if he wasn't wearing a six-shooter."

George Webb Slaughter carried Colts. Slaughter, who had been the messenger to the Alamo, was a cowman who also became a minister. He would travel sixty miles alone on horseback, across Indian country, to baptize—and he baptized over 3,000 persons. As protection, he toted two six-shooters. Once, at the village of Palo Pinto, there were so many Indians around that he kept a six-shooter and a carbine handy during the sermon. Every member of the congregation also was armed.

A cowboy called a six-shooter a "hog leg," or a "friend in need." Or a "smoke wagon" as in the sentence: "Both pulled their smoke wagons and got busy."

The result of such an incident—and such occasions were rare —might be that a man died of "lead poisoning."

The cowboy also called his Colt and its six cartridges "Judge Colt and six provisions of his statutes."

The cowboy carried a single Colt. Almost never, unlike George Webb Slaughter, two pistols. They would have weighed him down. The Colt often was in a holster on his left side. The butt (the hog leg) was forward. He could whip out the Colt by reaching across his body with his right arm.

He did practice drawing his gun quickly—not firing quickly. These dry runs went on all the time, and included, for the cowboy, practicing his grip on his gun. That meant drawing it fast, gripping it, and aiming it, all without shooting. He practiced his grip till he could point his Colt exactly and as easily as he pointed his finger. From elbow to muzzle was a single straight line.

To keep from firing his Colt accidentally, he often carried it with only five chambers loaded. The hammer of the Colt rested over the empty chamber.

On the whole, the cowboy was not the quick-on-the-trigger man he has been described as being. He drew his Colt (or his Winchester from a scabbard on his horse's neck) against an Indian out for his scalp or out for his horses or cattle, or against a cattle rustler or horse thief, or sometimes in a quarrel in a cow town, or when he was far away from the herd to kill a buffalo, antelope, duck, goose, wild turkey, or prairie chicken. Or if he broke his leg or lost his horse, he fired three shots as a signal for help.

He never fired near the cattle; that would stampede them. He never brought his hand near his gun—except to draw it. That meant that in a saloon quarrel he never, never fingered his gun—unless things had reached the last stage.

Because he had little practice with live ammunition—bullets were expensive—the cowboy was not, as a rule, a good shot. That he left to sheriffs, marshals, policemen, Texas Rangers, and soldiers.

A Texas Ranger, John Woodland, slept with his head on his saddle. He stuck his Colt under the fork of the saddle. That kept it dry. It also kept it handy: "If I hear anything in the night, I can slide my hand in and get it without rustling, quicker than I could take it out of my belt."

Woodland, like many a cowboy, was depending on his Colt. He felt he could. He had a good reason: at a time of inefficient guns—and, for that matter, of inefficient machines of other kinds—the Colts were dependable.

Not absolutely dependable—but almost. After six months of rough handling, wet grass, and neglects of camp travel, said Frederick Law Olmsted, "not once did a ball fail to answer the finger."

He went on: "Nothing got out of order, nothing required care; not once, though carried at random, in coat-pocket or belt, or tied thumping at the pommel, was there an accidental discharge." A Colt on one occasion was dropped into a bog. It was retrieved, and though it dripped water, not a single misfire resulted.

However, what made a Colt "almost" dependable was that, when you pressed the trigger, you might fire one shot, or you might satisfactorily fire any number up to five or six. With only a little practice, Olmsted said, you could knock the head off a nearby snake, or, with a fixed rest, you could hit a man at what was rifle range.

This accuracy and dependability ran up the price of a Colt. A five-shot, .38-caliber pistol had an original cost of $9. A six-shot .44 with a 7½-inch-long barrel cost $20. These prices soared on the Western frontier.

At any price, a Colt was invaluable. A cowboy got a sense of security from his: ". . . feeling you beneath my hand was like the hard grip of a friend." Wild Bill Hickok looked over his two Colts every morning and never let another man clean them. Wyatt Earp used long—twelve-inch—barrels and asserted they did not slow him up on the draw.

In the 1970s, a hundred years afterward, the six-shooter is still invaluable for sheriffs, policemen, soldiers, sailors, and bank robbers. But its greatest use is indicated by an exhibit in a Nebraska museum, where it is labeled: "The gun that won the west."

Mass-produced, the Colts armed almost every man in the West, and the fact that they did, and that most men were armed, was a great controller of tempers and a great preventer of quarrels. Besides, with every man armed with a Colt, there was no way of telling who would win a fight. "God made some men big and some men small," ran a saying, "but Colonel Colt evened things up."

The hero of this book—the largely anonymous young cowboy and his mount, one of several he would ride up the trail over a period of weeks and months.

A pair of not-so-anonymous cowboys and two of their more-than-usually docile longhorns. Col. George W. Saunders, on his horse, was part of the Long Trail virtually from start to finish. You'll recognize the man with the cheerful grin, standing beside him, as Will Rogers.

Principal Cattle Trails of the Period from 1865 to 1895

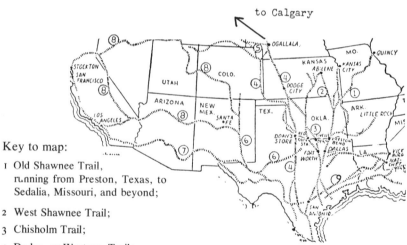

Key to map:

1 Old Shawnee Trail, running from Preston, Texas, to Sedalia, Missouri, and beyond;

2 West Shawnee Trail;

3 Chisholm Trail;

4 Dodge, or Western, Trail;

5 Montana Trail; 6 Goodnight-Loving Trail; 7 Main California Trail; 8 Other trails leading to California over which herds were driven; 9 Old Spanish Trail

This map shows the principal cattle trails, which between 1868 and 1895 carried millions of cattle from the breeding grounds of Texas to slaughter, and to the cattle ranges of the upper Great Plains. The Long Trail, never a single, formal trail, sometimes followed these established trails. More often, it crisscrossed them countless times as herds were driven north, east, or west.

The chuck wagon was literally the cowboys' lifeline since it provided water and enabled the outfit's cook to prepare meals miles from civilization. This photograph was taken about 1890 and pictures "hands" from the XIT (standing for ten—*X*—counties *I*n *T*exas) Ranch on a roundup.

Most supplies for the chuck wagons were bought at the start of the long drive since grocery stores were few and far between. Here, wagons from the Frying Pan Ranch load for the trip in 1885 from Tascosa, Texas, to Dodge City, Kansas.

Metropolitan, downtown Dodge City in 1873. The view here is from Front Street (!) looking east from Third Avenue. Santa Fe tracks, train, and depot are to the right across the street from the business buildings. Second building from the left was the U.S. Post Office.

A drawing of an early trail drive showing Texas longhorns en route to Ellsworth, Kansas, for shipment to market on the Kansas Pacific Railway. Note the positions of the cowboys "on guard" the entire length of the herd to forestall trouble, if possible, and to keep it to a minimum if it arose.

There were few settlers on the Great Plains in the earliest days of the cattle drives. What few there were scratched a bare subsistence from an arid land (the watermelons shown here must have been a rare treat) and lived in sod houses like this one.

Wichita, Kansas, end of many a cattle drive. This is what the railroad station looked like in 1880. The locomotive is typical of those which hauled cattle cars, though this one has passenger cars in tow.

George W. Littlefield was one of the trail drivers who became a wealthy rancher, settling in Texas. He valued education highly and made substantial financial contributions to the University of Texas.

Bottom left, Col. Charles Goodnight, one of the two men for whom the pioneer cattle route, the Goodnight-Loving Trail, was named. Long after the drives had concluded, Colonel Goodnight was photographed on his last ride on "Old Buttons" at Goodnight, Texas, in 1916.

Bottom right, Born in Willis, Montgomery County, Texas in March, 1842, Richard D. Cude was another of the Long Trail's pioneer cowboys. His family first came to Texas in 1834.

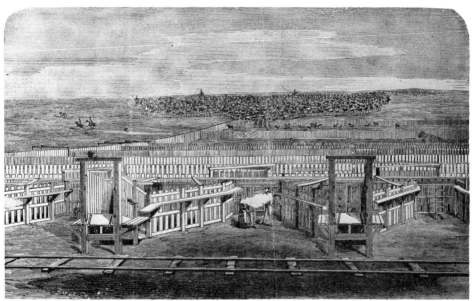

Cattle being herded for shipment, via the Kansas Pacific Railway, at Ellsworth, Kansas. Pens at trackside were typical of those used at railheads throughout the midcontinent.

Earlier methods of funneling cattle into railroad cars were somewhat more primitive and hazardous than the setup at Ellsworth.

Once loaded with live beef, cattle trains departed regularly and often for slaughterhouses to the east. Here, two steam off to Kansas City on the Kansas Pacific Railway line. Drovers' Cottage (right) was one of the few good hostelries the length and breadth of the Long Trail.

Meanwhile, back at the XIT Ranch, wind power was beginning to make the watering of stock a great deal easier than it had been in early trail days when getting 3,000 head of cattle enough to drink at water holes, creeks, and rivers was a mammoth job.

27

Barbed wire holds the longhorns

A FARMER, Joseph Farwell Glidden of De Kalb, Illinois, is said to have noticed that range cattle turned away from thorned cactus. He devised a fence of twisted wire, with barbs, that he used around his farm. It worked. An occasional barb, somewhere along a strand of wire, kept out cattle—or kept in cattle. It saved labor: before barbed wire, fences had been made by rails—chopping down trees. Or by gathering and piling rocks. Or, over years, by growing hedges. In any case, barbed wire saved seemingly endless physical toil.

There also were fences of smooth wire. Cattle easily broke through them.

Glidden in 1875 started a small factory with five boys stringing bales of wire. His first salesman appeared in Texas. H. B. Sanford (I also have the name as Sandborn), in Gainesville, sold the first barbed wire known to have been brought to Texas. Sanford was the founder of both the Frying Pan Ranch and the city of Amarillo.

In San Antonio, another salesman, twenty-one-year-old John Warne Gates, set out to peddle barbed wire. He built a barbed-wire corral. San Antonio cattlemen were skeptical. Gates insisted: "This is the finest fence in the world. Light as air. Stronger than whisky. Cheaper than dirt. All steel and miles long. The cattle ain't born that can get through it. Bring on your steers, gentlemen!''

Gates' corral fenced in a city plaza. Twenty-five of the meanest longhorns—the "worst fence busters"—in San Antonio were brought in. The longhorns, as expected, charged the wire. Their hides pricked by the barbs, they gave it up.

Before nightfall, Gates had sold hundreds of miles of what cattlemen would call "bob-wire." In time, Gates would be called Bet-a-Million Gates. One story is that, after he had grown rich, he bet a million dollars on which raindrop would go down a window fastest.

I. L. Ellwood made a fortune from barbed wire, and with it bought land. With Glidden he bought, near Lubbock, Texas, the Spade Ranch. Ellwood, Glidden, and the Spade became known for all-night dances that attracted cowboys from many counties.

An agency for barbed wire was established in Houston. A few years were all it took for ranchers to see the advantages of barbed wire. The Houston office soon was selling $750,000 worth of wire each year. Glidden by 1880 was opening a big factory in De Kalb. Every ten hours 202 machines produced 600 miles of fencing.

In Swenson, Texas, barbed wire surrounded the town square —and turned it into a corral to hold cattle before shipment.

All over the West, cattle learned to stop at barbed-wire fences. Barbed wire held in the longhorns—and put roadblocks across the cattle trails.

Barbed wire, fencing in wide tracts of pasture, reduced the number of cowboys needed to care for the cattle. It promoted the conservation of the range. It encouraged an owner to buy land—he could use it exclusively. It encouraged an owner to buy better breeding animals—with fencing, he would get their use exclusively.

Barbed wire began to go up in Texas, Oklahoma, and all the states farther north.

The days of the open range, the days of open grasslands from the Gulf of Mexico coast to Canada, were beginning to end.

Barbed wire would mean more ranches in the North, in Nebraska, Nevada, Wyoming, Montana, North and South Dakota, all the way to Canada, to fatten Texas cattle on the grass that grew, and dried to hay right where it grew, even behind barbed-wire fences. Vast areas became what they remain to this day: range country. Cattle country.

But even as barbed wire began to break up the Long Trail, Dodge City, Kansas, in 1874 and '75 was entering a ten-year hey-day as a cattle town—a longer turn than any other shipping point ever had.

The trail to Dodge City, George Saunders said, "as I remember passed up [in Indian Territory—Oklahoma] North Fork of the Red River and Croton Creek, and crossed the North Fork of the Red River at the Wichita mountains." Then it ran up the North Fork to Indian Camp. Then the trail crossed, in order, Elm Creek, Cash Creek, the Washita, the Canadian, Sand Creek, Wolf Creek, Otter Creek, Bear Creek, Wild Horse, and the Cimarron. "At the Cimarron," said Saunders, "Red Clark conducted a road house called Long Horn Roundup. The trail crossed Bear Creek, Bluff Creek at Mailey's Road House, Mulberry Creek, and from there ran to Dodge City."

Dodge City became known as the fastest and wildest of them all—where the cowboy had what he called a "hurrah time."

"Where do you want to go?" asked the railroad conductor. "To hell," said the cowboy. "Well, give me $2.50 and get off at Dodge City."

It had been a buffalo hunters' town. It became the cowboy capital. It provided necessities:

A jail. A well fifteen feet deep was a natural; into this cooler up to five drunks at a time were parked to sober up.

Saloons. To keep the well filled, they never closed. On his opening day, a proprietor threw away his key.

Women. The cowboys, when they arrived, were unshaved, bearded (if they were old enough), ragged, unwashed, tired from long days of wearying work. They had, they said, "come up the Chisholm Trail with the buffalo wild and woolly." They had not seen any women for weeks or months. Dodge City had a section of town where women entertained the cowboys. One establishment had a blood-red glass in its front door. This gave a name to the area, a name that spread to wherever such services were provided: the Red Light District.

A cemetery. Dodge City was one place where shooting became common. Those who died not in bed, but with their boots on, were interred in a graveyard that became known as Boot Hill.

A checkroom for weapons. With shooting on the rise, Colts had to be checked with town marshals. In order not to feel naked, cowboys soon obtained small pistols, the two-barrel .41-caliber derringers, that could be hidden in a pants pocket, boot, waistband, on a cord inside a sleeve, or even in the palm of a hand.

Not only cowboys were buried in Boot Hill. There were also children. Cowboy W. J. Burkett in 1883, when Dodge City was winding up as a cattle town, came upon a tombstone for Mary Hamilton, fourteen. Lines upon it read:

> Weep not for me my parents dear,
> I am not dead but only sleeping here.
> I was not yours alone,
> But God's who loved me best, and took me home.

28

A Long Trail to many places

1876. IN THE Long Trail country: On June 25, in Montana, Gen. George A. Custer and 264 soldiers of the Seventh Cavalry were killed to the last man at the Battle of the Little Big Horn—as the defenders of the Alamo in San Antonio had been wiped out, just forty years earlier. General Custer died with a smoking Colt in each hand. The Indians, united under Sitting Bull, were led in battle by Chief Gall and Chief Crazy Horse. Although the Sioux were victorious, the Little Big Horn would prove to be their last stand. . . . In Deadwood, South Dakota, an outlaw, Jack McCall, shot from behind and killed James Butler (Wild Bill) Hickok, who in 1871 had been the law officer in Abilene, Kansas. Hickok had his six-shooter partly out of his holster when he fell. . . . Texas A & M University was founded; a hundred years later it would be one of the world's great centers of cattle information.

AROUND THE UNITED STATES: In New York City, the West was becoming a popular topic for stage plays. One of the plays was *The Two Men of Sandy Bat* by Bret Harte. . . . A forty-year-old artist who had drawn battlefield scenes in the Civil War and had become a magazine illustrator was gradually making the long, slow switch to oil paintings and water colors: Winslow Homer. Bret

Harte also was forty in 1876; both Harte and Homer that year were already one year older than was Wild Bill Hickok when he died.

The Long Trail was shifting farther and farther west.

"We went as far, if not farther west, than any cattle had ever gone," said a cowboy from Fort Cobb, Oklahoma, J. F. (Little Jim) Ellison, Jr. He meant by that that the Long Trail itself was moving ever westward as farms and barbed wire and railroads and towns began to fill up the land toward the east.

Ellison said he crossed the Washita about eight miles west of today's town of Chickasha. "We passed through the Wichita mountains at the foot of Mount Scott," he said, "and saw lots of buffalo and antelope. Our first stop was at Dodge City, Kansas. We delivered part of those cattle north of Cheyenne, Wyoming Territory."

Dodge City, west of Abilene, west of Ellsworth, would be the last of the important towns in Kansas.

Ellison's outfit and one other drove about 100,000 cattle to Northern markets in 1876. These cattle, said Little Jim Ellison "were strung out from San Antonio almost to Dodge City." (Altogether, about 400,000 cattle that year passed Doan's Store on the Red River, cowboy A. E. Scheske of Gonzales, Texas, was told.)

Ellison himself drove also to Ogallala, Nebraska. "I held 7,000 head just south of Ogallala, across the Platte River, my camp being near a cold spring that boiled out of the ground. The water from this spring was the coldest I ever drank, so cold in fact that it could make your teeth ache."

On the railroad, Ogallala was 260 miles north of Dodge City. North of the northern boundary of Kansas, near the northern boundary of Colorado, it is in Keith County, southwest Nebraska. Ogallala lies on the South Platte River near its junction with the North Platte. The two rivers form the Platte, which eventually joins the Missouri, which in turn joins the Mississippi about fifteen miles above St. Louis, and turns the Mississippi its own muddy color. The Red Rock (Montana), Missouri, and Mississippi rivers together make a drainage system 3,741 miles long, almost as long as the Amazon system, 3,900 miles, in South America. The Missouri and Mississippi, draining two-thirds of the United States, are known for spring floods that made river crossings on their tributary rivers so difficult for cowboys and longhorns.

At no time had there ever been a single destination for the longhorns; and in 1874 and 1875 there were many. The cattle could plod to Dodge City for immediate transshipment to slaughter-houses. Or the cattle could go there, and then be walked on to somewhere else—for instance, northern ranches in Wyoming; on the Humboldt River in Nevada; on the upper Missouri or in the Black Hills. They could bypass Dodge City entirely and go to Indian agencies to feed the Indians. The cattle could even go to California.

Another man who drove far to the west in 1876 was D. S. Combs. "This was a real experience," he commented. "We started from San Antonio over an unknown route and where no road or trail was to be followed. We were the pioneers and made the first tracks that marked the Western Trail. We reached Ogallala, Nebraska, after about three months' straight drive, passing through some hard country and often forced to go long distances without water." Food was hard to get, too. "Our meals consisted of just whatever we could find that would do to eat."

A. D. McGehee of San Marcos, Texas, told a story of another occasion when Combs had no known trail to follow: "I fell in with D. S. Combs and about daylight one morning we landed at Burlington, Iowa, and started up the street to get breakfast, and a toddy was suggested. After going up the street for some distance, not knowing that Iowa was a dry state at that time, we stopped on the corner of a street and looked about as strangers would do, when a man standing on the opposite side, without asking a word, but, I think, from Combs' droughty look, sized us up and said: 'Go back two doors and go in a back room and you will find what you are looking for.'

"We followed instructions," McGehee concluded. The man's directions were accurate.

Although it was the year of General Custer's defeat at the Little Big Horn, the Indian troubles in 1876 were fading. Jasper (Bob) Lauderdale saw with his own eyes a sight that summarized the end of the Indian wars. Lauderdale, twenty-two years old, was the boss of a herd. The herd belonged to George Hindes, a cowman who had come from Alabama and driven a small herd at age twelve, and now was an owner at thirty-one, and to another man named

J. W. Murphy. Bob Lauderdale drove the cattle in the spring to Dodge City, Kansas.

"On this trip," he recalled, "I saw old Sitting Bull and about 1200 of his bucks and squaws in charge of Government troops; these were the Cheyenne and Sioux Indians, who had massacred General Custer and his men and were being taken to Fort Reno. There were about 2000 horses with the Indians. The troops had pack mules so well-trained that you could not make them break line. They moved in single file and were taught this to enable them to travel through the mountains.

"The Indians were traveling in their usual way, poles tied to the necks of ponies like shafts in a buggy, but much longer (the ends of the long poles dragged on the ground behind the ponies), and in willow baskets lashed to these poles the old bucks and squaws rode who were too old to ride horseback—their tepees and supplies were also carried in this manner. Squaws with their papooses strapped to their backs rode horseback, and in passing through this camp I saw one old buck dressed in moccasins, breech-clout, a frock tail coat, and an old-fashioned preacher's hat."

A career of any kind was a rare thing a hundred years ago. But a cowboy could make a career for himself, and might obtain a measure of security in his job at a time when such security was rare. One who did was R. G. (Dick) Head, born in Saline County, Missouri, and a Confederate soldier at sixteen. In 1876 he was in the middle of his career.

A year after the Civil War, he had begun to work for Col. John J. Meyers, the man who had driven cattle north without a destination in 1867, and had gone to Abilene, Kansas, thereafter. Head began working for Colonel Meyers for the standard cowboy's wage, $30 a month.

He received frequent raises till the third year. Then he was given charge of all Colonel Meyers' trail business, and received $1,800 a year plus expenses. He held that position for some years after Colonel Meyers died in 1874.

29

A trail driver
sets up as a rancher

AFTER OLIVER Loving died, back in 1867, Charles Goodnight had acquired another partner, John Dawson. Dawson had lice. The other men with him soon acquired lice. Goodnight, among others, could not sleep. He wanted to stop for a day to wash. Because it was costing $75 a day to operate their outfit, Dawson did not want to take the time out. Said he: "Turn your shirt wrong side out. It will take them all night to get back through and you can get a good night's sleep."

Goodnight in 1876 acquired yet another partner, an Englishman, John George Adair. Adair in 1874 had come over and hunted buffaloes. He succeeded in killing only his horse. But he liked the West. He was given the name then given to English investors in the West, a "velvet breeches."

In 1876, nine years after Goodnight and Loving had driven the Goodnight-Loving Trail, Charles Goodnight and John Adair, as partners, established in the Palo Duro Canyon in the Texas Panhandle the JA Ranch. The Palo Duro Canyon was cut by the Red River—I believe by the Prairie Dog Town fork of the river.

The Panhandle is the north section of Texas, between Oklahoma and New Mexico, which looks on the map like the handle of a frying pan. It also is "where the wind blows prairie-dog holes inside out." There is nothing between you and the North Pole to stop the wind and the cold except a barbed-wire fence.

The Panhandle is also endless, treeless green (belly-deep grass) or brown prairie that Capt. R. B. March in 1849 had said "must remain uninhabited forever." Its distance and loneliness, he thought, would prove too much for human beings to bear.

In the Panhandle in Goodnight's day, there were, however, Comanches. To get along with the Indians, Goodnight signed a treaty with one of their chiefs, Quanah Parker. Goodnight used to know his mother.

It came about this way.

Quanah Parker was the son of a white woman, Cynthia Ann Parker. As a small girl, she had been captured by the Comanches—in 1836, the year Goodnight was born, and the year the Republic of Texas was born. She grew up with the Comanches, and bore the son who took her name. Then, after twenty-four years, in 1860, she had been recaptured by whites in a fight with the Indians.

On hand when she was recaptured was Charles Goodnight.

On the JA Ranch in the Panhandle, sixteen years after that, in 1876, Goodnight signed his agreement with Cynthia Ann's son Quanah.

Panhandle ranches were so vast that on some of them a cowboy would leave the ranch house and work for six months without returning—and without leaving the ranch. The JA Ranch at first spread over five counties; later over seven. Men worked with feverish energy to stock the ranch, and herd after herd of cattle were driven to it. On 1,300,000 acres, the JA Ranch eventually had 300,000 cattle.

Goodnight, at twenty, in 1856 had started with seventeen cattle.

Goodnight on the JA sought better cattle. He brought to the ranch high-grade Herefords. Seeking to improve beef, Goodnight crossed the Herefords with Longhorns and with Shorthorns. Goodnight also crossed buffalo with Polled Angus (Shorthorn) cattle. The result: The first herd of cattalo. His efforts at crossbreeding led to Goodnight's being called the Burbank of the Plains.

Once, as he traveled the Staked Plains of the Panhandle,

Charles Goodnight had seen a herd of buffalo that he figured was 25 miles wide and an incredible 125 miles long.

In the 1870s, the buffalo were being hunted for their hides. A construction camp for the Fort Worth and Denver City Railroad was housed in a collection of buffalo-hide tents. Even a hotel had all of its walls of buffalo hides. This buffalo-skin city would become today's city of Amarillo.

Buffalo bones bleached the land; they were gathered, and thousands of tons of bones were shipped as fertilizer.

Goodnight on the JA Ranch kept and preserved buffaloes. He is credited with saving from extinction the buffalo of the Midwest's south plains.

30

The rattlesnake and other neighbors

DURING THE years of the Long Trail, there were in Abilene, Kansas, more prairie dogs than anything else. They lived on the Great Plains from Mexico to Canada. The prairie dog—not a dog, but a rodent—weighs one to three pounds, and is twelve to seventeen inches long. Its burrows, which may tunnel fifteen feet down into the ground, whole networks of them, all up and down the Long Trail provided holes for a cowboy's horse to stumble into—and maybe snap a leg and throw the cowboy so that a stampede might trample him. There still are prairie dogs on the Great Plains, though their numbers are fewer; there are protected prairie-dog towns in Texas at Lubbock and Odessa.

Besides buffaloes and prairie dogs, many other wild animals abounded around the cowboy, every step of the Long Trail. Many of the creatures were new and strange to the men and women pushing into the unfamiliar land of the midcontinent. Some of the animals were so strange as to be unbelievable. They could help or hinder the cowboy or the woman back home in the dugout, and they did both.

Along the trail, there were animals that, like the longhorns themselves, were not generally found over North America: big-

179

horn sheep, mule deer, pronghorned antelope, otter, beaver, and mink. In Texas alone, there were—and are—eight species of skunks. These could inconvenience the cowboy, the woman, or a horse.

There was the big, gray timber wolf.

One day in 1875, Louis Schorp, out riding the range, heard a cow bellowing and noticed her running about. He found that three wolves were after her calf. He chased away the wolves. "I have been on the range more or less since 1870," Schorp said, "and this is the only time I ever saw wolves attack a calf."

Nevertheless, there seems little doubt that the timber wolf, also known as the lobo, the loafer, the loper, or the buffalo wolf, became a killer of cattle (mostly calves) and sheep, and found both of them easier prey than wild animals. The wolf, nearly three feet high, over 150 pounds, had a mournful, drawn-out, smooth cry that resembled the howl of a large dog—but sounded more eerie. The wolf could outdodge a horse.

Individual wolves made names for themselves. There was Geronimo; the Osage Phantom; the King of Cedar Canyon; and Three Toes. Three Toes had had a foot crippled in a trap. He was said to have killed thousands of cattle. One pair of wolves was said to have killed twenty-one cattle in two months. A huge, silvery gray wolf, Old Snowdrift, avoided government hunters for months.

The timber wolf had an assistant: the doglike or wolflike coyote, two feet high and twenty to fifty pounds heavy. A couple of coyotes would travel with a wolf. They would lead him to prey, and then eat off the prey the wolf killed. The coyote's wild call—a yelp, bark, and growl all in one—has been written as "yip, yip, yip, yowr, urf, ooooo." Said Mrs. Vielé, in west Texas with the U.S. Army, just before Long Trail days: "Their dismal howlings sounded like the moaning of the sea waves, and lulled me to sleep every night during our stay in Texas." Two coyotes on opposite hills could sound like a dozen. Cowboys learned to imitate the coyote's night howling, and did so when celebrating.

Red deer were common, and provided food to hunters at home and cowboys or cooks along the trail if a man could shoot one. The red deer buck attacked men. Once a hunter, after—he thought— killing a buck, laid down his gun. The buck kept running at him and kept him away from the gun, time after time, till he (the buck) could move away.

One of the oddest animals was hard to see, and once you saw it, still harder to believe. This was the nine-inch-long horned toad or horned frog—truly a horned lizard, related to the iguanas.

The horned frog is hard to see because it is the color of sand, rock, or the ground. But if you can manage to see the horned toad, it looks like a dinosaur—like a small version of something that should have died out a few million years ago. It has horns. It has spiky scales running down its back. Its sides are fringed. Using the fringed sides, and tilting itself side to side, and pushing, the horned frog can quickly dig into and bury itself in the sand. It can live indefinitely without food or water.

In all of Texas except the very center, and in every state of the Long Trail, there was heard the bullfrog's sonorous, bass, foghorn-like jug-o'-rum call from ponds, lakes, and bayous.

Flitting through the moonlight, zigzagging beneath the bright stars, beginning at twilight when the fireflies glowed, were the bats.

The bats, the only mammals that fly, lived in caves or roosted in trees in Texas, Mexico, and New Mexico. They thrived, as do many birds, by gobbling insects, though some bats live on fruit and nectar of cactuses.

After a rain, near a river, a cowboy might awaken and find a water dog snuggled up to him. In other words, a mud puppy, also called a water puppy, also called a hellbender—a reptile with shiny, smooth skin, halfway between a frog and a lizard.

Huge sea turtles in Long Trail days waddled out of the sea to scrounge out nests in the sand and lay their eggs amid the water birds of Galveston beach.

A surprising small dog, kept by the Mexicans, was described by Willy Hughes: "They are hideously ugly, though small, and haven't a bit of hair on except a sort of narrow ridge of bristles along their sides. They look as though they had been shaved, but are really born so." That was the dog known as the Mexican hairless.

There were two wild hogs. The three-foot-high, white-collared peccary, or javelina, was a native. It killed and ate rattlesnakes and, like the longhorn, could be tamed.

The other, not native, the Spanish had brought, the long-tailed, tusked razorback. Explorers for Spain, including Columbus, let loose on islands and in unknown lands pigs, cattle, horses, and sheep to feed and take care of men who might come later. The razorback ate rattlesnakes, acorns, and prickly pears. When it was domesticated it produced sowbelly (bacon or salt pork).

The Mexicans possessed another small animal, a little donkey, the burro. Its virtues were those of its ancestors, the wild asses: surefootedness, persistence, ability to go for a while without water or food, ability to carry a load. Like the longhorns, burros escaped and established themselves in the wild.

The porcupine sometimes seemed to the cowboy to be everywhere. Because he had to pick out so many sharp quills from his horses' hind legs, the cowboy thought incorrectly that the porcupine could shoot out its quills like arrows.

The bony-shelled, nine-banded armadillo, at first limited to southwest Texas, starting in the days of the Long Trail has migrated all the way northeast to the Red River. Nothing else like it is known in North America; it is a northern representative of a varied South American group. The armadillo has no teeth and has lost most of its hair. It has a narrow head, large ears, and short legs. Its shell—hinged, in segments—lets it, when frightened, roll up into a ball. It digs for insects with a long, sticky tongue. The armadillo, like the wild longhorn, is active at night when it does its digging in order to eat spiders, insects, and scorpions, all abundant in Texas. But the most curious thing about it is its reproduction: the females always produce identical triplets.

Of all the snakes, of which there were plenty, the chicken snake was the most common nuisance. It is not poisonous, but it has an almost unlimited capacity for eating the eggs of chickens or domesticated or wild turkeys. "They don't leave us a single egg," complained Tim Hughes. "One of them ate seventeen out of a nest one day, and the same brute ate ten turkey's eggs that the old hen was sitting on."

The two-foot-long coral snake, of Texas and Arkansas, with its rings of bright red, gold, and black running around it, has a powerful poison that can kill a person in twenty minutes (according to a Mexican story) or in twenty-four hours (a cowboy story). It rests by day, comes out at night, and is therefore only rarely seen—and rarely bites. Another species, the nineteen-inch-long Arizona or Sonora coral snake, lives west of Texas in Mexico, New Mexico, and Arizona.

The yellow- or orange-and-black king snake could—and can— kill a rattlesnake. It twists itself around the rattler, sinks its fangs beneath the rattler's jaws, and squeezes, or constricts, the rattler to death.

One cowboy, sitting in the grass and resting, was startled when a snake crawled up his back, over his shoulder, then across a knee. He did not know what kind it was.

Joe Hough and Philip Paxton did not know what they met in an open forest, at the foot of an oak: a pair of moccasins. Paxton later described them: "Hideous . . . abominable . . . demonic eyes glaring . . . bifurcated tongues darting in and out." The Western cottonmouth moccasin, a snake of the pit viper family, olive brown, six to nine feet long, is found in trees or bushes near water. When it opens its mouth, it shows white inside—the cotton-mouth.

It is poisonous. Joe Hough felt a sting in his thumb and thought he was snake-bitten. He wasn't sure.

His resulting oaths, just to be sure he had covered all the pos-sibilities, mentioned all the snakes, reptiles, hornets, mosquitoes, fleas, ants, and horned toads he knew of.

It turned out that he had been stung by a hornet.

Inside prairie-dog holes, right along with prairie dogs, there lived burrowing owls. The cowboy called them squinch owls. Also in the prairie-dog holes right alongside the prairie dogs and the squinch owls there were said to be rattlesnakes. The snakes were said to eat the young prairie dogs and the squinch owls were said to eat the rattlesnakes.

Charles Goodnight said this was not so. No prairie dog, he said, would enter a burrow with a rattler in it.

Of all the dangerous varmints in Texas and elsewhere on the Southwest frontier, and up the Long Trail, the rattlesnake was the most dreaded. There were, and are, ten species. Like the long-horns, they lived all over Texas. Cowboys saw them hanging from branches, or saw their tracks on dry trails, or saw them coiled on the ground. The cowboys used their skins as hatbands or to decorate saddles.

The up-to-eight-foot-long, up-to-twenty-pound Texas diamondback rattlesnake, says an authority, John Crompton, is probably the most dangerous snake in the United States.

The diamondback was what the cowboy meant by the word *rattlesnake*. It has big reddish-brown diamond-shape markings.

Besides his bow legs, a trademark of a cowboy was that he looked carefully around for any diamondbacks before he sat on the ground. Waking in the morning, he lay still for a moment to see if any rattlers were on his blanket. If so, he slid quickly out of the blanket.

A hefty rattler killed in Long Trail days had thirteen rattles; another, as thick as a man's arm, had nineteen. Nobody ever has described the sound of the rattles—about the best you can do is "r-r-r-r-r-r-r-r-r-r-r."

A rattlesnake's poison is powerful for a long time. Once a rancher put on boots that had been his father's. His father had died ten years before. The rancher's leg began to swell. He remembered that his father, wearing the boots, had been bitten by a rattler, and he found one of the snake's fangs broken off in an eyehole of a boot. The fang had scratched the rancher.

A rattler's strike is slow, but it was fast enough for a cowboy, E. C. Abbott (Teddy Blue)—the one from Cranwich Hall, England. At a Denver bar there was a rattlesnake in a big glass jar. A man offered to bet drinks for the house that no man could keep his finger on the glass while the rattler struck.

Teddy Blue knew the jar was of thick glass. He could see that. He took up the bet. He held his finger there. The rattler struck. "And away came my finger."

He still thought he could to it, though. He tried until he had lost $17. Then he gave up. "Since then," he said, "I've never bucked the other fellow's game and it has saved me a lot of money."

There was a standard cure, at the time, if a rattlesnake bit you. To the outside of the bite you applied a poultice of chewed chewing tobacco, over which you poured whisky. Internally, you drank whisky, swallowing a tumblerful at a time.

The internal treatment was observed to produce the quickest visible results.

Out milking, one woman was bitten on her ankle. She rushed home and promptly drank a pint of whisky.

It worked. Or something did. She recovered.

Another prescribed cure was to at once cut open the bite made by a rattlesnake—you could use the needlepoints of the yucca to do it—and suck out the blood and thus with it suck out the poisonous venom. This was not much help if you had been bitten in the middle of your forehead or your back, while you were sleeping alone on the prairie.

It was no comfort on the Southwest frontier to be nicknamed— as were some questionable characters—Rattlesnake Pete. But at least one woman in Texas had a rattlesnake that acted friendly. It periodically thrust its head through the adobe floor of her house. It did not bite her. She said she preferred it to the armies of wasps, gnats, fleas, etc., that did bite. The rattler even gave her a little companionship in a lonesome land.

The early Texans put their beds two feet away from a dugout wall to avoid insects. Mrs. Vielé, in west Texas, said: "Walking was impossible." The reason: "Scorpions, tarantulas, and venomous snakes lurking in the scanty vegetation." One cowboy woke up in the morning and found a scorpion curled up near his forehead —he thought the scorpion sought to obtain warmth.

Everything in west Texas, said the first men and women to arrive in the Big Bend, "either sticks, stings, or stinks." After a fight between two insects, one community, between Bonham and Sherman in Long Trail days, was named Bug Tussle.

Texans may not like their bug collection, but they always have been proud of having the biggest and worst anywhere, such as mosquitoes that—Texans say—a man can ride. A long poem by an anonymous author so pleases Texans that thousands of copies on postcards have been sold. A couple of the poem's many lines: .

The rattlesnake bites you, the scorpion stings,
The mosquito delights you with his buzzing wings.

But Texans do not have a complete monopoly on nasty insects. Some of their more unpleasant neighbors they share with other Southwestern states—New Mexico, Arizona, and Oklahoma—and with Sonora, Tamaulipas, Coahuila, and other states of Mexico.

The insects often were troublesome and dangerous. "Wasps, bees, hornets, and other winged insects," said the National Geographic Society in July 1967, "cause more fatalities in the United States than any other wild creature, including rattlesnakes."

The scorpions, which are also called vinegarroons (they smell like vinegar when you stir them up), turn out to be not so poisonous as once was thought.

The tarantulas, the great (ten inches across the legs) hairy spiders of the Southwest, had a bite like the scorpion's, but it was not especially harmful. Cowboys would put a couple of tarantulas into a bowl and watch them fight it out.

Millions of tiny red ants invaded corncribs, stables, and cabins, and piled up dirt three or four feet high outside buildings. One night two men slept in a bed above several lines of red ants marching across the floor. One man's trousers were dropped onto the floor. The next morning, half asleep, the man put them on. A thousand burning stings told him he had the classic case of ants in his pants. He rushed to a nearby creek and jumped in to cool off.

Texas was divided into two parts—ant country and roach-and-flea country. Red bugs—chiggers—in both parts caused furious itching and scratching.

Willy Hughes told of a man named Townsend and the red bug: "He had to get up in the middle of the night and go and get a bathe in a stream, they worried him so."

Willy told of another insect: "There is a beetle out here, called the tumble-bug in polite society, that rolls a ball four times as big as itself. A green English fellow, just out the other day, asked 'Why was that ball pushing that bug about?' "

One insect brightened evenings: the firefly.

The cowboy's experiences with wild animals of the trail was as varied as the animals themselves. A pronghorn antelope frustrated a cowboy named Shelby, who was on a drive with Virgil Johnson and A. Huffmeyer.

Shelby bet $10 he could catch an antelope, the 3½-foot-high, 140-pound creature that crosses the plains with a poetry of motion at a pace that may reach fifty-five miles an hour. On its rump there is a great circular white patch that spreads to warn other antelopes of danger. It can see as far as a man with eight-power binoculars.

Shelby chased and chased an antelope. He made its tongue hang out, and he made it pant. But it stayed ahead of his pony, and he never caught it. A cowboy on a fresh horse did rope the tired antelope. Shelby's horse was so tired that it did not get rested for over two weeks.

And Shelby lost $10.

Another Long Trail wild animal affected history. This was the panther, puma, catamount, painter, or mountain lion, the biggest cat in North and South America. It sped up the building of one of today's big cities.

Cowboy C. H. Rust had said that Fort Worth was where the panther laid down and died. Another version of the remark was that Fort Worth was so dead that when a panther dozed on the main street no one disturbed him. This so enraged and delighted the local citizens that they banded together and called themselves Panthers and their town Panther City. Firemen obtained a panther cub as a mascot. The citizens, organized into Panther Clubs, went to work, and with pick and shovel built a right-of-way for a railroad, and got the railroad, the Texas and Pacific. The first train arrived July 19, 1876. Fort Worth went right on from that day to become one of the United States' principal cities and a major cattle and meat-packing town.

One utterly mysterious wild animal puzzled cowboy Hiram Craig. His cattle in 1876 grew so thin that his men could not eat them. So Craig's cowboys went hunting buffalo. The buffalo thundered past them. The buffalo were led by a mysterious red animal that did not look like a buffalo. What then could it be?

Craig killed it.

It was not a buffalo, but a big red steer that once had belonged to John Chisum and that had returned to the wild.

Some cowmen visit
a world's fair

THE UNITED States in 1876 was one hundred years old. To celebrate, there was held a great world's fair, the Centennial International Exhibition in Philadelphia.

The Centennial was a sign—a sign marking one of the important turning points in the history of mankind. It was a sign that there soon would come changes that would end the days of the cowboy and of the Long Trail.

For all of man's history—that is, for thousands of years—he had been absolutely dependent on muscle power for his transportation and for much of his energy (he had to paddle a canoe, he had to saw wood).

At first, man had had only his own arms and legs. Gradually, he had learned to ride, or to be hauled by, oxen, asses, camels—and eventually horses. On land, he had had, for transportation, only his own muscles or the muscles of animals. (On the water he had acquired power from the wind in the sails of a ship.)

The Centennial Exhibition of 1876 showed that man was ceasing to be dependent on muscles—his own or an animal's—for transportation or for energy.

Instead, he was beginning to be able to use the power of

machines. Man was combining metal, lubrication, and fuel to provide new transportation. At first, this mechanical transportation consisted of steamboats on the water and, on land, the railroads that every year were reaching like fingers farther and farther into the Long Trail country.

Men were so accustomed to the use of muscle power and the horse for transportation that they perfectly logically came up with a name for their own new source of transportation over land. Their name for the locomotive: the iron horse.

The change from a live horse to the iron horse—the change from muscles to metal machines—was not sudden. It was gradual. It had begun in 1805, with Oliver Evans' steam wagon-and-dredge; other foundations had been laid by the steamboats of John Fitch and John Stevens and Robert Fulton, and the changeover had been furthered in 1830 by Peter Cooper's little locomotive, the Tom Thumb. The 1876 exhibition showed man nearing the end of the transition—he had come to the turning point—from animal or muscle power to machine power.

With the horse still on the Long Trail and predominant in man's thinking, there was exhibited at the 1876 fair what was considered the ultimate in family transportation, and what was actually heralded as the greatest peak man ever would reach in family transportation: the most elaborate, most perfected horse-drawn carriages. Advertisements soberly said that the carriages never would be surpassed. One carriage, described in the exhibition catalog as "as luxurious as possible," had elliptic springs. It remained necessary for there to be a horse in front, providing energy.

The cowboy had used muscle power—the horse's—to travel from the Gulf of Mexico to Canada. Men in covered wagons—the prairie schooners—had used the horse to go about as far.

Along with the latest-model horse-drawn transportation, there was on exhibit at the 1876 fair a transportation device that both (1) depended on muscles for power and (2) introduced mechanics into transportation.

This link between the old world of the horse and the new world of mechanical power was the bicycle.

Imported from Europe and shown at the fair was the high-wheeled bicycle—one big wheel (the front), one small wheel. Albert A. Pope of New England saw it and began to manufacture it.

The bicycle would be the last leg-power method of transportation. But it was also a mechanical device, and for millions of Americans it would be the first mechanical device they ever had known.

The bicycle would teach millions of Americans something about mechanics. It ever-so-lightly prepared them for automobiles.

The iron horse—the locomotive that already was hauling the cowboy's longhorns to St. Louis and Kansas City and Chicago and other markets, and that already was hauling passengers to the West from the Eastern seaboard—was on exhibit in 1876. The iron horse in 1876—the year General Custer died at the Little Big Horn—already was pretty far advanced.

The Baldwin Locomotive Works, Philadelphia, showed a passenger locomotive of the kind that was bringing new farmers to the Midwest and hauling cowboys home and longhorns to market. The locomotive had a wheelbase of 44 feet 2 inches including its coal-carrying tender; the locomotive alone had a 22-foot-5-inch wheelbase. Its four big driving wheels each was 5 feet 2 inches in diameter. Its four small truck wheels were 2 feet 4 inches in diameter. The total weight of the locomotive was 75,000 pounds. The total weight on the driving wheels was 51,500 pounds.

Also shown at the exhibition were improved railroad-car axles, bridge spans and girders, model bridges, railroad switches, and signals.

From Germany, there was something else: Longen & Otto's Patent Gas Engine—a forerunner of the automobile. Its motive power was obtained "by the direct action of the force of the explosion of a mixture of gases on the surface of the piston." But the first automobiles, by Germany's Benz (1885) and Daimler (1886), were still almost ten years away.

Related to the steam locomotive, there were on display steam-rollers to flatten roads, and a "farm locomotive engine"—a steam tractor.

Machinery on display in 1876, for purposes other than transportation, would mass-produce over the next century the goods that would change the cowboy's world—and everyone else's.

Machine tools—machines that make machines—were on exhibit in profusion: turning-lathes, drill presses, hydraulic forging machines, steam hammers, punching and shearing machines, riveting machines, and others for working metals or for other uses.

Still other exhibits showed how the cowboy's world was at a turning point.

The cowboy had traded four or five cattle for that rare, almost unobtainable, item—a clock. The exhibition's catalog said the United States had become noted for the manufacture of inexpensive clocks, over a million annually.

The cowboy's mother or wife had had to make her own thread from the wool on a sheep's back or from a boll on a cotton plant.

The Clark Thread Company of Newark, New Jersey, and Paisley, Scotland, demonstrated a thread-winding machine that wound thread on spools.

The cowboys' mothers and wives had to make clothes by hand, with their homemade thread, from cloth, which they wove, or from leather or other animal skins.

Power looms, the 1876 catalog said, made weaving "a new art."

Some spectacular results of science were shown at Philadelphia.

A mineral, copper, was on display in its metallic form. Another mineral, asbestos, previously believed only a curiosity, had been discovered to be useful. H. W. Johns of New York exhibited asbestos. It was fireproof, and would make an excellent roofing material. It was to cover steam boilers and pipes.

Science at the Centennial Exhibition of 1876 directly and drastically affected the longhorns and the cowboys. There was on display a menagerie owned by a German who studied animals, Karl Hagenbeck. He showed a breed of cattle from India, the Brahmas. Tick fever remained a deadly problem with Texas cattle. Cowmen —including Captain King and Captain Kenedy, who had worked with Brahmas—had noticed that Brahma cattle did not have ticks. Furthermore, Brahmas were prolific, hardy, and quick to mature. Colonel James Alfred McFaddin bought a herd of Brahmas. At a later world's fair, in 1893, McFaddin acquired a magnificent Brahma bull, called Prince, and a fine Brahma cow. Prince became the kingpin of the McFaddin herd. McFaddin and his son, A. M. McFaddin, ended with fine beef-producing Brahma cattle—immune to ticks. For the McFaddins and for many other cattlemen, the Brahmas replaced the longhorns.

Colonel and Mrs. McFaddin were to live and work with

Brahma cattle for a long time. When she died, in June 1911, they had been married almost fifty years. He died, at seventy-six, in Victoria, Texas, on June 25, 1916.

Besides Brahmas, another breed—Herefords—was shown in 1876. W. B. Ikard, like the McFaddins a cowman from Texas, visited the fair and saw the dark red, white-faced Herefords. Before the year was over, he had brought the first purebred Herefords to Texas. Charles Goodnight, Col. C. C. Slaughter, Judge O. H. Nelson, and in west Texas near Marfa, the Mitchell family, helped develop Herefords to a very high quality, so high they would replace Longhorns and eventually become three-fourths of all the cattle in Texas.

The 1876 exhibition showed that the Brahmas and Herefords were on hand to replace the Longhorn. It showed that the Iron Horse was at hand to replace the four-legged horse. It showed dozens of machines that would reduce drudgery, muscular toil.

32

The trail to Wyoming

1877. AROUND THE United States: The first long-distance telephone calls ever were made, over lines between Salem, Massachusetts, and Boston, and between Chicago and Milwaukee. . . . Both the American Library Association and its magazine, the *Library Journal,* were one year old. . . . Way back in 1610, an astronomer, Johannes Kepler, had predicted that Mars would be found to have two moons. At the U.S. Naval Observatory in Washington, D.C., Asaph Hall proved Kepler all along had been right.

ALONG THE LONG TRAIL: A rancher, C. J. (Buffalo) Jones, and the Indian fighter John B. Slaughter, in addition to Charles Goodnight, crossed buffalo with cattle to obtain cattalo. They used Brahma cattle. . . . Roadside conveniences were established along the trail in Texas. Not, perhaps, what you might think. A cowboy relieved himself squatting on the ground. The conveniences were trailside pens—corrals—into which you could drive your cattle and leave them a while. . . . S. W. Swenson, a Swede for whom Swenson, Texas, is named, was selling cattle by mail to buyers in the North who fed and fattened them. . . . New Texas ranches belonged to Leasial B. Harris, M. J. and S. R. Coggin, W. C. Parks,

J. A. Poole, Thomas A. Bugbee, the Harold Brothers, Hank V. Cresswell (the Bar C), W. H. Bates and David T. Beals (the LX), and W. B. White (the OM).

Herds were being driven through to Wyoming. Ben Drake was with a herd of Blocker cattle to Wyoming. Jerry M. Nance of Kyle, Texas, drove 2,100 cattle to Cheyenne. Early in the trip he had to get them across the rising Brazos River above Waco, Texas. "It was so wide that all of the cattle were in the river swimming at the same time, and it looked as if I had no cattle at all, for all we could see was the horns."

Further north, at the North Canadian River, Nance and his men stripped to their skins to drive the cattle across. They were caught by a hailstorm. They broke for the wagon. When the hail stopped, it was two inches deep on the ground.

Between Ogallala, Nebraska, and Cheyenne, they saw a little stone dam—a tiny thing—an effort to store a little bit of water, long before today's huge dams in the arid West. Who built it Nance never learned.

They had left Hays County, Texas, just southwest of Austin, April 15. They reached Cheyenne, Wyoming, in July—three months on the trail, a fast trip.

Cheyenne, 6,000 feet (over a mile) high, surrounded by grazing land, had been founded in 1867 when a branch of the Union Pacific Railroad reached the area.

"Our first trouble was at Haze Prairie, where we had our first stampede." W. C. Fielder, speaking, had been on his first drive at the age of nineteen.

Afterward, one cowboy, W. F. (Zeke) Hilliard, had a black eye.

It looked as though during the stampede he had, in his fright, run against the spindle of the wagon axle.

Hilliard insisted he had not been frightened.

The men with him considered and consulted each other.

The verdict was that the wagon had become frightened and had run over him.

"The saddest sight I saw on the trail," said Fielder, "was at a place where we stopped to camp. We spied a little mound of fresh earth and a pair of new-made boots sitting on it. It showed the last resting place of some poor cowboy.''

Near Red River, G. W. Mills was asleep, ''sleeping as only Texas cowboys can.'' Not a cowboy on the trip was yet twenty-three. Less than twenty feet from him, just on the other side of the chuckwagon, a panther stood up on its hind legs and began to eat the carcass of a yearling. A shot from another cowboy chased the mountain lion—then only did Mills wake up. Later that night Mills heard ''the most horrifying yell, or more of a scream, that I had ever heard in all my life''—the panther. Mills and another cowboy were riding in opposite directions around the herd, on night herd. ''From then on until daylight we just rode around together.''

Later, on Salt Fork, Mills saw ''unbelievable doings of the lightning; it beat anything I ever saw. The lightning would hit the side of those hills and gouge out great holes in the earth like a bomb had struck them.''

Near Tascosa in the Panhandle in 1877, George W. Littlefield started the LIT Ranch. At one point it was 260 miles across. The LIT later was held by the Prairie Cattle Company, owner of three vast ranches: The JJ in Colorado, the Cross L in New Mexico, and the LIT. The Prairie Cattle Company, Tad Moses reported in the 1947–48 *Texas Almanac*, was said to have owned ''all outdoors.'' The Prairie would be in business until 1917, its last herds not liquidated until 1919.

The Matador Ranch, near Matador and Channing, Mr. Moses wrote, had about a million acres within fences.

Charles Goodnight in 1877 met an old friend: Old Blue.

Old Blue had been, in the Pecos River country, a leader of the herd for Goodnight. The steer had been obtained by Goodnight from John Chisum. When the rest of the herd had been sold for beef, Old Blue, three years old, had been given a yoke and hauled wagons.

When he was six years old, he was back with Goodnight. From 1877 on, Old Blue, with a bell around his neck, faithfully led cattle from the JA Ranch in the Texas Panhandle to Dodge City. He sometimes made two trips a year. He was not sold; he returned home with the cowboys, sometimes having to travel thirty miles a day to keep up with them. This went on for eight years. Then Old Blue was released, in the Palo Duro country, and eventually died, age twenty. His horns were mounted above the JA Ranch's office door.

P. E. Slaughter delivered a small herd of steers to W. E. Crowley. Crowley had no checkbook, not even a scrap of paper. He did have a roof of cypress shingles. He pulled a shingle out of the roof and wrote a check upon it.

The bank honored Crowley's check.

33

Conversation on the Long Trail

THE LANGUAGE spoken on the Long Trail was English—with variations.

The cowboy could express himself, and he got better at it as he went along. On ordering a steak rare: "Just cripple him and drive him in. I'll eat him." On a saxophone: "I used to own a saxophone, but traded it off for a cow. Made about the same noise and gave milk besides." At a wedding, when the bridegroom promised to endow his bride with all his worldly goods: "There goes Sam's shotgun. Somebody stole his dog last week." On the wind of the plains that never, never seemed to cease: "Does it blow this way all the time?" "Hell, no! It blows the other way about half the time."

On a cowboy who had gone to Texas from the East in a hurry: "Without remembering to bring his name with him." Such a cowboy had G.T.T. (Gone to Texas).

An Indian fighter, Bigfoot Wallace explained his nickname in terms of his shoe size: "12's fit me best." Another version is that his nickname came after he killed a thieving Indian and brought back the Indian's big foot to prove it. Wallace called a pretty Virginia girl he met a "deadener" and a "knee-weakener."

Of a man suspected of rustling calves, the cowboy said, "He's always willin' to stake 'em to a brand with his own iron."

The Texas climate was described as healthy: "Out west, you lived a long time—even horse thieves had to hang five minutes longer than anywhere else."

The word "tenderfoot" originally had meant an ox with sore feet from a long pull. It came to mean someone who had made the long trip from the East out to the West. Tenderfoot also meant a beginning cowboy, because an experienced cowboy's foot had grown tough from rubbing all day against his boots. Greenhorn, which meant the same thing, Samuel J. Sackett says, is after the young cattle whose horns begin growing in the spring when plants begin to turn green. The word "greenhorn," much older than the Long Trail, originally did refer to the immature horns of young animals.

Spanish mustangs supposedly had learned to buck when they tried to toss mountain lions off their backs; they became bucking broncos. A bucking bronco, said Ramon F. Adams, "warped his backbone and hallelujahed all over the lot." The bronc was "a beast with a bellyfull of bed springs." He was a "gut-buster." He was a "real hunk o' death." He was a "cutey little grave-digger." He would "stamp you in the ground so deep you'll take roots and disappear." Or he would "throw you so high in the air the birds will build nests in your hair before you light."

A man sticking onto a bucking horse was "sitting that bronc as easy as a hoss-fly on a mule's ear."

A man who could not hang on "couldn't ride a covered wagon."

How a cowboy should treat his partner at a dance—he called the girl a "calico"—from a poem by Col. C. C. Walsh of San Angelo, Texas:

Every gent salute yer heifer—
    Show how th' baboon grinned.

And at an intermission in the dance:

Start up the trail—drift—two by two—
    Refreshments have their charm.

A tall bad man: "He's just as long as a snake and he drags the ground when he walks." A fool: "He don't know dung from wild honey." Vomiting: "Airing the paunch." A small town: "A wide place in the road." When a man played a deuce (a two) in a card game: "Laying down his character." To ride a horse: "To fork him." When a man doesn't know the answer: "I ain't got any medicine." A delicate situation: "Hair in the butter." A Negro: A "headlight in a snowstorm." Crazy: "Plumb locoed." That was from the Spanish word *loco*, meaning mad or crazy, and from the locoweed of rainy Aprils, with its lovely purple flowers, the poisonous American hemp, a kind of marijuana. When cattle or horses ate it, they sometimes lost their eyesight or went into paroxysms of nervous twitching.

To get through a bad time was to "tough it out." To start out was to "hit the grit." To pick up wages was "to get my time." A man good at roping could "sling the catgut well." Said the cowboy, describing muddy water: "You have to chew it before you can swallow it." On the early cow hunts, the men who rounded up— or "popped"—wild longhorns out of the chaparral and brush were called brushpoppers.

A steer—a word the cowboy rarely used—was a "male cow who had been operated on so he could never be a family man." The cowboy instead often called his animals beeves.

Any cattle he drove, the cowboy called cows—not only the females. A cow, by the dictionary, is a female two years old or older. But on the Long Trail all cattle were cows—including steers.

A young cow that had not had a calf, after her first birthday, was a heifer. A young bull, on his first birthday, became a yearling. A motherless calf was a dogie.

The cowboy took many words from Mexican Spanish: Lasso (from *lazo*), lariat (from *la reata*), rodeo (from *rodear*, to round up), *segundo* ("second in command"), *bronco*, *loco*, and others. A man was the Spanish *hombre* (pronounced "ohm-bre"), mispronounced by the cowboy "umbry" or "ahmbry."

When he had no blankets and no sugan (a quilt), a cowboy, lying on his stomach and covering his stomach with his back, slept in what he called a Tucson bed. Cowboy John James Haynes told how he walked the last of his trip home after the Civil War. He traveled, he said, by "ankle express."

A name for a cowboy saloon: the Road to Ruin. A cowboy

town: Tombstone, Arizona. Its newspaper: The Tombstone Epitaph.

A quiet cowboy: "Sayin' less than nuthin'."

When a cowboy felt like cussing when women were around, he tried to remember to say "doggone."

He had a way to be a good cowboy: "Keep one eye on the boss, and two on the herd."

And the cowboy explained how anybody could understand a cowboy's way of talking: "All you've got to do is to know in advance what the other fellow means and then pay no attention to what he says."

34

More and more
Texas ranches

1878. AROUND THE World: The United States signed a treaty of friendship and trade that has resulted ever since in an American interest in the Samoa Islands in the Pacific Ocean. At Pago Pago, the United States acquired rights to base naval ships. . . . Edward Muybridge set up a series of coordinated cameras. He took photos of a horse in motion—a step toward movies.

ALONG THE LONG TRAIL: Leigh Dyer, who had found the location for the Goodnight and Adair JA Ranch in the Texas Panhandle, established another ranch. This one was sold to Gunter, Munson & Summerfield, and the brand became GMS. Jot Gunter, who later ranched in Duval and McMullen counties, was to give his name to the Gunter Hotel. In San Antonio, the Gunter was to become famous for reunion meetings of Long Trail drivers. . . . Other ranches were established by: a cowman named Brennan near Fort Stockton. George Crosson in Presidio County. M. Halff & Brothers, the MN on the Pecos, the Circle Dot near Marathon, and the ¿Quién sabe? (Spanish for "Who knows?") in the Fort Stockton country. R. L. McNulty, the Turkey Track near Adobe Wells. He later sold it to the Hansford Land & Cattle Company; W. T. Coble bought the old headquarters and used the branch in 1916. A. M.

Britton & Associates, the Matador Cattle Company. A Scottish syndicate later bought it and renamed it the Matador Land & Cattle Company, Ltd., and added other ranches to its land. The Espuela (Spanish for "spur") Land & Cattle Company, Ltd., started by J. M. Hall, one of the brothers who had started the Cross L brand of the Prairie Cattle Company in New Mexico. The property was acquired by the Espuela Company of Fort Worth, then sold to a British syndicate. About 1888 this syndicate owned about 60,000 cattle and 500,000 acres of land. The Swenson interests of Stamford, Texas, bought the ranch in 1907 and sold all the cattle in the Spur brand to W. J. Lewis of Dallas and Clarendon in 1910.

At a time, around a hundred years ago, of no automobiles, no airplanes, no motorcycles, no trucks, no buses, for a man to see a self-propelling vehicle of any kind was an awe-inspiring thing.

Cowman J. C. Thompson never quite got over it.

"I shall never forget," he said, of his trip up the trail in 1878, at age seventeen, "that it was on this trip that I saw a railroad train in motion. We were approaching Dodge City when I looked across the Arkansas River and saw a real locomotive pulling a train of cars. I can shut my eyes now and see that picture far across the plains."

To Thompson, who had spent most of his years in the warm South, a Northern winter could be almost as startling as a locomotive.

"I intended to stay in Montana that winter," said he, "but after finding out you could not get outside the house for seven months without snowshoes ten feet long, it was TEXAS for me."

The cowboy's experiences up north provided him with a new phrase for his vocabulary. Damp, foggy weather he described as "cold as a well-digger in Montana."

George W. Brock, eighteen, of Lockhart, was working for Mark A. Withers in Fayette County, when he saw something new. Brock noticed a strange heifer trying to join his herd of 300 cows. The heifer was a Jersey—the first Jersey Brock ever had seen. Jerseys, originally from the Jersey Islands in the English Channel, were to be another breed that would replace the Longhorns.

Trail boss Virgil Johnson, with about two thousand steers and cows, decided to drive straight for the Indian Territory's Wichita Mountains—seventy-five miles—which he could see in the distance. This would save miles of travel—and time. But there was no water for cattle for two days. On the third day the herd had strung out over two miles. About noon the big lead steers smelled water. They threw up their noses and ran. They ran across a ridge. Sure enough, there was a little stream. Johnson camped there a day and a half, cowboy A. Huffmeyer of San Antonio remembered, to rest stock and men.

Huffmeyer on this trip saw a wild turkey, chased it, and killed it with the butt end of his quirt. That night, the cook served wild turkey.

Branch Isbell, who in 1871 had gone up the trail with Amanda Burks and her husband William, and who in 1872 had been rebuked by a girl, in 1878 was still having trouble with girl friends.

He was working on a ranch in Mitchell County.

"Once when I was returning from a trip to Belle Plain, a hundred miles away, where we went almost monthly for our mail," he said, "I was harbored for the night by a gentleman named Altman, who had a few cattle, and as bright and handsome a daughter as one might encounter in any country.

"Their house was a one-room shack, but no place ever covered two warmer hearts. They gave me a hearty welcome and entertained me royally in every way. When it came time to retire for the night, a wagon sheet was stretched across the room behind which I was assigned to a pallet on which a real feather bed had been placed. Before my departure next morning, Miss Emma (I hope she is alive and happy yet, and that God has ever blessed her), inquired if I had enjoyed my bed. Thinking to give her a cute reply, I answered that my rest had been unbroken except for one brief interval during which my 'goosehair' surroundings had caused me to dream that I was a goose. Like a flash the retort came: 'The truth will prevail even in a dream.' "

Isbell remembered—and recorded—that remark forty-four years afterward.

A one-time cowboy had become a rancher in western Nebraska. He was Capt. James Cook and he was a great-grandson of an English sailor of the same name. The first Capt. James Cook, in the late 1700s, had completed the exploration of the Pacific Ocean that, around the lifetime of Columbus, the Portuguese and Spaniards had begun. In the late 1800s, on the ranch of the great-grandson James Cook, there were discovered so many outcrops of fossil bones that the place was to become famous in paleontology and to give men many of their ideas about prehistoric animals. Cook's son, Harold J., made the ranch a headquarters for visiting bonediggers; his wife, Margaret, helped. Cook's ranch, in the 1970s still a goal for fossil hunters, is now part of the Agate Fossil Beds National Monument, 3,150 acres on the Niobrara River, a treeless area of plains, grass, wild flowers, bluffs, and badlands.

"My first trip up the trail was in 1878," said W. M. Shannon, "with Bob Martin from Refugio County with 1100 two-year-olds and upwards. Our chuck-wagon was drawn by two yoke of steers.

"We started our herd about the 15th of March, crossed the Colorado below Austin, went by Round Rock and Georgetown. On the North Gabriel we had a heavy rain and hail and our cattle stampeded, drifted back and mixed with one of the Kokernot herds. Next morning I was five miles from camp with a hundred steers. It took us two days to separate the cattle and get started on our way. We went by Waco, Cleburne, and Fort Worth and crossed the Trinity River. We crossed the Red River at Red River Station and took the Chisholm Trail through the Indian Territory. We got by the Indians without any trouble.

"At Pond Creek we saw our first buffalo, and it seemed as if the plains were literally covered with them. . . . We crossed Bluff Creek into Kansas and passed Newton about the last of May. There was a blacksmith shop, a store and a few dwellings there at that time, but the railroad soon came and Newton quickly grew to be a large town.

"We crossed Holland Creek and went to Abilene and there the cattle were sold, and we all hit the back trail for Texas with our saddle horses and chuck-wagon. . . . On my way back I met my old friend, D. S. Combs."

Shannon died November 2, 1921.

Herd after herd of cattle moved north over the Long Trail. It was frequently called, as it had been by W. M. Shannon, the Chisholm Trail.

When cattle were lost from a herd, the herd following would pick up the lost cattle, drive them on, and eventually return them to their original herd.

Ike Pryor's herd went up the trail a few weeks ahead of Bill Jackman's. One day Jackman's outfit picked up a steer that had belonged to Ike Pryor. They drove the steer along. One afternoon, about forty Indian warriors, with their squaws, drove up to Bill Jackman. One gave him a letter:

"To the trail bosses.

"This man is a good Indian. I know him personally. Treat him well, give him a beef and you will have no trouble in driving through his country.

"[Signed] Ike T. Pryor."

Jackman at once gave the Indian a steer: Pryor's.

Pryor was quickly thereafter informed of his loss—by Jackman's cowboys. They could hardly wait to tell him.

A young man named Hughes, son of a once comfortable but now impoverished English family had G.T.T. (Gone to Texas), but, unlike some others, he had not had to go in a hurry, nor had he to leave his name behind. By the winter of 1878–79 he had reached the sparsely settled West. He and three companions one evening rode alone and came upon a wagon holding two girls, about six years old—alone in the desert. Their horses had run off, and their father had been out looking for the horses since daybreak. "We asked them if they were not frightened," Hughes said. " 'Oh, no,' they said." Hughes asked if they had any water. " 'No.' Then what will you do for it? 'Starve, I guess,' said the eldest; as much as to say, You ought to know that."

Their father returned—without the horses—and with boots whose soles were tied on with string. Hughes and his companions gave them water and rode on.

Whisky was illegal many places in Texas, Hughes learned; where it was illegal, a custom was being established that would last: it was sold as medicine. Its square glass bottles had labels, "two table spoonfuls, &c." The medicine's name: Stomach bitters.

35

He never got away from the birds

ALONG THE sands of the Gulf of Mexico shore, the cowboy came upon a long-billed, long-legged shorebird, more common then than it is today, the curlew. The cowboy saw it both along the edge of the Gulf, on prairies, and near water. He sang about it; in "A Home on the Range," a line says, "the curlew I love to hear scream."

The stars at night are big and bright (as goes another song, "Deep in the Heart of Texas"), the stars hang low over a man or woman's head, and with the full bright Apache or Comanche moon they light up the night. Against the moon, along with countless flurrying bats, a man could see the silhouettes of flocks of birds flying, or the shadow of the solitary great horned owl. From the start of the Long Trail along the Gulf, by night as well as by day, birds were the most visible wildlife to the cowboy on the Long Trail as they have been the most visible animals to travelers of all times and places. From Texas all the way to Kansas, Nebraska, Wyoming, Montana, the Dakotas, and Canada, the birds were his constant and continual companions.

Along the Gulf, along with the curlew, he found gulls, herons —the great blue, the little blue, the white heron and the white egret, and brown and white pelicans. Up from Brownsville, in the Rio

Grande valley, thoroughly familiar to a cowboy, there appeared tropical birds that occur no farther north, white-winged doves, the red-billed pigeon or blue cock, the Inca dove, and the Mexican ground dove, which I imagine is the same as the chubby, pinkish-brown-and-gray ground dove of Central America.

The mourning dove, with its familiar doleful cry, is common over much of the United States, but it funnels through Texas on its migrations in incredible numbers, and a cowboy would have seen it countless times. So too he would have known its relative, the passenger pigeon, that once swarmed in such vast flocks their very hugeness made them easy prey for hunters and so the pigeon became extinct. John Fitzhenry, the policeman in San Antonio, was one man who remembered seeing some of the last of the passenger pigeons.

A cowboy had an unusual opportunity to become a bird watcher: He did not know it, but there are within the borders of Texas a whopping 500-plus species of birds. Some of them are found nowhere else, at least not in the United States: the Sennett thrasher, the Colima warbler, the couch jay, and the small, long-tailed green jay, with a blue crest and marks of yellow. The golden-cheeked warbler breeds only in Texas.

At the very beginning of the Long Trail, near Mexico, in the dry, mesquite and milkweed and cactus country of southwest Texas, where so many wild longhorns roamed and were captured, the cowboy saw a bird walking ahead of his horse, and saw it run along beside wagons or coaches. He helped give it a name: the roadrunner. Another name for it is the chaparral cock. Two feet long—the tail is one of those two feet—the slender, brownish-black-and-amber roadrunner could actually run faster than a horse-drawn buggy. (An automobile speedometer once clocked it at twenty-six miles an hour.) As it runs, it extends or flutters its short wings, something like an ostrich. It hardly seems to leave the ground. It gets lots of thorns in its feet and picks them out with its strong bill. A member of the cuckoo family, with a small, shaggy crest, and long legs, it spends so much time on the ground that it has been called a pedestrian. To stop quickly, while running, the chaparral cock thrusts its long tail up and over its head. It can fly—for about an eighth of a mile—and it can glide, with its stubby wings out, across a gully or down a hill. In its nest, on the ground, there can be at one and the same time both newly laid eggs and young it is feeding.

It never leaves the barren plains or thorny cactus, it never migrates from its land of scorpions (which it eats), elf owls, coyotes—and rattlesnakes. Very nimble, like the mongoose that kills cobras in India, the roadrunner can circle and dance around a snake, rush in and peck at it and batter the snake with its beak, and is said to peck out the snake's eyes. It can kill a rattlesnake this way. The University of Texas zoologist Osmond P. Breland says, "One road-runner was seen to kill a rattlesnake three-and-one-half feet long, after which it ate the snake's brain and nothing else." If it eats a snake too large to swallow whole, the bird strolls about unconcernedly with the snake's tail dangling out of its mouth.

In the days of the Long Trail, the roadrunner served some people as medicine: a Mexican cure for boils was to kill, cook and eat a roadrunner.

No cowboy or anyone else who has seen a scissor-tailed flycatcher has failed to think it is almost as unusual a bird as the roadrunner. With its fifteen-and-one-half-inch-long forked tail, like a pair of scissors, the flycatcher is common around Austin and breeds from southern Texas to southern Nebraska. A bird of the open lands, it flies high and circles and floats and turns easily—one of the most graceful of all birds in the air.

The yellow-breasted meadowlark, with its cheerful but plaintive, bubbling or slurping whistle, was heard and seen by cowboys on many a mile of the Long Trail, from the Gulf to Canada, from Nebraska east. An eleven-inch-long, brown-streaked bird, with a black V on its breast above the yellow, and with white outer tail feathers, it walks in grassy fields (it is one of the few birds that walk), or flutters (with rapidly vibrating wings) or sails over fields. Atop a tree or fence post it turns its yellow breast to the rising sun and with a clear, loud, melodious song welcomes the coming day.

The prairie chicken the cowboy encountered from Texas to Kansas. Once L. B. Anderson, with a herd, encountered too many. He had camped in the only spot he could find that had grass not burned off by a prairie fire.

"I think every prairie chicken in that whole country came there to roost," he said. "They were there by the thousands. The next morning, when these chickens began to leave, the noise they made frightened the cattle and caused them to stampede. The three thousand beeves ran over that rough country in every direction, and they went several miles before we were able to check them. Several were killed and about a hundred got away."

A quail, or bobwhite (from its call that sounds like Bob Whiiiiiiiite), was the object of a hunt the cowboy arranged especially for the benefit of new arrivals in the land of the Long Trail. Out in the wilds, the tenderfoot or greenhorn would be given a large sack to hold. The other men along would tell him to stand there, and they would drive quails into the sack. Then the others would leave him and return to a campfire for coffee and yarns.

A while later, perhaps an hour or more, it would dawn on the tenderfoot that he had been left holding the sack.

The cowboy had no way of knowing it, but as his cattle plodded north, at ten miles a day, up the Long Trail, they were most of the way beneath what we today call the Central Flyway, a superhighway for birds that carries much of North America's winged traffic—and in North America there is the heaviest north-to-south and south-to-north bird migration on earth. Two-thirds of the birds in the United States migrate, and the Central Flyway carries the most crowded traffic west of the Mississippi and east of the Rocky Mountains. It is busy nearly all year. Some birds start south in July, while others start south only after snow falls in December. Similarly, northward passages begin at different times.

The robin redbreast really did begin his trip up the Long Trail early in the spring; he earned his reputation as the first harbinger of spring. The black-headed, gray-backed, red-breasted robin made lots better time than the longhorns: he went north at up to forty miles a day, keeping right up with the thaws that brought out earthworms. He got as far north as the cattle, and farther: to central Alberta, Canada; and he has even been seen only a hundred miles south of the northernmost point on the continent of North America, Point Barrow, Alaska.

In the autumn, the robins band together in great flocks and, instead of eating earthworms, feed on wild berries. They eat more wild fruit than any other bird; they distribute the seeds widely. They distribute and plant nearly all the wild fruit in the United States. There is simply no telling how many cowboys, farmers, pioneer women or children owed something to eat to the American robin.

Later in the spring, barely ahead of the cowboys and the longhorns, came the cheery, warbling bluebird with its rusty breast. It ate some wild fruit, but mainly insects, and arrived in the spring as soon as insects became available.

Other migrants that traveled the trail with the cowboys were the rose-breasted grosbeak, the indigo bunting, the goldfinch, the chipping sparrow, and thirty of the fifty-seven species of waterfowl in North America, including brant and snow and white-footed and Canada geese. And most species of wild duck—canvasback, redhead, pintail, mallard, gadwall, baldpate, green-wing teal, bluewing teal, the wood duck, and the rare tree duck. Many winter today on the High Plains of Texas in the National Muleshoe Wildlife Refuge, at Muleshoe (a name from Long Trail days), Bailey County.

From the Houston area into Canada, the cowboy saw the catbird, black and dark gray, a bird smaller than the robin. The catbird likes the thickets and swampy woods as well as human habitations, and the cowboy often saw it as he took a drink from a farmer's well.

Constant entertainment for the cowboy was provided by the black, brown-headed cowbird that hangs around cattle and buffaloes and eats insects on their backs, or just sits there. The cowbird also eats insects churned up by the hoofs of the cattle. It is a blackbird, and it joins other blackbirds in huge flocks to migrate south: the common blackbirds, the iridescent purple grackles with boat-shaped tails, bronze grackles, and Brewer's yellow-headed and red-winged blackbirds. The redwings move in flocks that, like cattle herds, have a leader: when he turns, all do.

One of the remarkable things about birds on the Long Trail was that there were so many big ones. Hawks were far more common than today: red-tailed, rough-legged, or Swanson's hawks, goshawks, copper hawks, duck hawks. The wild turkey, twice as big as our domestic ones, was in many states.

The black crow was in the midcontinent when the first European man—the Spaniard—got there in the 1500s. It was there when the cowboy opened the Long Trail, cawing, eating grain and small birds, and amazing men with its cleverness. For one thing, it learns to stay out of gunshot range. It migrates, in large flocks. Its roosts are used for centuries. When he got to Nebraska, the cowboy saw huge roosts; one in Peru, Nebraska, contained a hundred thousand crows.

The red-necked turkey buzzard, as long as thirty-two inches with a wingspread up to six feet, sailed over the Long Trail; on the ground it gorged itself upon dead bodies of sheep, cattle, many wild things, and men—then it flapped its wings and bounded into the air. Probably two or three live per square mile. The buzzards, or vultures, patrol an area thoroughly; when they find something dead, they descend; others see them, and every vulture for miles around comes to join the feast. After a drought killed a lot of cattle, the cowboys noticed, the buzzards became so fat they could hardly fly.

In the upper Midwest and Canada, during the summer, as far from the sea as possible, the cowboys came upon the rosy-tinted, black-headed, gray or mainly white Franklin's gull. The explorer for Spain, Ferdinand Magellan, probably saw it first, sometime late in the year 1520, and he then would have seen it at the southern tip of South America in a narrow strip of water that became known as the Strait of Magellan. In the northern springtime, the gull travels north, leaves the sea, and moves inland in the Midwest and Canada. Today, in plowed fields, it picks up worms and grubs and grasshoppers. And in the spring as he plows, the farmer hears a flutelike po-lee, po-lee from the bird that he calls the prairie pigeon and that has come to him possibly all the way from southernmost South America.

The Americas are the great home of woodpeckers, some of them big ones, and anywhere along the Long Trail, Gulf to Canada, where there were trees, woodpeckers were numerous—often flaring their trademark, red color—the red-headed, the hairy, the downy, the red-bellied, the red-cockaded (in the pine trees), and the flickers. The woodpeckers of east Texas woods included the large, crow-sized, pileated woodpecker that throws chips as big as a carpenter might. It has a conspicuous red crest and white wing feathers that are seen in flight. A modern tale from Nacogdoches, in east Texas, is that a pileated woodpecker, imprisoned inside a carton, easily got out of it (with its bill) then pecked a three-inch-square hole in the wall of a house and flew away.

In mountainous country, from across the Pecos River in Texas to northern Alaska, is the range of the American golden eagle—a vaster range than even the buffalo or the wild cattle or wild horses ever roamed. The golden eagle, like the bald eagle, nests in tall trees or big cliffs. The golden eagle is on his guard even in sparsely settled regions. Well he might be: His feathers made Indian head-dresses. But on Western ranches he became so accustomed to cattle drives and their riders that he paid little attention to cowboys on horseback.

Far more plentiful in the cowboy's time than today, from central Mexico to all over the United States, there was the bald eagle, a bird that quickly got used to cattle drives and horsemen—and ignored them. Like the golden eagle dark brown and six feet across the wings, the bald eagle has a head and neck covered with white feathers.

Among the other Long Trail birds were tiny ones, many kinds of wrens. And the sooty chimney swift that zigzags over the sky, from Texas to Iowa, chasing insects. And the barn swallow, the tree swallow, the bank swallow, and the purple martin, fond of wide rivers, grass, and meadows. The sparrows included the white-throated, swamp, and song sparrows; and many more. On the eastern edge of the Long Trail, the golden-winged, worm-eating Kentucky warbler—and other warblers—flitted about the treetops.

A cattle driver and rancher, Willy Hughes of England, in Texas was fascinated by his first hummingbirds. Hummingbirds are unique to the Americas. With their whirring wings, they can fly backwards. They are the smallest animals with backbones on earth and they are the smallest of all migratory birds. The bee-sized ruby-throat flies—nonstop—500 miles across the open Gulf of Mexico between Texas and South America.

Miscellaneous other birds along the Long Trail were the wood thrush with its flutelike song; on the western trails in Texas, and again farther north, the most brilliantly colored of American birds, the red, black, and gold western tanager; the shrike or butcher bird, a meat eater; and the brown thrasher, which somewhat resembles the wood thrush. At twilight, along with the chimney swifts, and after dark, the night riders among the cowboys would have the company of the gray or blackish nighthawk, a cousin of the whippoorwill, that carried on its wavy, up-and-down flight among insect swarms. Many a night a cowboy heard the cry of the little screech owl, and many a night he heard the hoo-hoo-hoo of the great horned owl.

The cowboy saw, along the Gulf of Mexico, where grow tropical magnolias, holly, palms, asters, poinsettias, and crepe myrtles, the seed-eating, bright red cardinal, a grosbeak, with a crest on his head and a black bib and mask, and his tawny female. In the spring, when the cowboys and longhorns started north, the red-birds would be beginning their nests for the first of as many as four broods they might raise in a long summer. In the winter, among the evergreens around the northern ends of the Long Trail, some cardinals always stayed on—their scarlet glowing against the glittering white snow. The cowboys could hear as well as see the redbirds.

In spring and summer both male and female sing, in a clear whistle—sometimes in unison. Along with the redbirds, hanging on amid the Northern snows, were the black-capped chickadee, the nuthatch, the sooty snowbird or junco, the bluejay, and the downy and hairy woodpeckers. These winter birds, when they could, thrived on the thousand seeds in the face of a sunflower, abundant in many states, but reaching dinner-plate size in Kansas. And if a top hand among the cowboys trekked farther north, into Canada, he perhaps might encounter, down from the Arctic, the white snowy owl.

Of all the birds, the favorite perhaps of the cowboys, their women, and all Texans, was a dark-and-light gray bird, ten inches long, with white tail-edge feathers, the mockingbird. It sang to the cowboy from the Gulf Coast a good way north. Its song, which varies, sometimes mimics the calls of other birds of the Long Trail (robin, wood thrush, bluebird, wren, cardinal). The sweet, liquid, thrushlike song is heard at night as well as by day and during both nesting and nonbreeding seasons. The song gave the mockingbird its nickname, "nightingale of the south." That it leaped up and down, apparently for joy, from a fence or telegraph post, possibly additionally endeared it to Texans. At any rate, the state legislature, where the cowman and his family had some influence, years ago adopted the mockingbird as the state bird. And only recently, at a meeting of descendants of the old trail drivers in San Antonio, one of them said that a mocker made a cowboy's heart stand still.

36

The superest cowboy who never lived

JUST EXACTLY as you would expect, along with the Long Trail there grew up a mythical supercowboy who did everything right, and did it big, and his name was Pecos Bill. The cowboys, who added to his story as they went up and down the trail, said he was born about the time when Sam Houston discovered Texas (they ignored the Spaniards), and he cut his teeth on a Bowie knife. As he was being carried across Texas in a wagon, along with seventeen or eighteen brothers and sisters, the infant Bill fell out. His parents missed him five weeks later.

Coyotes raised him.

He and his squatter-hand ate all the buffalo in west Texas.

Bill rode an Oklahoma cyclone as it leveled mountains and removed the trees from the Staked Plains of the Texas Panhandle. Pecos Bill dug the Rio Grande. He staked out New Mexico, and made it his ranch. Arizona was his cow pasture. His rope was long enough to reach from the Rio Grande to Big Bow, Canada; when he threw it up, he could bring down eagles and buzzards.

He saw a maiden, Slue-foot Sue, riding a catfish twice as big as a whale down the Grand Canyon. He married her.

His bronco throwed all other riders, and so was named Widow

Maker. Pecos Bill's bride, Slue-foot Sue, rode Widow Maker, who pitched her up almost to the moon. When she landed, back on earth, her life was saved by her steel-spring bustle. But the spring in her bustle kept her bouncing for three days.

To dig fence holes, Bill rounded up prairie dogs; they like to dig holes. When Bill wanted pets, he invented two suitable to his character: tarantulas and centipedes. He also put horns on the toads and thorns on the trees.

He used a rattlesnake as a lariat to spin at the poisonous, beady, under-two-feet-long Mexican and Southwestern lizard known as the Gila monster. Reminding you of Davy Crockett, he hugged to death two grizzly bears.

He did not invent stealing cattle. King David of the Bible had done that. Pecos Bill improved methods.

His mother once killed forty-five Indians with a broom-handle. When he was three days old, she weaned him on moonshine.

There was a rumor that his father was a liar.

It took a tenderfoot in cattle country about ten days to judge what he heard about Pecos Bill—or anyone else: "If the story sounds like the truth, it is undoubtedly a lie; but if it sounds like a lie, it may be true."

Bill fought a mountain lion, the biggest one in the West, till the lion pleaded: "I'll give up, Bill; can't you take a joke?"

Bill took up with human beings, acquired their vices, and sank to the uttermost depths, the cowboys said: Pecos Bill became a cowboy.

He asked the toughest cow outfit he could find who was boss. A big man with nine Bowie knives and seven pistols in his belt replied: "Stranger, I was; but you be."

To give added kick to his toddy, he dropped into it fishhooks and barbed wire. And from it he died.

37

All kinds
of weather

1879. AROUND THE United States: A government agency was established that would survey the country and provide a great deal of valuable information to Americans, the U.S. Geological Survey. . . . More machines were coming in. Farms were being mechanized, as they obtained twine binders, spring-tooth harrows, and centrifugal cream separators. . . . Thomas Edison developed the first practical electric light bulb. . . . Near Lancaster, Pennsylvania, and in Utica, New York, stores opened—the first of a chain that would prove successful in the Midwest, the United States and abroad. Their founder: F. W. Woolworth.

ALONG THE LONG TRAIL: New ranches included C. C. Slaughter's Long S holdings in Borden County, on the South Plains; John Beckwith's, south of Marathon; H. H. Campbell's (he laid the foundation for the Matador below Quintague by buying cattle from John Dawson, Coggin, Wylie, and others). Other pioneer cattlemen included a Scot, Murdo MacKenzie, who managed the Prairie and Matador syndicates, Bassett Blakely, J. M. West, H. F. McGill, J. C. McGill, J. D. Jackson, T. D. Hobart, A. P. Borden, who imported Brahma cattle, Charles P. Taft, Frank Hastings, J. P. Norris, R. R. Russell, Lee Russell, A. M. McFaddin, who boosted the Brahmas, James Callen, Julian M. Bassett, the Landergin brothers, John and Pat, Cyrus Lucas, J. H. P. Davis, John M. Shelton, J. M. Dobie, W. W. Jones, Ed C. Lasater, who became interested in Jersey cattle, W. Q. Richards, Dennis M. O'Conner, L. C. Brite, E. F. Williams, D. W. and J. W. Godwin, John N. Simpson, William E. Hughes, R. B. Masterson, George W. Evans, John Z. Means, T. D. Love, J. F. Newman, J. H. Parramore, C. W. Merchant, John H. Wood, J. G. Lowe, William and Robert Adams, Jerry and Robert Driscoll, and A. C. Jones. . . . A couple of lines by Berta Hart Nance:

> Other states were carved or born;
> Texas grew from hide and horn.

"I started in 1879," said Ben Drake, "but got done up just about the time we reached the Territory." He meant that he became ill. He was taken to an Indian camp, and left there. "While there I ate dry land terrapin and dog meat cooked together and was glad to get it." He had to stay in the camp for three months. "Then the chief went to Texarkana and got someone to come after me. A United States marshal brought me to Austin in a buggy."

Bossing a herd for Jim Ellison, Dick Withers drove 5,000 cattle—two herds combined—past Doan's Store on the Red River, through Dodge City, Kansas, and on to Ogallala, Nebraska, and from there on to Sidney Bridge on the North Platte. "The largest herd ever seen on the trail," Dick Withers described it.

G. W. Mills drove for M. A. Withers. A new trail to Dodge City had been worked out, starting at the Cimarron. It was marked by a buffalo head set up every half mile. After reaching Dodge City, Mills headed for Ogallala. Thirty miles from Ogallala, Mills and his companions camped, a mile from a spring that forms the head of a stream called Stinking Water. "I had an experience with lightning," Mills said, "that I know rivals the experience of any man who ever went up the trail." That was something. One cowboy spat tobacco and saw a ball of fire leap from his mouth. Other cowboys saw the points of the cattle's long horns blaze with light.
"The storm hit us about 12 o'clock at night," Mills said.

"There was some rain, and to the northwest I noticed just a few little bats of lightning. Then it hit us in full fury and we were in the midst of a wonderful electrical storm. We had the following varieties of lightning, all playing close at hand, I tell you: It commenced like flash lightning, followed by the peculiar blue lightning. After that show it rapidly developed into ball lightning, which rolled along the ground. After that spark lightning; then, most wonderful of all, it settled down on us like a fog. The air smelled of burning sulphur; you could see it on the horns of the cattle, the ears of our horses, and the brim of our hats. It grew so warm we thought we might burn up with it, and M. A. Withers and Joe Lewis, old-timers, told me afterwards that they never had seen the like in all of their experiences. The cattle did not give us so much trouble as the constant flashes keeping them moving so much."

The Frenches drove steers to the Cheyenne Agency. The cattle were to be food for the Sioux Indians. "One day early in December," recalled C. C. French, "an Indian carrier came to our camp with a message from the commander of the post saying that if the mercury went 28 degrees below zero he wanted 250 steers that day, to commence killing for the Indians' winter beef. We delivered the steers and the Indians killed them all in one day. The meat was exposed to the cold for a few days and then stored in an immense warehouse to be issued out to the Indians every week. . . .

"It was no uncommon sight to see a squaw at one end of an entrail and a dog at the other end, both eating ravenously. When the killing was completed, we had about 600 steers that had to be crossed over the Missouri River on the ice, which was then about 28 inches thick across the channel. After this was done we had to deliver the horses to Fort Thompson. At this time the government thermometer at Peeve recorded 72 degrees below zero. On our way home we were in that fearful blizzard which froze the bay at Galveston and ruined the orange trees in Florida.

"I have never liked cold weather since that time."

38

Lost—and
dying of thirst

IN 1879, a cowboy named Samuel Dunn Houston, of San Antonio, drove cattle all the way from southern Texas to Ogallala, Nebraska. Then he was hired to drive a herd of 4,000 cattle from the King Ranch on to the Red Cloud Agency, North Dakota, an Indian agency. The King cattle, like Houston himself, had come all the way from the Texas Gulf Coast.

"Everybody in town," said Houston, "was out to see the big King herd go through. I threw my hat back on my head and I felt as though the whole herd belonged to me."

When the lead cattle had crossed the South Platte and walked all the way to the foothills beyond it, the tail-end cattle still were going into the river. Cowboy Sam Houston was riding point—on the left-hand side of the herd near its front. "I told my partner, the right-hand pointer," he said, "that we were headed for the North Pole."

One night about ten a big black wolf, or so the men thought, got too close. The cattle ran. Houston and the other cowboys turned them into a mill. The cattle broke out. That went on till 3 A.M. when the 4,000 cattle were finally quieted.

At the Red Cloud Agency, there were 10,000 Indians. The

cattle were weighed, and it took all day, said Houston, "ten steers on the scales at one time." As the cattle were weighed, the agents called the Indians by name and gave one to each family.

That night the cowboys watched as the Indians, who had killed a dog, ate it. "Every Indian on the ground had a bite of that dog." Then they danced around the carcass. The Indians invited the cowboys to have some. "We were not hungry," Houston remembered.

Houston wanted to get home. "I was very anxious to get on the trail road and go down in Texas to see my best girl."

At the Dillon Ranch, on the Niobrara River, he heard of an Indian trail across the Laramie plains that would cut two hundred miles off the way back to Ogallala. Houston decided to take that trail, which he did not know—alone. It would be a shortcut. The trail to Ogallala was, by the shortcut, 175 to 200 miles. The first lake was 65 or 70 miles away. The second watering place was beyond that.

Houston's foreman, Tom Moore, told him: "You are a fool. You can't make that trip, not knowing where the fresh water is, you will starve to death."

Next morning, Houston, alone, headed out. He told the boys "if they heard of a dead man or horse on the old Indian trail, across the plains, for some of them the next year to come and pick me up."

Houston thought he was on "the best horse that ever crossed the Platte River." He thought the horse carried him sixty-five to seventy miles the first day. He began to look for the lake. He found an alkali lake, but no water to drink.

With blankets, a slicker, and saddle blankets, he made a bed and lay down. "Red Bird (my horse) was also jaded."

Next morning, he looked on both sides for the lake. What he found, instead, were big alkali lakes. "But I knew there would be a dead cowboy out there if I should take a drink of that kind of water."

He saw elk, antelope, deer—and wolves.

At noon he rested.

His tongue began to swell, and kept swelling, till he could not spit.

By midafternoon, he "saw a large lobo wolf about one hundred yards away and he seemed to be going my route. I would look in his direction quite often. He was going my gait and seemed to have me spotted. I took a shot at him every little while, but I kept on going and so did he."

That night, still with no water, he camped on the edge of another alkali lake. He said he "made my bed on my stake rope so I would not lose my horse."

The moon came up.

About nine o'clock a wolf howled.

Houston started awake.

"I looked up and saw him sitting about twenty feet from my head just between me and the moon. I turned over right easy, slipped my gun over the cantle of my saddle and let him have one ball. He never kicked. I grabbed my rope, went to him, cut him open, and used my hands for a cup and drank his old blood. It helped me in a way, but did not satisfy as water would.

"I went down to the lake and washed up, went back to bed, and thought I would get a good sleep and rest that night, but found later I had no rest coming."

A herd of elk waked him at midnight.

He saddled Red Bird and rode till dawn.

"I was so tired I thought I would lay down and sleep awhile."

He thought he had passed the second lake.

He slept a little, rode on till noon.

It was his third day on the trail.

"I thought I could walk around, and the first thing I saw was an old dead horse's bones. I wondered what a dead horse's bones were doing away out there, so I began to look around some more and what should I see but the bones of a man."

The man and the horse had tried the same trail.

They had perished "so I told old Red Bird that we had better go down the trail and we pulled out."

About 4 P.M. Houston, now walking and leading Red Bird, came to a high sand hill. From its top he could see cottonwood trees. To get a little shade, he sat down underneath Red Bird. Then he saw cattle, horses—and a man.

"I didn't know whether he was an Indian or not. He was in a gallop and as he came nearer to the horses I pulled my gun and shot one time. He stopped a bit and started off again. Then I made two shots and he stopped again a few minutes. By that time he had begun to round up the horses, so I shot three times. He quit his horses and came to me in a run. When he got up within thirty or forty feet of me he spoke to me and called me by name and said, 'Sam, you are the biggest fool I ever saw.' I couldn't say a word for my mouth was so full of tongue, but I knew him. He shook hands and told me to get up behind him and we would go to camp. He took his rope and tied it around my waist to keep me from falling off, for I was very weak. Then he struck a gallop and we were at camp in a very few minutes. He tied his horse and said, 'Now, Sam, we will go down to the spring and get a drink of water.' "

They came to the spring. Said Houston, "the finest sight I ever saw in my life."

Sam tried to get to the spring. But he was so weak his friend could hold him back with one hand. As he did, his rescuer said, "Now, Sam, I am going to be the doctor."

He took an old tin cup and put just a teaspoonful of water in it. "Throw your head back," he ordered Sam. He poured the water on Sam's tongue.

"After a while he increased it," Houston remembered, "until I got my fill and my tongue went down. When I got enough water then I was hungry. I could have eaten a piece of that fat dog [the one the Indians ate] if I'd had it."

Houston's friend was a cowboy who had ridden with him many times, Jack Woods.

Jack got Houston to lie down while he got ready to cook some of the meat of a calf he had killed the day before. Houston could not wait. He sneaked around to where the rest of the calf was hanging, and with his pocketknife cut off bits of raw meat and ate them. After fifteen or twenty minutes, Jack caught him: "Sam, I always thought you were crazy, now I know it. Come on to supper." Sam still could eat a lot more.

"After finishing supper, I never was so sleepy in my life. Jack said, 'Sam, lay down on my bed and go to sleep and I will go out and get your horse and treat him to water and oats.' He got on his horse and struck a gallop for the sand hills, where my poor old horse was standing starving to death."

On the next day, Jack told Houston about a man named Lumm who had tried to cross the plains. He said, "He and his horse's bones are laying out on the plains now. Perhaps you saw them as you came along.''

Houston said he had.

He stayed with Woods five days, helping him take care of the horses every day.

"On October 29," Samuel Dunn Houston remembered, "I saddled my horse and told Jack I was going to Texas. He gave me a little lunch, and I bid him good-bye and headed for the North Platte.

"I reached Bosler's ranch at 12:20 o'clock, had dinner, gave the boss a note from Jack Woods, fed my horse, rested one hour, saddled up, bade the boys good-bye and headed for Ogallala on the South Platte, forty miles below.

"I reached Ogallala that night at 9:30 o'clock, put my horse in the livery stable, went up to the Leach Hotel, and there I met Mr. Dillon, the owner of the Niobrara ranch, sold my horse to him for $80, purchased a new suit, got a shave and haircut, bought my ticket to Texas, and left that night at 8:30 o'clock for Kansas City.

"On November 6th I landed in Austin, Texas, thirty miles from my home, and took the stage the next morning for Lockhart. That was where my best girl lived, and when I got there I was happy.''

Samuel Dunn Houston had reached the Red Cloud Agency, North Dakota; had gotten lost on the way back; had nearly died of thirst and hunger.

"This," he wrote, "was the end of a perfect trip.''

39

The longhorns graze on Northern ranches

THE 1880s. AROUND THE WORLD: A U.S. patent was granted for a safety belt—to prevent people from falling out of horse-drawn buggies. Nevertheless, the era of the horse was fading. After thousands of years riding horseback, or being hauled by horses, men were turning to mechanized transportation instead. The safety bicycle arrived in 1881; Americans, by the hundreds of thousands, learned from it some simple mechanics. At Baltimore, in 1885, the first electric streetcars in the United States appeared. The big breakthrough, though, was made in Germany: at Mannheim, in 1885, Karl Benz—as his wife followed behind and clapped her hands—drove around his yard, at one mile an hour, a tricycle (three-wheeled) carriage. Its one-cylinder engine used as fuel a form of liquid gas. On the night he had finished his engine, Benz and his wife had not had sufficient money for supper. Also in Germany the next year, 1886, Gottlieb Daimler produced the first four-wheel gasoline-engine car, the first of the hundreds of millions. At the Universal Exhibition in Paris, in 1889, the 984-foot-high Eiffel Tower (a step toward the first skyscrapers) was opened, and the first automobile to be exhibited—ever—was on hand: a Benz.

A step was taken, in 1880, toward controlling a disease that summer after summer after summer weakened people of the Gulf Coast. The malaria parasite was discovered. Not until seventeen years later would men know that a mosquito transmitted the malaria parasite to a human being.

ON THE LONG TRAIL: Charles Goodnight in 1880 organized the Panhandle Stockmen's Association. It would combat cattle thieves. . . . A spur of the Santa Fe railway reached Caldwell, Kansas, on the southern border of the state—the farthest-south of any Kansas town where the longhorns met the railroad. The town of Caldwell became known as the Border Queen. . . . The University of Texas opened, in 1883, and its situation looked precarious: there were only about six high schools in the entire state—and scarcely enough high school graduates to attend the university.

In the northern Midwest, the ranges and ranches were being stocked with cattle.

The first ranches in the north of the midcontinent area had been established by men en route to the goldfields of California in 1848–49, but who dropped out on the way. Where they stopped, they settled. They captured and broke wild horses of the Great Plains. They obtained domesticated cattle from the pioneer farms to the east of them, and they bought longhorns from Texas.

In Laramie, Wyoming, J. W. Iliff had bought lame, footsore animals from among early cattle going to California. His herd grew. Eventually, Iliff fed construction crews building that first railroad track across the United States, the Union Pacific. Iliff became one of the best-known ranchmen in Colorado.

Col. J. D. Henderson, before the Civil War, had established a store on the trail to California, and had bought lame cattle from covered-wagon travelers. He located on an island in the Platte River.

Edward Creighton of Omaha, Nebraska, had begun grazing cattle in 1859. D. J. Jenkins that same year had pushed a wheelbarrow from Colorado to Nebraska and had established a ranch there.

By 1860, scattered ranches had been established in Nebraska, 150 miles beyond the Missouri River, on the Overland Trail. The Overland Trail ran from Westport or St. Joseph, Missouri, to Wyoming, then branched to Oregon and California. In 1861, the Pony Express carried mail across the continent on the Overland Trail. In the first half of the 1860s, except in midwinter, there were always upon it 4,000 to 10,000 covered wagons. Concord stagecoaches ran along it, carrying nine passengers inside, six on top. The coaches changed to fresh horses or mules at stations ten to fifteen miles apart. A stagecoach reached California from Missouri in seventeen to nineteen days.

Barring Indian attacks, that is. Otherwise, somewhere on the trail there would be six dead mules or horses, a burning stage-coach, and the bodies of the driver and up to fifteen passengers so full of arrows they looked like pincushions.

As the longhorn drives from Texas increased, both Iliff and Henderson bought large numbers of Texas cattle. So did many other men. So did companies from the United States and overseas organized for the purpose of ranching. The new ranchers and their hands filed for homesteads up and down the streams and rivers. Here their cattle had water—and the cattle could graze for miles on either side of a stream on the grass that grew thick in the Northern states.

A homestead was 160 acres. Every individual steer, however, needed as much as 16 acres of its own to graze. Therefore, it took many homesteads to provide grazing for a herd of cattle—this despite the abundance of the grass.

Accordingly, ranches were measured not in acres but in sections. A section is 640 acres, or one square mile.

The cattle on the ranches had to be young ones because they would spend two or three years being fed and fattened on the grass before being shipped to market.

A result of the cattle drives up the Long Trail and of the establishment of ranches was an increase, between 1870 and 1880, in the numbers of cattle in many states. E. E. Dale records it: Kansas, from 374,000 to 1,534,000; Nebraska, from 80,000 to 1,174,000; Colorado, from 70,000 to 790,000; Montana, 37,000 to 428,000; Wyoming, 10,000 to 521,000; Dakota Territory, 12,000 to 141,000.

"These figures," said Dale, "are startling and reveal clearly what was taking place on the Great Plains."

In the summer of 1881, two-thirds of the 384,000 longhorns driven north were yearlings or two-year-old steers to be fattened on Northern grass.

The Northern Pacific Railroad reached Miles City, in Custer

County, Montana—and well north of Denver, Colorado, and Cheyenne, Wyoming.

Cattle accordingly were driven onward to Miles City. The problem here was foothills that the longhorns had to cross. A Montana cowman, Granville Stuart, said that the magpies broke their wings flying over the ridges. Another problem was a cold, fast stream, on which Miles City was located, the Yellowstone River, that eventually, Teddy Blue said, would drown more cattle and more men than any other river. Cowboys wanted to be able to say they had trailed to the Yellowstone. It made them looked-up-to.

There was another reward for reaching the Yellowstone and Miles City. As the cowboys trailed onward, so did girls. The young and pretty prostitutes the cowboys had met in Abilene, Dodge City, Ogallala, Denver, Cheyenne, and elsewhere—Texas Queen, Texas Rose, and others—moved to Miles City.

Teddy Blue met one of the girls—and another person—in Montana in 1883. The other person was President Chester A. Arthur who took a ride on the Northern Pacific to help open it. His train, Blue said, "came through all decorated with flags."

The girl Teddy Blue met at a stagecoach station near Miles City, also in 1883. She had traveled with the Wild West show of Buffalo Bill. She had also been a madam in charge of Texas Roses and Texas Queens, she had been known for wielding a Colt pistol, and her name was Calamity Jane. From her, Blue borrowed fifty cents. He said he would repay her when next he saw her. She said to forget it. Nevertheless, when he did run into her the next time, at Gilt Edge, Montana, he walked up to her and gave her half a dollar. That was twenty-four years later—in 1907.

The trail went beyond Miles City.

The Long Trail, now traversing the Northern grasslands, grew longer till it stretched to its farthest point. The Long Trail that had begun on the hot, humid Gulf of Mexico coast, among the palm trees of tropical Brownsville, Texas, and, as Jim Daugherty and J.J. Meyers had done, had crossed Oklahoma to meet the newly laid railroad tracks in Kansas; the Long Trail that had begun, with men like Charles Goodnight and Oliver Loving and Bill Wilson and Jesse Chisholm in the cactus desert of west Texas' Pecos River country, and had wound north through New Mexico to army posts and Indian agencies and railroad-track-laying crews, in Colorado;

the Long Trail that had gone on and on from Kansas and Colorado to provide the stock for new ranches in Nebraska, Iowa, South and North Dakota, Wyoming, Montana, and even across the Rockies to the Pacific Coast; the Long Trail at last reached its point farthest north. On through Montana the longhorns plodded, on across the U.S. boundary, on to Calgary. Onward to another nation, Canada; on to Calgary—to a region of mountain valleys and plains and the foothills of the Rockies. This was as far as the longhorns were to go on their tough hoofs and string-bean legs on the Long Trail—to Calgary, as far north as grazing remained good, the farthest-northern tip of the wide land of grass.

The land of grass, the cattle country, was a wide, wide land.

The land of grazing and ranches was as large as western Europe, from European Russia to and including Great Britain. It covered one-third of what is now the United States. From south Texas to Calgary on the Bow River, Alberta, Canada, the cattle country covered, south to north, a distance of 1,600 miles, or approximately the distance from Moscow to London, or 2,000 miles or more the way the cattle walked. Its width, from the Rocky Mountains to the east, was 400 to 600 miles. Also part of the cow country, but west of the first range of the Rocky Mountains, there were valleys and deserts and semideserts in the Great Basin, New Mexico, and Arizona.

By the 1880s, twelve million cattle at one time were pastured on the grass of the midcontinent.

A single rancher had a wide domain. His ranch house might not be impressive or even large. But from it he presided over a territory, which his cattle ranged, larger than the land of many a European duke, prince, queen, or king.

As the cowboys came from anywhere and everywhere in the world, so did those later cowboys, the ranchmen. Said E. E. Dale: "No scientific attempt has ever been made to determine the original homeland of the western ranchmen and their riders, but it seems likely that they came from virtually every part of the country."

They also came from Europe. From France, Antoine de Vallambrosa, Marquis de Mores, set up a ranch on the Little Missouri River in Dakota Territory. He built an elaborate château on a hill overlooking the Bad Lands. He fenced in his ranch. He founded the town of Medora, and for a time supported a stage line from Medora to Deadwood. He sought to be the most important cattleman in his part of Dakota, and he competed with a rival, a young American who was just out of the New York state legislature, and who had established in North Dakota the Elkhorn Ranch, Theodore Roosevelt.

A Norwegian named Olson, who had gone to sea at age fourteen, established a ranch near Laramie, Wyoming. He brought books to his ranch, read them, and put notes in their margins. He named his milk cows after Dickens' characters.

From Germany to Colorado came Walter, Baron von Richthofen, ancestor of the aviator of World War I who was to become known as the Red Knight of Germany.

From France there was Pierre Wilbaux. He owned a ranch partly in Montana and partly in Dakota. His ranch house, a showplace, became called the White House or the Palace. Wilbaux was host to hundreds of guests from around the world. He retired from the cattle trade in 1904. The town of Wilbaux, Montana, is named for him.

England exported to the cattle country the Marquis of Tweedsdale, who is believed to have owned 1,751,000 acres; Lord Dunmore, who owned 100,000; Lord Dunraven, who held title to much of today's Estes Park, Colorado.

From Scotland there had arrived Murdo MacKenzie. He became manager of the Matador Land and Cattle Company in 1891, a company that at one time had more than 100,000 cattle, which it kept in Texas and Montana. MacKenzie had better cattle: his Herefords came to be known as among the finest cattle on earth. Except for a short time, MacKenzie would manage the Matador for almost forty years.

From Scotland there came also John Clay, Jr. He helped establish several companies: Western Ranches Limited, the Wyoming Cattle Ranch Company, the Cattle Ranch and Land Company, and the biggest Scottish ranching venture on the Great Plains, the Swan Land and Cattle Company. The Swan firm, combining properties owned by Americans, Alex H. Swan and Joseph Frank, at one time owned according to its books 89,000 cattle. John Clay managed the Swan company, and later organized the John Clay Live Stock Commission Company that became one of the biggest in its field.

Other Scottish-financed companies included the Prairie Cattle Company, with ranges in Colorado, Kansas, New Mexico, and Texas—a total of 8,000 square miles of pasture, on which 140,000 cattle grazed. And the Hansford Land & Cattle Company, Powder River Cattle Company, Texas Land and Cattle Company. Furnishing money to companies in the United States were the Scottish-American Investment company under S. J. Menzies and the Scottish-American Mortgage Company under Duncan Smith.

English and Irish capital financed the Espuela, or Spur, Ranch; the Carlisle Cattle Company in Wyoming; the LX Ranch in northwest Texas. The English also financed the American Pastoral Company, the Rocking Chair Ranch, and one that became famous, the XIT.

The XIT, or Capital Syndicate Ranch, 160,000 cattle, covered a breathtaking three and one-half million acres, much or all of it fenced, and spread down the western Texas Panhandle, running south from Oklahoma and along the New Mexico line. Its brand, XIT, stood for ten—X—counties *In* *T*exas, which the ranch was said to cover. But when anybody counted the counties, they never could find more than nine.

Back of the XIT and the Capital Syndicate was the Capital Freehold and Investment Company in London. It sold lands, and helped finance the building of the state capitol in Austin, in return for land given by the state of Texas.

English money also had been behind the JA Ranch, established in the Panhandle by John G. Adair and Charles Goodnight of the Goodnight-Loving Trail.

Like earlier immigrants who had G.T.T. (Gone to Texas), many young Englishmen now arrived to run English ranches in the north, and, while they were companionable, they might be social outcasts back home. They might have left behind a gambling debt or a girl or something else. In the West, as the earlier arrivals had been known to do, they forgot their names. They also forgot their titles, if any. And they otherwise tried to conceal their identity.

They did not always succeed. There was, for instance, the time when news of the result of the Oxford-Cambridge boat race reached a cowboy in Montana, and produced from him the cry: "Thank God, we won!"

At their peak, Europeans owned the thirteen largest ranches

on the Western plains. By the 1940s, this had been reduced to two —one of them a sheep ranch, the Swan holdings in Wyoming; the other the Matador Land & Cattle Company, Ltd., of Motley, Dickens, Hartley and Oldham counties in Texas, slightly less than a million acres.

The interest of Europeans in U.S. cattle was due to the profits to be made in the business, and to the possibility of shipping more and more beef to Europe. Back in the days of the British Colonies in North America, before the American Revolution, salt and pickled beef and live cattle had been exported, largely to the West Indies, from Georgia and other British colonies. Cattle and pickled beef had been exported from Texas to Cuba after 1845. In 1875 over 33,000 Texas cattle had made the four-day Gulf-of-Mexico trip from Indianola or Galveston to Cuba. This trade faded. An effort to ship live cattle from Texas to Britain failed.

Then came a turning point.

John L. Bate of New York worked out a way to refrigerate meat for shipping. It included keeping carcasses of cattle cool (thirty-eight degrees Fahrenheit) by using fans driven by steam. On Bate's first shipment of meat across the Atlantic, however, the steamship company refused to provide the steam. Bate hired men to turn the fans by hand. The meat reached Europe in fine shape. After that, steamships carried millions of pounds of beef across the Atlantic, on the Cunard, White Star, Anchor, and other steamship lines.

The Long Trail already had brought down the price of beef to the American public. Now it would reduce the price of beef in Britain.

Even as meat from the United States was partly replacing beef raised among Scotland's heather-clad hills as the roast beef of Old England, there was criticism in Britain that the meat from the United States was inferior in quality. A dinner was held in London. The guests were prominent, and so was the entrée: a huge, red roast of beef that did not stay prominent as it vanished down the guests' throats. The dinner-table talk was practically unanimous that British beef need fear no competition. At the end of the meal, the host delivered the crushing blow: The beef was American.

40

The day he wasn't killed

A COWBOY FROM Oklahoma City, Fred Sutton, in 1881 was in New Mexico rounding up cattle for Jesse Evans when he had what he called his "most interesting incident." He was *not* killed by a slight, 135-pound, hazel-eyed young man, Billy the Kid.

This was, for Fred Sutton, an achievement. For Billy the Kid (born William Bonney in New York City in 1859) had by 1881, when he was twenty-two years old, murdered one man for every year of his life, most of them in 1880. This was, somebody pointed out, "not including Indians and Mexicans," of whom Billy had killed at least four.

The sheriff of Lincoln County, New Mexico, Pat Garrett, was detailed to bring in The Kid, dead or alive. Lincoln County is north of El Paso, Texas, and west of the Texas Panhandle and the Goodnight-Loving Trail, and Fred Sutton and Jesse Evans' roundup were in the area. Sheriff Garrett came to their camp to get help. Sutton joined a posse to go with Garrett.

Sheriff Garrett, Sutton, and the other men in the posse located Billy the Kid and surrounded the ranch house in which he was holed up. "A halt was called for a parley," Sutton said. Billy the Kid asked for Sutton and Jimmy Carlyle to come to the house to talk. "Leaving our guns behind, Jimmy and I went to the house, where we found as tough a bunch of outlaws, gun fighters, and cattle thieves as ever infested a country, or were ever congregated in a space of that size.

"After an hour spent in propositions and counterpropositions, we agreed to disagree, and started back to our own crowd with the promise of not being fired on until we reached them." But Billy the Kid and his associates fired anyway. "An avalanche of lead," said Sutton. The shots missed him. They struck and killed Jimmy Carlyle. They did more—they also killed a ranchman, George Hindman, and another law officer, William Bradley.

With three of its members dead, the posse had to withdraw. Billy the Kid escaped. But the killings influenced the Southwest. Sheriff Pat Garrett returned to the trail of Billy the Kid. "In the summer of 1881 he located him at Sumner, New Mexico," Sutton said, "and killed him first—reading the warrant to him afterwards."

A short time later, Pat Garrett himself was killed by an outlaw by the name of Wayne Brazel, at Las Cruces, New Mexico. New Mexicans put up a monument over Sheriff Garrett's grave.

Fred Sutton concluded: "I do not know of a more exciting time for yours truly than when Billy the Kid and his grand aggregation of murderers and cow thieves opened fire on poor Jimmy Carlyle and me, and do not know why I was not killed, but such is the case, and in a few weeks we were on our way to Dodge City by way of the Chisholm Trail."

On that trip to Dodge City, Fred Sutton knew a quiet, blue-eyed, twenty-two-year-old cowboy named Burt Phelps. One day the other cowboys saw Phelps reading a small edition of the Bible. Phelps, a modest and retiring lad, became a favorite of other cowboys—all except one named Driscoll. Driscoll kept calling Phelps "mamma's boy."

Driscoll, a man with already one or two notches in his gun, was looking for trouble. One night Burt Phelps threw a handful of wood on the fire.

A coal flew up into Driscoll's face. Driscoll reached for his six-shooter.

Before he could get it out, Phelps had his own gun in Driscoll's face. He took Driscoll's gun, smiling as he did, removed the shells from it, and handed it back.

Some nights later, the owner of a ranch house called out to Phelps to lend him his gun as a man wanted to use it to kill a wolf. Phelps, knowing the rancher was a friend, lent him his gun.

The next day Driscoll and Phelps met at a water hole. Driscoll drew his gun. Before he could fire, Phelps had snapped twice from the hip. His pistol did not fire.

Driscoll fired. Phelps fell dead.

The man who had asked the rancher to borrow a gun so he could shoot a wolf was, of course, Driscoll. While he had Burt Phelps' six-shooter in his possession, Driscoll had removed the loads from it.

About Phelps, Fred Sutton said: "Where he came from no one knew.

"On a gently sloping hill overlooking the valley of the Red River is an almost forgotten grave that contains all that is left of the mortal remains of poor Burt Phelps, and in the inside pocket of his coat is a little Bible, on the fly-leaf of which was written, 'From mother to her boy.' "

Cowboys, who met their share of bad men, had a saying: "The only time twelve honest men ever got together was at the Last Supper and one of them was a traitor."

41

A wild white mustang forever roams free

THE WILD mustangs that neither the ranchers nor the cowboys could capture became legends. They became legends that caused awe, wonder, and admiration, on the parts of both the cowboys on the Long Trail and the ranchers of the wide, wide land where many of the mustangs roamed.

In March 1882, the Ghost of the Staked Plains—a milk-white, wild mustang stallion—moved over Texas, and was located by buffalo hunters. With relays of horses, they chased him for almost three hundred miles, over four days. On the last day they drove him over a cliff edge where he fell into alkali slush that would swallow him forever.

He had not broken his stride.

He has not broken his stride to this day:

As the Spaniards had sought mythical cities of gold in the West, so the cowboy and rancher looked for—and sometimes have seen and pursued—a mythical stallion: the Great White Mustang, a horse with long, flaring mane and tail and the speed of the wind. The Great White Mustang, since 1882, has vanished for years, but has always reappeared and been seen again. There is no reason I know of to suppose that the Great White Mustang ever has died. In the mind of the cowboy and the rancher, he will live forever.

About 1882, another wild horse called the Ghost—this one steel blue with a silver tail—was captured in a roundup of wild horses. He attacked four men, then leaped over a high corral fence and escaped. He roamed the Montana Badlands. Cowboys, ranchers, and ranch hands saw him by moonlight, his tail and mane appearing to glow. In a week, he would be seen hundreds of miles away. For years he wandered over the Badlands, then vanished.

As recently as 1971 near Texas' Fort Hood, a wild stallion reared on its hind legs to challenge helicopters and avoided capture. He was one of an estimated ten thousand wild horses remaining in the West.

He was named Born Free.

And he was left alone to run forever with the ghosts of—or the descendants of—the Great White Stallion and of the steel blue stallion with the silver tail.

42

Hail on July 4
—and other items

COWBOY WILLY Hughes, the Texas rancher from England, said he'd met hail "as big as hen's eggs." Others in the 1880s ran into such hail. G. W. Mills was opposite Fort Dodge on the Arkansas River: "On the Fourth of July, 1880, about 2 o'clock in the evening, the awfulest hailstorm came up a man ever saw. The hailstones nearly beat us to death; it knocked over jackrabbits like taking them off with a rifle. It even killed a few yearlings and many fleet antelopes, but the cow hands had to stick to their posts, although we nearly froze to death—on the Fourth of July. The ice lay about four inches deep on the ground next morning."

E. A. (Berry) Roebuck of Lockhart, Texas, who was sixteen when he "entered the trail life," was caught in a cyclone and hailstorm in Indian Territory "one night while I was on guard." Said he: "The wind was so strong at times it nearly blew me out of the saddle, and the hail pelted me so hard great knots were raised on my head."

A white high-crowned, wide-brimmed Stetson hat was becoming popular among cowboys.

At La Grange, Texas, Hiram Craig had to lead his cattle across a river, and had to strip bare to do it. The spectacle of cattle swimming a river had become an attraction, and people gathered to watch. Some of the people were women.

Craig was embarrassed.

At the head of the Colorado River, Hiram Craig saw a roundup said to be the biggest ever. It was a C. C. Slaughter roundup, and brought together 10,000 cattle in a herd that measured half a mile on each of the four sides.

One night in 1882, just north of Red River crossing, the trail was so busy there were eleven trail herds in sight—33,000 cattle altogether. That night a terrible storm arose. "The worst that I ever experienced," said W. M. Magiller of Williams, Arizona. "The thunder, lightning, and rain was awful. All the cattle were turned loose except small cuts we were holding. The following morning cattle were dotting the plains in every direction as far as the eye could see." It took the 120 cowboys on hand ten days to sort out the cattle—all 33,000 head of them.

Magiller's herd went on to Cheyenne.

A herd of cattle arrived in Wyoming and was met by Governor Bush. A cowboy, Gus Black, along the way north had picked up the horns from a dead cow. Black now fitted the great long adult-size horns over the just-sprouting horns of a small yearling. He told the governor that it was just a yearling. The governor looked at the long horns. He said he would bet that it was four years old, and did bet $1,000.

Black roped the dogie and took off the false horns.

Black told the governor to keep his money. Governor Bush set up whisky and cigars for everyone.

In 1882, M. A. Withers, who had driven cattle to Abilene back in 1868, was driving again, this time with G. B. Withers and Gus Johnson. A storm hit. Lightning struck and put out one eye of G. B. Withers; it burned the plush off M.A.'s hat but did not harm him. But it set Johnson's undershirt on fire and it melted his gold shirt stud, tore up his hat, and killed him.

Driving to Denver, Thomas Welder of Beeville, Texas, was among cowboys who took 2,000 cattle to drink along a small stream, Sandy River. There were so many cattle, and the stream was so small, that the cattle actually drank the river dry.

A half-owner of the CN outfit (Cody and North), Buffalo Bill Cody, offered $100 to any cowboy who could rope a jackrabbit.
A cowboy named Jesse Reeves did.

On July 4, 1884, at Pecos, Texas, cowboys from two neighboring ranches competed in cow-country events: roping, racing, and riding.
The occasion was the first known rodeo.

At Fort Sill, Indian Territory, L. B. Anderson had a new experience: "I saw my first telephone. It was a crude affair, and connected the agent's store and residence, a distance of several hundred yards. The apparatus consisted of one wire run through the walls of the store and house with a tube at each end through which you had to blow to attract attention of the party called, and then you could talk over it as well as any phone of the present time." (Anderson was recalling the event long afterward.)

Charley Colcord, a cowboy who rode what he still called the Chisholm Trail, introduced one day to Medicine Lodge, Kansas, a new device never before seen there: the toothbrush. "The punchers all wanted to borrow it till pay day," Fred Sutton—the cowboy who had not been killed by Billy the Kid—remembered, "and after that day came, for a short time, each rider had a white-handled brush sticking out his top vest or shirt pocket."

Jeff D. Farris of Bryan, Texas, who had driven for Col. Jim Ellison of San Marcos, was an experienced cowboy and tried something else: "I married the sweetest woman in all the country." They had five boys and three girls, all but one of whom they would raise to adulthood—a remarkable record at the time.

George W. Saunders, now a trail boss, hired in 1885 an English tenderfoot named Lambert. Lambert asked Saunders to let him ride a bucking horse. Saunders let him.

Once aboard, Lambert addressed the pony: "Gaddup, Old Chap, I've rode worse 'orses than you." The pony stood still, humped up. Saunders told Lambert to hit the pony's head with his hat. Lambert did. "At that same instant," said Saunders, "the horse and the Englishman went straight up in the air with their heads toward the north, turned in the air and came down with their heads toward the south." As he hit the ground, Lambert yelled: " 'Old the blooming rascal. 'E made such peculiar movements I lost my balance."

In 1888, Dick Withers drove 3,520 cattle four years old and over. He went via Dodge City and made it to Deadwood, South Dakota. He delivered 3,505, an amazingly low loss.

"That was the most enjoyable trip I ever made," he said. "Those steers walked like horses, and we made good time all the way."

Withers, the brother of Mark A., originally from Lockhart, Texas, liked the Northwest so well he settled, as the cattle country spread there, at Boyes, Montana.

James M. Daugherty in 1887 made his last drive up the trail. On his first, in 1866, he had been tied to a tree by Kansas Jayhawkers while they discussed how best to kill him. By 1887, Daugherty had taken cattle to Kansas, Nebraska, the Dakotas, Montana, Wyoming, Utah, and Colorado. He had grown a handsome moustache and looked like an English country squire or a successful American businessman. He was successful indeed. He had become the sole owner of one of the largest and best-equipped ranches in Texas, the Figure 2 Ranch, in Culberson and Hudspeth counties. Daugherty, one of the best-known of cattlemen, was widely called Uncle Jim.

In 1887, on his last trip up the trail, after years of driving cattle, L. B. Anderson drove horses. They were, he said, Spanish mares from Mexico. As a small boy he had been brought to Texas in a mule-drawn wagon. Grown-up, he was to be on the Long Trail for most of its important years, and his experiences amounted to a history of the Long Trail.

At twenty, in 1869, he had made his first drive, and had returned home with—still intact—$10 sewed into his pants.

He had been attacked, in 1870, by Sioux Indians, who stole all his outfit's provisions and most of its horses, and left its men to hunt buffalo and antelope.

He had seen, in the next year, 1871, Newton, Kansas, right after the brand-new railroad track to it had been laid.

He had seen, in 1874, the buffalo as a solid moving mass covering the plains.

He had seen, in the 1880s, at Fort Sill, Oklahoma, his first telephone.

In 1888, Anderson, retired from the trail, was married.

From then on, he said, he tried to like Jerseys or other cattle as well as he liked the Longhorns. He never quite could.

Thirty years after 1888 he would say, "the call of the trail is with me still, and there is not a day that I do not long to mount my horse and be out among the cattle."

Capt. John T. Lytle, a cowman from McSherrystown, Pennsylvania, at sixteen years of age had gone to work as a cowboy on the ranch, southeast of San Antonio, of an uncle, William Lytle. From 1873 to 1888, he sent a total of 450,000 longhorns up the Long Trail to Kansas, Colorado, Montana, etc. Altogether, he handled livestock worth $9 million, a record. He had three partners, John W. Light, T. M. McDaniel, and Capt. Charles Schreiner. His S-L and L-M brands became famous. Captain Lytle died in Fort Worth in 1907. The town of Lytle in Atascosa County, near San Antonio, is named for him.

Captain Lytle's partner, Capt. Charles Schreiner, had been born in Alsace-Lorraine February 22, 1838. At fourteen, in 1852, he reached the village of San Antonio. At sixteen, in 1854, he became a Texas Ranger and served until 1859. At the time the longhorns still were running wild, in 1859, he entered the cattle business. For four years during the Civil War he served in the Confederate army. By 1869 he was in banking and running a general store in Kerrville,

Texas. With Captain Lytle as a partner, he sent over 150,000 cattle up the trail. He was to stay in banking, merchandising, and cattle till 1918—a long stretch—building a fortune of several million dollars over the years. A two-year college, Schreiner Institute of Kerrville, Texas, bears his family name.

The director of admissions at Schreiner Institute, William James Campion, says that the residents of Texas' hill country, around Kerrville, in the late 1970s still see glowing balls of fire on dark, moonless nights—the restless spirits of a Spaniard, Esteban, and his son, Juan, who looked for treasure in Bandera Pass. The pass, Campion says, has been guarded for over a hundred years by a headless horseman. A great place for Indians to swarm upon and scalp travelers, it was dreaded by the Pony Express. A Pony Express rider named Ben one day was killed by an Indian arrow and was decapitated. When the mail did not reach Kerrville, a posse sought, and brought in, his body. A legend grew that Ben's ghost would protect treavelers through rugged Bandera Pass. The ghost may ride a white horse; a pool of blood on the ground may indicate the ghost is nearby; in any case, on starlighted, moonlight nights people still hear the sound of hoofs in Bandera Pass.

After the headless horseman began to ride, there never was another Indian raid in Bandera Pass. And never has been.

Once, for the Schreiner Ranch, a trail driver, Jones Glenn, worked in a roundup. Glenn became lost, wandered two days with nothing to eat, found a ranch where the woman told him a tornado was coming but brought out a plate of biscuits. She and her husband went into the storm cellar. Glenn, hungrier than he was afraid, did not go underground; he stayed at the table and reached for a biscuit. The tornado struck; it blew every last biscuit away, together with the ranch house.

The wife and her husband emerged from the cellar. Glenn saw there was nothing to eat, got set to leave, and asked which direction was north. The rancher said that it had been over that-away, but he didn't know where the twister had put it.

43

A cowman handles cow thieves

At MOBEETIE, Texas—in the Panhandle, near Oklahoma—Col. Charles Goodnight attended a cattlemen's meeting, and heard that a number of cattle thieves were in town.

Goodnight and other cattlemen had their cowboys, on their best horses, enter the town. The cowboys were armed—for once—with two six-shooters and with extra shells. They rode or strolled quietly about; they did not draw their guns; they uttered no threats —in fact, no words at all.

At the courthouse, Colonel Goodnight announced that he knew about the cattle stealers, and that there was evidence enough to hang them.

The cowboys cleared the loafers and hangers-on out of the courthouse. This meant that the loafers and hangers-on would wander about the town, and they would spread the word of what Goodnight had said.

Then the cowboys visited saloons and dance halls, not drinking a drop, just standing around, presumably looking for cattle thieves, but making no effort to capture them.

There were fifty armed cowboys moseying around town altogether.

No one appeared to want to challenge them.

What with the uneasy rumors spreading out from the courthouse, and the threatening appearance of the cowboys, the cattle thieves sneaked out of town and took to the hills.

The cowboys let them go.

Later, a man was seen riding out of town—presumably a messenger to the outlaws. He would tell them that the cowboys still were sticking around.

The cowboys let him go too.

That was part of the game—to scare the outlaws.

Next day the war of nerves continued. The cowboys rode back into Mobeetie and asked for men they knew had fled the town.

Then they searched the town—for men they knew were not there.

They said they might ride out to the hills.

Another horseman rode out to inform the outlaws—and, presumably, to frighten them further.

The cowboys let him go, too.

Eighteen cattle rustlers were known to have fled Mobeetie, due to the silent searching by the cowboys.

Only three were known ever to come back to Mobeetie.

Cattle thievery by the Mobeetie mob never amounted to much afterward.

Colonel Goodnight's bluff had worked.

44

The entire midcontinent changes

BESIDES HIS high, wide-brimmed, white Stetson to protect his head against rain, hail, or sun, the cowboy of the 1880s was obtaining other new wearing apparel that made him considerably better dressed than the scraggly cow hunter he once had been. His spurs now were smaller, and they might be hand-forged and silver-inlaid. His shirts had changed into the fancy Western shirts with pockets that he wears (or dresses up in) today. He wore striped or checked pants made in Oregon City, good to ride in. His Colt pistol, which at one time had a twelve-inch barrel, now had one only six or seven inches long. Its handle was of ivory, pearl, or black rubber.

The Long Trail was changing as much as the cowboy's dress.

It reached its busiest years. John Blocker said that in 1883 and 1884 half a million cattle passed through Ogallala, Nebraska. Some of the longhorns went further north. Many others walked only to Dodge City, Kansas, and were shipped from there by rail.

One cattleman, Col. Dillard R. Fant, in 1884 sent 42,000 cattle up the trail. Their value was $12 to $20 a head. It took 200 men and 1,200 saddle horses to drive them.

A hundred thousand cattle, plus 120 million pounds of beef, were shipped to England in 1884.

All this meant that 1883 and 1884 were the busiest years the Long Trail ever would know.

One change on the Long Trail made things easier for the cattle drivers. Only around ninety years ago, in 1885–86, after many decades, Americans on the North American continent ceased to fight a tough enemy, the Plains Indians, admired for their competence on horseback by those experts on horseback, the cowboys themselves. When, in 1886, the chief of the Apaches, Geronimo, surrendered to U.S. troops, the Indian wars were considered over. That was 110 years after the Declaration of Independence, and the birth of the United States.

If Indians rarely blocked the way, however, barbed wire did so increasingly.

George W. West, from Tennessee, and John Blocker, from South Carolina, drove cattle north in 1885 and ran into fences that ranchmen had put up to keep other men's longhorns from crossing their land. West and Blocker spent over $100 (a good deal in those days) wiring Washington to get orders for fences to be cut to let their herd through. Finally the orders came. With help from the U.S. Army, the cattle began to move.

Within a few minutes from receipt of the orders, lightning struck the telegraph instruments and put the line out of commission.

That was one of the last times the fences gave way to the cattle. From then on, it usually would be the other way round.

Ranches, north and south, were vast. In Cameron County, Texas, Captain Mifflin Kenedy had established the Kenedy Pasture Co., whose ranchlands were thirty miles long by twenty miles wide.

They had to be vast. With the number of cattle being prepared for market, with the number of acres of grass a steer requires for grazing, and with the water it needs, a ranch had to take in a lot of acreage—and had to shut out other cattle to support those already upon it. With ranches crowded with cattle, in 1885, a drought struck. Around Wichita Falls, Texas, not a drop of rain fell for eighteen months. Cattle died, 15,000 belonging to one rancher alone. Other cattle were rushed early to market. The prices of cattle fell. Ranches went bankrupt. It became clear that the ranges had to be preserved. This meant more fencing, more barbed wire.

That year, 1885, the trail through Kansas was closed. From then on, the cattle plodded farther to the west—in Colorado, to Northwest ranches and ranges. In 1886, John Blocker partly or entirely owned 82,000 cattle on the trail at one time. By 1893, he would be delivering as far from Texas as Deadwood, South Dakota, 9,000 longhorns.

The year 1888 is given by the authoritative *The Trail Drivers of Texas* as the year when fences barred the entire way, and most cattle were traveling by train—which the book called the Iron Horse.

William Baxter Slaughter made his last drive—and the only buffalo drive he ever heard of—when he moved 104 buffaloes from Dalhart, Texas, to Fort Garland, Colorado. The buffaloes gave him less trouble than had cattle. They had been domesticated by feeding them with cottonseed cake; Slaughter provided it each night. The buffaloes ate it, lay down till midnight. Then they got up. They got up on all their four legs at once—unlike cattle, which rise from the ground on their hind legs first. The buffaloes then grazed on buffalo grass, and licked up the waste cottonseed cake that was left. Then they bedded down again till daylight, "at which time I would be up (for I had an alarm clock) and head them on north." That alarm clock itself was a change on a trail that had had few if any timepieces in the past.

Some cowboys now were turning into ranchers. One who did was Mark A. Withers, who set up near Lockhart, Texas. G. W. Mills—who had encountered the July 4, 1880, hail at Fort Dodge—visited the Withers spread and described it. "On a flowing stream," he said. Ranches, north and south, fenced in water, river or creek locations; they had to. The Withers' stream was Clear Fork; it was fed by springs. Trees lined the creek, said Mills, walnut, pecan, hackberry, elm, wild plum. "And dipping into its crystal waters were the weeping willows." The creek had fish: silver perch, channel cat, bass. Away about three hundred yards, on top of a gently sloping hill, was the ranch house. It overlooked beautiful country, Mills said.

The longhorns on the ranch still were wild. Four acres of corrals, divided into pens, held them for branding. The pens were post-oak rails, said Mills, "built to endure and were very strong as cattle in those days were wild, and in this exciting work none but well-built pens could hold them.'' The longhorns tried to go over the fences or break them down. Old, spreading live-oak trees shaded the corrals.

A cowboy's job was changing. He was more likely to drive horses up the trail. John B. Conner of Yoakum, a cowboy since he was nineteen, saw men capturing wild mustangs. They ran the mustangs for days, keeping them just in sight, and keeping them from rest and watering places. Finally they ran down the horses and captured them. But wild horses gave way to trailed ones. ''After ranches were established throughout the northwest,'' said George W. Saunders, ''these ranchmen learned that our Spanish ponies were better for their range work than their native horses.'' Later there was a demand for Texas brood mares. Texas ranges were overstocked with horses, and they were almost worthless—exactly what the situation had been regarding longhorns when the cattle drives began. Said Saunders, ''I drove 1,000 [horses] in two herds to Dodge City in 1884. It was claimed that 100,000 went up the trail that year and more than 1,000,000 went up the trail from the time the horse market opened until the trail closed.''

As horses were driven north, Jim Dobie, Frank Byler, the Boyce brothers, and others guided herds of them. Their cowboys, not surprisingly, had a wide variety of choice as to what horse they would ride. ''When applying to any of the above-mentioned men for a trail job,'' one cowboy recalled, ''it was useless to ask what horse one might ride, for the reply would inevitably be 'Throw your rope and whatever it falls on, fork him.' ''

George Gerdes and five other men took horses up the trail in 1884. ''I was born when quite young,'' he said, ''in 1863, at a little jumping off-the-road place called Quihi, Medina County, Texas.'' As a boy he drove wagons; and knew what it was to hook up as many as sixteen animals (oxen, mules, or horses) to a wagon to pull it out of the mud. His group drove 450 horses from Castroville, through Bandera, Kerrville, and across the Red River at the old Doan Store. In Indian Territory, they met Indians, who said ''How'' and asked for sugar and tobacco and stole twenty-five ponies. They reached Dodge City. Said Gerdes: ''The first thing we did was to go to town, get a shave, and a haircut, and tighten our belts by a few good strong drinks.'' At Dodge City they met George W. Saunders.

George Gerdes went to work near Pueblo, Colorado, where he found a regular event he liked: a dance that started every Saturday afternoon at two o'clock and that lasted till dawn Sunday morning.

Many of the horses taken up the Long Trail, including some specimens too poor for work on ranches, found a ready market. They pulled horsecars.

They were followed by street cleaners with brooms and shovels to collect their manure.

After appearing in Baltimore in 1885, electric streetcars gradually were introduced in other cities. They replaced the horse-drawn cars.

There went a market for horses.

Some cowboys, as the land was fenced in, became what were called fence cutters. They would ride along the barbed wire, often after dark, and cut it. Garland G. Odum, who had about 100,000 acres fenced in in east Texas, had wire cutters in one night clip about forty miles of his fence.

Fence cutting passed, and barbed wire took over. And along with it would come something else. Windmills.

Water always has been in short supply in Texas and in the United States' West (hence today's huge dams). Cattle primarily will not graze more than five or ten miles from water. As land was fenced in, by barbed wire, not only was rangeland—grazing, food, grass—made unavailable to traveling herds of cattle, so also was water.

An owner of fenced-in-land would do something about water that he could never do on public grassland: he could dam a ravine to hold rainfall. Or he could install a windmill.

Windmills pumped water—life-giving water—for men, women, children, cattle, horses, and farms, and crops.

They used the first power—the first energy—that man ever used except for his own muscles and the muscles of animals: the wind. Men had used the wind at least as long ago as prehistoric Stone Age times, in the sails to move ships.

Windmills were the first mechanical devices to spread on ranches throughout the cattle country. In arid west Texas, and on the wide plains of the Panhandle, windmills were erected to take advantage of winds that in some locations were almost constant. The windmills made possible deep wells, deeper by far than ever before; they pumped up the water, and brought water where no water had been.

Pumping water from a well into a steel tank, a single windmill could deliver water to 300 cattle. Windmills added millions of usable acres to the cow country: they provided water for parched cattle, people, and land.

Before the windmills, said the first 1968 issue of the magazine *Kansas!*, water had to be pumped from a well or dipped from a stream and perhaps carried a long distance. Besides ranchers, the windmill helped millions of farmers. They helped the railroads as they arrived and their locomotives had to have water. The clank-clank-clank of the windmill, after the cow's moooo, became one of the common sounds of the midcontinent.

To the clank, clank, each windmill added its own distinctive noise: a wheeze, rattle, or squeak.

Gasoline engines and electricity in time were to replace the windmills. But some windmills remain, still pumping water.

Others simply remain.

They stand from fifteen to forty-five feet in the air—doing nothing but creaking in the wind.

W. S. Hall, back in 1865, had been a man who, when 7,000 of his cattle were stolen and taken to Mexico, did not even bother to chase them—so worthless were they at that time.

In Rockport, Texas, Hall, a cowman born in Maine, established a business that would help make cattle drives unnecessary. He slaughtered cattle and, preserving his meat with salt, shipped it to New Orleans, New York City, and even to Europe. This and refrigeration on transatlantic ships and on railroads reaching down into Texas, the land where the cattle drives began, would eliminate the need for the long walk north. And all these things would cause the cattle to change: the longhorns, with their ability to walk a long way and take care of themselves, were replaced on Northern ranches by superior (in some ways) cattle, the Shorthorns or Durhams, Herefords, black hornless Aberdeen Angus, Jerseys, and in time others. All did better on ranges under fence than did the longhorns. In the 1880s, all were becoming familiar sights on the plains.

Something else involving the longtime preservation of food was happening. It would have a profound effect on the cowboy and rancher, the farmer, their families, and in fact on almost everyone in the world.

Food in tin cans was becoming more widely available.

Before food could be preserved, the hot summers of the United States had meant that meat and milk and fruit and vegetables continually spoiled. You ate meat where the steers were slaughtered. You drank milk where the cows were milked. Because they quickly rotted, you ate fresh fruits and vegetables where—and at the time of year—they were harvested. The earliest salting, refrigerating, and condensed milk had been by no means enough to supply food to the armies in the Civil War. A result was greatly speeded-up research on how to can foods, and the result was that tin cans showed up on the Long Trail and elsewhere.

Never, in all history, had food been kept or preserved well. Now tin cans made food last. (So would refrigeration, and so would glass—but Mason jars were easily smashed on the Long Trail.) Canned food gave people more variety and more taste in their food than they had had. Cowboys on the Long Trail, out of tin cans, had better food. E. C. Abbott (Teddy Blue), working for the D H S Ranch of Granville Stuart, was enthusiastic: "I'd never seen such wonderful grub as they had at the D H S. They had canned tomatoes all the time, canned peaches even. . . ."

Canned tomatoes were especially helpful. Drinking alkalized water, a cowboy might "rust his boilers," and alkali dust might cut his face. The juice in the cans of tomatoes both assuaged a cowboy's thirst and counteracted the effect—on his insides—of the alkali. The canned solid tomato he could wipe across his face to heal the bleeding cuts. He would also rub the tomato on his pony's alkali-cracked lips.

The cowboy had ready-at-hand a can opener. He fired his six-shooter at the top of a can.

Canned food would be consumed also by sailors, pioneers anywhere, explorers, and the families of the new farmers in the Midwest. It would also provide a market to farmers for crops, and would determine in many cases what crops they grew.

Farms were being established and people were moving onto

farms in Long Trail days, but in time both refrigeration and tin cans would enable more men, women and children to live in cities and not on farms—when families no longer had to raise their own food, and had to eat it fresh.

Unsung and largely overlooked, the tin can affected history as few things or events ever have.

45

The terrible winter

TEXAS LONGHORNS up the Long Trail continued to move northwest. Barbed-wire fencing-in of ranges reduced the amount of pasture land available. Most of the pasture that was left had too many cattle on it. Much of the land in the North belonged to the Federal government; there was no way a cowman could lease it for a long term.

With more cattle in the North, and less land for them to graze on, and that land crowded, there came along what would be remembered as the terrible winter of 1886–87.

Winter swept down from Canada and the Arctic. Between the Texas Panhandle and the North Pole, as I have said, there was nothing to shut out the wind except a barbed-wire fence. Between the North Pole and Wyoming, Montana, the Dakotas, Colorado, Kansas, and Nebraska there was not even that much. On Christmas Eve the storm started. From the Arctic, white, snowy owls, five feet in wingspread—they go south only when driven by frigidity and loss of food—flew silently over Montana. Heavy feathers almost hid their beaks and feet; their yellow eyes gleamed. The Indians said "heap snow coming." They were right.

Snowstorm succeeded snowstorm. For two months.

259

The wind chased the cattle into canyons. Here they died by tens of thousands. A rancher said that "when an animal lies down its legs freeze." Cattle walked out onto the ice of frozen rivers. They could not drink the ice; they desperately sought water; when they found it, they fell in, or were pushed in. Cowboys, riding to rivers through two feet of snow, their horses' feet bleeding from the heavy crust of snow, saved thousands of cattle by breaking the ice so the cattle might drink.

A cowboy in Judith Basin, Montana, commented that "fools go way up in the Arctic Ocean hunting after the North Pole and it ain't over half a mile from here."

On January 14, at Fort Keogh, Montana, the temperature was sixty below zero.

Virtually every cattleman, large and small, on the Northern plains was destroyed financially. In western Kansas and Nebraska, in Colorado, Wyoming, the Dakotas, and Montana, it was the same story.

Antoine de Vallambrosa, Marquis de Mores, the Frenchman who had built a château overlooking the Bad Lands, abandoned the château and the cattle trade and went back to France. His rival also gave up the Elkhorn Ranch, leaving it partly covered with the bones of perished cattle—Theodore Roosevelt returned to New York and decided he would reenter politics instead.

In Wyoming and Montana many men lost nine out of ten of their cattle.

The cattle business would recover after 1886–87—but it would never be quite the same again. How hard the winter was on the cattle was summarized by a man who painted pictures of the West and of the cowboys, Charles Russell. Russell had started the winter in charge of 5,000 cattle owned by Eastern investors. When his bosses wrote and asked him how their animals had done, he painted a picture of what the cowboys called a die-up and sent it as the answer. The picture showed, in deep snowdrifts, a single, gaunt steer, obviously about to die. Beneath the picture, Russell had written: "The last of five thousand."

46

The cowboy with no bad habits

IN THE spring of 1888 Samuel Dunn Houston of San Antonio was driving cattle for the Holt Live Stock Company of New Mexico and Denver, Colorado.

Houston, the trail boss, had driven cattle almost every single year since 1876. He had been the one, in 1879, who almost died of thirst when, by himself, he had taken an unfamiliar Indian trail back to Ogallala from North Dakota.

"I expect," he said, "I have made more trips over the cow trail from southern Texas and New Mexico than any man in the country."

But in 1888 something different was going to happen to him.

He was in the land of the Goodnight-Loving Trail, in northeast New Mexico, south of the Colorado line, and he could put his hand out and almost touch Texas and Oklahoma.

He left his herd outside and went in a few miles to Clayton, New Mexico, to look for two or three cowboys to hire.

There were no men in Clayton. A friend told him about a kid who wanted—as did so many boys—to go up the trail. "I put out to hunt that kid," Houston said, "and found him over at the livery stable. I hired him and took him to camp, and put him with the horses and put my rustler with the cattle."

The youngster did fine. Besides looking after the horses, on the darkest, stormiest nights he got up and rode night herd and stayed with the cattle. He seemed to have no bad habits, no use of tobacco, no swear words. "His name," said Houston, "was Willie Matthews, he was 19 years old and weighed 135 pounds. His home was in Caldwell, Kansas"—that southernmost point in Kansas where cattle were loaded into trains—"and I was so pleased with him that I wished many times that I could find two or three more like him."

Houston and his herd reached Hugo, Colorado, on the Kansas Pacific Railroad on the way to Wyoming.

The kid came to Houston, said he was homesick, and quit. Said Houston, "I had to let him go."

The cowboy with no bad habits had been with the outfit almost four months.

At sundown Houston and some of his cowboys were sitting around while others were nudging the herd onto the bed ground. "I looked up toward town," Houston said, "and saw a lady, all dressed up, coming toward camp, walking. I told the boys we were going to have company." He couldn't imagine why a woman would be approaching a cow camp. She did, though. She drew near, and he got up to receive his guest.

Everyone was watching.

"When she got within about twenty feet of me, she began to laugh, and said, 'Mr. Houston, you don't know me, do you?' "

Houston was speechless.

When he recovered he said, "Kid, is it possible that you are a lady?"

He said he thought of all the bad language the men had been using on the trail.

The only amenity the cowmen had to offer a girl was a tomato box to rest on. They drew up a tomato box for her chair. She sat. Said Houston, "Now I want you to explain yourself."

Willie, the girl, did. Her father had been a trail driver, and ever since she was ten or twelve years old, she had wanted to go up the trail. She had borrowed an outfit of her brother's. She had borrowed a pair of his boots. On her own pony, she had ridden to Clayton looking for a job. "Now, Mr. Houston, I am glad I found you to make this trip with," she said. "I am going just as straight home as I can and that old train can't run too fast for me when I get on it."

Houston left one man with the herd. Everyone else went to the station at Hugo to see the girl off.

Houston returned home to a ranch on the Pecos River. Later, Willie and her father both wrote and thanked him for his kindness. They invited him to visit them.

"She was," Houston said, "a perfect lady."

Five years later, in the fall of 1893, Samuel Dunn Houston retired from the trail. "I came back to my home to die," he said. Around thirty years later he was still living. "I live in San Antonio," he said, "with my good wife and three nice daughters, and keep my gun at the head of my bed to keep the young, up-to-date cowboys away."

47

When cowboys rode trains

COWBOYS LOADING cattle into cattle cars prodded them with long, spiked prod poles. A new word was entering the English language and came to mean cowboy: cowpuncher. So did another word: cowpoke.

The Southern Pacific Railroad, building east, reached El Paso on May 19, 1881. It met the Texas and Pacific, and another transcontinental line began operation (after the Union Pacific, 1869). Both tracks were built with the use of black powder but largely by men with picks and shovels and wheelbarrows and resulting aching arms, legs, and backs. Muscles—not machines—still were the source of most energy.

Other tracks were laid throughout the 1880s, and the story of the Long Trail throughout that decade was a story of getting the longhorns to where they could take a train to market.

Sometimes, especially en route home, the cowboy himself took a train. He was less at home than he was on a horse.

According to "Cattle Clatter" in the *San Antonio Express,* and to George W. Saunders, a cowboy walked into a sleeping car one night with a bundle of blankets. He asked the Pullman conductor if there was any place where he could lie down.

The Pullman, one of the early ones, had lower and upper berths.

The conductor said sure there was; the cowboy could have either an upper or a lower. Not knowing what was meant by an upper or a lower, the cowboy said any place would do for him.

The cost of an upper berth was then, and was always, lower than the cost of a lower berth. A passenger had to climb a ladder to the upper. He simply stepped into the lower; the lower was more convenient.

This the Pullman conductor tried to tell the cowboy. As is the case with many an explanation, this one made the situation more obscure.

Explained the conductor, confusingly: "The lower is higher than the upper. The higher price is for the lower. If you want the lower you will have to go higher. We sell the upper lower than the lower. In other words, the higher the lower. Most people don't like the upper, although it is lower on account of its being higher. When you occupy an upper you have to go up to go to bed, and get down when you get up. You can have the lower if you pay higher. If you are willing to go higher it will be lower."

The cowboy, according to George Saunders, that night slept in the aisle between the rows of berths in the Pullman.

Once in a while a cowboy rode a freight—instead of a passenger train. He called that "saving money for the bartender."

Jack Potter of Kenton, Oklahoma, in 1882 drove cattle to Wyoming. That left him 2,000 miles to get home—by train. He had never been on a train, and it was strange to him. He had never even slept in a hotel. Potter was the cowboy who, one night in a farmer's hovel, had slept leaning against the wall with two small boys. He had "never taken a bath in a bath house, and from babyhood I had heard terrible stories about ticket thieves, money-changers, pickpockets, three-card monte and other robbing schemes, and I had horrors about this, my first railroad trip."

He proceeded to do his best. His money he tied up in his shirttail. He bought a trunk, and in it put his worldly possessions: "One apple-horn saddle, a pair of chaps, a Colt's .45, one sugan [a blanket], a hen-skin blanket, and a change of dirty clothes."

He boarded a Union Pacific train at Greeley, Colorado. The conductor took his ticket, punched it, and gave him a red slip, which he tucked into Potter's hatband. Potter did not know that the conductor was supposed to collect part of the ticket, as he had. He jumped to his feet, tried to chase the man. "Give me back my ticket!" he shouted. But Potter did not know how to walk on a moving train.

The train crossed a bridge. Potter thought part of the bridge was about to hit him on the head. "I dodged those bridges," he said, "all the way up to Denver."

He had checked his trunk through. This meant that it would be transferred from train to train till it reached its destination. At Denver he saw his trunk being unloaded—but he did not understand what was meant by its being checked through. He tried to get it back. No one would give it to him. Finally it was explained that the trunk would get to San Antonio by itself.

In a Denver bathhouse he took a bath. "I commenced undressing hurriedly, fearing the tub would fill up before I could get ready. The water was within a few inches of the top of the tub when I plunged in. Then I gave a yell like a Comanche Indian, for the water was boiling hot! I came out of the tub on all fours, but when I landed on the marble floor it was so slick that I slipped and fell backwards with my head down. I scrambled around promiscuously, and finally got my footing with a chair for a brace." He fanned himself with his Stetson hat. He looked at his toenails, which he thought were falling out, "but I found them in fairly good shape, turning a bit dark, but still hanging on."

He went that night to the Tabor Opera House. Going to bed back in the hotel, he tried to blow out the light—gas. Then he tried to fan it out with his hat. Neither worked. The gas burned all night. He slept with his hat over his eyes. Later it dawned on him what happened to people who blew out the gas.

At Denver, Jack Potter got a cowboy ticket to Dodge City, Kansas, and cowboy ticket on to San Antonio. The rate to San Antonio was a reduced one, $15. He checked up on his trunk, watched the baggage men put it aboard the Santa Fe train, then he climbed on. There were more bridges, and he kept dodging them. An experienced traveler saw his predicament. He made Potter sit with his back to the front of the train so he would not see the bridges as the train approached them. It worked.

At Dodge City, he noticed the noise of a dance hall and a six-shooter duel between a cowboy and a gambler. "Lots of smoke, a stampede, but no one killed."

Next morning he wandered around Dodge City. "The first acquaintance I met here was George W. Saunders."

As that night he waited for the train in the Dodge City station, he noticed that another cowboy, Dog Face Smith, was more nervous about trains than he was. "Pretty badly frightened," he described Smith.

Potter's cowboy ticket was a long one. The conductor tore a bit off. Said Potter: "What authority have you to tear up a man's ticket?" Said the conductor: "You are on my division. I simply tore off one coupon and each conductor between here and San Antonio will tear off one for each division."

Potter wondered if his ticket would last out till San Antonio.

Potter and Dog Face Smith and other cowboys by 3 A.M. had gotten to bed. Another train passed them and its whistle was sounded. "That bunch of sleeping cowboys arose as one man, and started on the run with old Dog Face Smith in the lead," Potter said. Before he was fully awake, he said, he thought he was in a cattle stampede and yelled, "Circle your leaders and keep up the drags." The cowboys tried to circle, fell into each other, trampled on a man trying to sell newspapers, and he "jumped through the window like a frog." The train crew came in and quieted the cowboys.

At Emporia, Kansas, Potter and Dog Face Smith transferred to the Missouri, Kansas & Texas Railroad for Parsons, Indian territory, where they would change again to the main line for Denton, Texas. Another hazard hit Potter: A girl asked him for his autograph. He did not know what to write in her album. She insisted. In desperation, he wrote a verse he had heard as a small child: "It's tiresome work says lazy Ned, to climb the hill in my new sled, and beat the other boys. Signed, Your Bulliest Friend, Jack Potter."

He finally reached San Antonio. He looked for his trunk—and found it. He thought the railroad had assigned a man to take care of it all the way there. He even wrote the Santa Fe, back in Denver, a letter about it. "I want to thank you very much," he wrote, "for the man you sent along to look after my trunk."

48

The cowboy marries the farmer's daughter

THE 1890s. Around the World: Wilhelm Conrad Roentgen invented X rays. . . . The Shaw Plastics Corporation of New Jersey sent gimmicks to an eighteen-year-old tinkerer in Italy, who with them invented radio: Guglielmo Marconi. . . . Students at Yale College in 1890 adopted the first mascot of a football team, a bulldog named Handsome Dan. . . . At a fair (1893) in Chicago, Eva Tanguay kicked high her elegant legs and sang Ta-ra-ra-boom-de-ay. . . . The kinetoscope of Thomas Alva Edison opened (1894) on Broadway: the first movies.

ALONG THE LONG TRAIL: At Wounded Knee, South Dakota, U.S. troops, in their final battle with Indians, defeated the Sioux. . . . Among the ranchers using a windmill was C. C. Slaughter. New Texas ranches were run by Lord & Nelson, with the 96 brand; Coleman and Company, the Shoe Bar; Curtis and Atkinson, the Diamond Tail; Alfred and Vincent Rose, the RO (later owned by W. J. Lewis); the Western Land and Livestock Company, a twelve-by-ten-mile ranch; the IOA (for Iowa); William D. Lee and D. A. Reynolds, the LS; the Nave McCord Cattle Company, the southern XIT (its land later would be sold to John B. Slaughter, the man who spent so much of his life fighting Indians); the St. Louis

Land and Cattle Company; T. A. Childers and J. W. Merrill and his father; J. B. Slaughter, the Square and Compass Ranch that became the U Lazy S. . . . In the Panhandle, the man who had sold the first barbed wire in Texas, H. B. Sanford, and J. F. Glidden, the inventor of barbed wire, operated the Frying Pan Ranch. Other ranches around this period were near Sanderson, that of Charles Downie, who handled sheep as well as cattle. The Union Beef Company, ranging from Toyah to where the Pecos meets the Rio Grande. The Pecos Land & Cattle Company. J. W. Snyder and Col. D. H. Snyder, the Renderson Ranch; the Colonel's lead steer had led cattle across the Mississippi River to the Confederacy; he had stopped killing calves in 1868 on the trail to Colorado. Later the Snyders sold to I. L. Ellwood and Son; Ellwood had grown wealthy selling barbed wire. Colonel Snyder described the cowboy's character: The cowboys, he said, placed their faith "in God, their trusty six-shooter, and the chuck-wagon." Other ranchers: L. W. and J. W. Kokernot; W. H., George E., John M., and Buck Cowden; W. H., George E., and John M. later owned the great JAL spread in Texas and New Mexico. J. M. Shannon. Clay W. Mann. John W. Henderson. A. S. Gage. Cyrus Lucas. A. W. Dunn. Ben and George Wolcott. W. G. Rusk. Nelson Morris. W. H. and Dave Brunson. Frank and Ed Crowley. Fred Cowden. C. B. Holt. W. E. Connell. T. J. Martin. Sam Holoway. John Scharbauer. The Swenson brothers, from the SMS near Fort Worth, sold by mail feeder calves and yearlings.

The trail now was becoming more and more blocked by farms. "Leaving Ogallala (Nebraska)," said George W. Brock of Lockhart, Texas, "we went up the south side of the Platte River to Julesburg Junction.

"Going up the river our only trouble was to keep our stock off the farms. They had no fences and it took very careful watching to keep them out of those patches." With fences not yet having reached the area, the farmers, as elsewhere, were marking the boundaries of their land by plowing a furrow around it.

When the cattle stepped across a furrow and crossed their land, a farmer demanded damages. He often got them. "To let your stuff get on those patches," said Brock, "meant the highest price grazing that a Texas horse or steer ever got."

Between Ellsworth, Kansas, and the North Platte in Nebraska, said A. F. Caraval, his cattle had to go for three days without water and "some were almost perishing." They gave a farmer two cows and calves for allowing the cattle to drink on his land.

Driving across Texas from the Pecos River, Jerry M. Nance recalled, he took advantage of one change along the trail. Ten miles west of Midland he watered his 2,000 cattle at troughs filled with water pumped into them by a windmill.
The rancher who owned the windmill charged five cents a head.

The cowboy on the Long Trail was being put out of business by the railroads (which carried cattle to market), and by the fences of the ranchers and farmers (which blocked the trail). The new settlers, largely farmers, spread fast. Into the Dakotas, Nebraska, Montana, Kansas, Colorado, Oklahoma, Texas, and all the Midwestern states the settlers came in swelling numbers. The ranchers fenced in vast areas of land. The farmers fenced in land in small (to the cowboy) allotments—160 acres for a homestead.
The farmers plowed and turned over the soil. The cowboy had thought God had laid it right-side-up in the first place.
There was another difference between cowboys and farmers: Many of the settlers had been Union soldiers and did not like Texas people, and, said Teddy Blue, "their love was returned plenty."
The cowboy, his job vanishing, joined the army, went to Alaska to seek gold, built ships in San Francisco, worked in the lumber mills of Puget Sound, in the factories of Chicago, in the mills of New England. Some, who stayed on the range, now had to repair barbed-wire fences. They became what once they had sneered at—"pliers men"—so named for the tool they used to repair the fences.
Many a cowboy became a rancher. A few cowboys homesteaded themselves and became farmers.

The cowboy, despite his differences with the farmer, could not help helping the farmer. He provided the cattle that provided the dung that fertilized the soil. He provided cattle for milk. And he brought the oxen that hauled many a farmer's plow.

The farmer, to break the stubborn Midwest soil—sod a thousand years old, maybe older—needed a heavier plow than farmers had used back east, in New England, New York, and elsewhere. A heavier plow, accordingly, was devised. It often was hauled by oxen—oxen that originally had been Texas longhorns. And when the grass roots had been broken, the dark, rich soil was deep and fertile and had a vegetable mold that helped it produce abundant grain and other crops that today are helping to feed men, women, and children throughout the entire world.

The farmer, in his turn, could not but help the cowboy. He gave him a meal, shelter for a night in a sod house, or water to drink.

The farmer and the cowboy helped each other another way.

The young cowboy, lonesome for women, discovered—when he visited a homesteader's dugout to ask for a drink of water, for instance—the farmer's daughter, about his own age, sixteen to twenty-one or so. Somehow—though her father might be a natural enemy to the cowboy—the girl seemed attractive. Lovely. Sometimes beautiful. Always magnetic. She had an appeal.

She had something her father or her brother did not have.

The cowboy became thirsty again the next day. He rode up to the settler's place and maybe jingled his spurs as he did so. He might have happened to put on his white fur chaps, the kind he wore against Northern winters, if he had any. He gave the girl's younger brother fifty cents for opening the gate. If he had managed to get to a town, he might be bringing a two-pound box of candy for her.

Soon thereafter the little brother and his playmates were seen playing cowboy in the backyard. The girl's mother, as mothers do, worried—but thought maybe the cowboy was generous and good looking. The girl's father, as fathers do, worried—he did not like the cowboy's profession, but he wanted his daughter to be happy. But the older man and the younger cowboy had something in common. They could feel it without seeing it clearly. The settler had come to the West to get a better break—a living. So, earlier, starting in the 1830s and 1840s, during the Republic of Texas, had many a cowboy's family. And that was why the cowboy had made the Long Trail. It is hard to blame a man for trying to better his family's lot. And it is hard to blame a man for being motivated by the same forces that motivate you.

The cowboy courted the girl—which he called "sittin' her."

In some areas, the cowboy and his girl friend attended dances. In other areas, where dancing was forbidden, they played games instead—Miller Boy, Down to Rosers, and Shoot the Buffalo, while the fathers and mothers looked on.

A song said Texas boys knew how to court: "Hug them a little and kiss them plenty." But the title of that song was "All Her Answers to Me Were No."

The cowboy told her he loved her a bushel and a half. I don't know if that's cowboy talk or farm talk. It is what Connie Burge of Houston calls purr talk.

The girls, at least those in Missouri, were warned in a song: "Don't you wed with those Texas boys."

In due course, the marriage took place.

After the wedding, the girl had her influence. Just as a curly-headed girl had tamed cowboy J. L. McCaleb, so were many thousands of cowboys domesticated. ("He thought that she was his'n/ But he found out that he was her'n.") The cowboy settled down on a ranch, farm—or even in town. As the next step, churches, schools, and more small towns were established and grew. Many a cowboy always had been a reader, of books and papers and even the labels on tin cans and everything else in print. Now, with his wife, he helped bring the component parts of civilization to the Great Plains.

The one-room schools the cowboy and the farmer's daughter at first established were in their day as good as any schools on earth. Today the schools that have followed them are as good as any others—or better. Today's universities, the eventual outgrowth of school systems, in the Northwest, Midwest and Southwest provide an excellent education. School and public and university libraries are outstanding. The library at the oldest university in Texas, Baylor, dating from 1845, in Waco—a town that saw so many cattle herds—has the world's best collection of the work of poet Robert Browning. In a collection that has grown slowly, a rare book or two at a time, a collection little-known to Dallas citizens, the Dallas Public Library owns a first edition of Samuel Johnson's dictionary, plus a fourth edition, printed in 1685, of William Shakespeare, plus a papyrus fragment of the ancient Egyptian Book of the Dead.

The farmer's daughter—the cowboy's wife—or her mother often had brought out to the Great Plains a piano or a harpsichord or a singing voice. Today some of the best music is in the midcontinent area. Some of the best symphony orchestras, for instance. And the university bands of the midcontinent, marching and sitting, are unsurpassed in the world. As the cowboys worked off steam dancing or chasing antelopes, so today's university students work off their exuberance and energy by dancing and by a folk-art form all their own in the halftime shows they put on at football games. There is nothing in the world that I know of just like this folk art. Much of it commemorates the Long Trail and the cowboys: the Kilgore Rangerettes, the Hardin-Simmons University Cowboy Band, the Mustang Band of Southern Methodist, and the University of Texas Longhorn Band, with its song, "The Eyes of Texas," sung to the tune of "I've Been Working on the Railroad," known to both cowboys and railroad workers.

In addition, today some of the most important art collections in the world are in Chicago, Omaha, Kansas City. Some of the best live theaters and natural history and science museums are in the midcontinent.

Education, art, religion, music, reading, rest, recreation, leisure, and civilization—more of all these things than the cowboy knew—all of them are part of the heritage left by the farmer's daughter, often the cowboy's wife.

One of the most important weddings in history was the one between the cowboy and the farmer's daughter.

Its effects go on and on.

With many a cowboy sittin' and marrying the farmer's daughter, things looked up for Branch Isbell. Isbell first had gone up the trail as a young tenderfoot, in 1871, with William Burks and his wife Amanda. In 1871, Isbell had been rebuffed when he wanted to dance with sixteen-year-old Lizzie Hinnant. In 1878, he had had a misunderstanding with Emma Altman.

He had read law, obtained a license, and been elected county attorney of Scurry County, Texas, and later was county judge.

In the 1890s, he did better with a girl friend.

At forty years of age, for the first time, he married. His bride was Mrs. S. W. Courley. She was one of the pioneer women who brought education to the Midwest and to pioneer children—she was a teacher. In that era of short lives, and early deaths, she had —at thirty—lost her husband. "She was ten years my junior," said Isbell, "and a daughter of J. S. Abbott, a Baptist minister, well known in Gonzales and adjoining counties for many years. She blessed my life more than seven years and died at her sister's home near Lockhart in May 1898." She died, that is, at around thirty-eight—a good average long life in those days.

49

Nearing the end of the trail

AT THE Red River crossing, on the Texas-Oklahoma boundary, Doan's Store was thriving. There, one day in 1884, five women and a man had held a picnic—partly because they were lonesome, and partly to celebrate the store's part in the Long Trail. The picnic would become an annual affair. It grew. The crowd became thousands, the dinner became what C. F. Doan called "a sumptuous affair," and the politicians of the area converged on it every two years to sell their candidacies.

The Doans had built, in 1881, a new home. It would stand till it was burned down in 1922. Said owner C. F. Doan: "Here, my old adobe house and I sit beside the old trail and dream away the days thinking of the stirring scenes enacted when it seemed an endless procession of horses and cattle passed, followed by men of grim visage but of cheerful mien, who sang the 'Dying Cowboy' and 'Bury Me Not on the Lone Prairie' and other cheerful tunes as they bedded the cattle or when in a lighter mood danced with the belles of Doan's and took it straight over the bar of the old Cow Boy Saloon."

In 1890, G. W. Scott of Uvalde, Texas, was one of the cowmen driving to Colorado 2,221 two-year-old steers and 64 horses. There were eleven men altogether, including the cook. A storm and a stampede struck. The steers, he said, went "in all directions, running over wire fences and going across creeks that happened to be in their course." In that one night, thirteen steers were killed by lightning.

Jerry M. Nance had had his own trouble with storms. Hail struck his cattle and cowboys. "We had one bald-headed man in the outfit, and when the hailstorm was over he was a sight to behold. He had welts and bruises all over, and lots of hide had been peeled off. The hail had beaten the grass into the ground and killed lots of jackrabbits in the vicinity."

At one time, Nance had about two thousand cattle in a pasture near Colorado City. A cyclone hit. It "was only about one hundred yards wide, and went through about a mile of pasture, leaving everything trimmed clean in its path. Even the mesquite switches had all the bark pulled off. Deer, rabbits, owls, snakes, and many other animals were to be found in its wake. So were the bodies of about 150 steers."

In 1893, Hiram Craig took his son, Walter A. Craig, eight years of age, along on a cattle drive. "He had his own horse, leggings, and spurs," said father Hiram, "and made a splendid little hand in daytime. I caught him asleep but once. He was on his horse under a tree and two other grown men were down on the ground and asleep. He was too young to do any night herding."

Another menace had hit the cattlemen: sheep. The range had been as open to sheep as it had been to cattle and horses. The sheep were moved in. The sheep ate the grass to its roots. Their sharp hoofs chopped up the roots so that the grass died. They walked mile after mile, and cut a wide, desolate path across the plains. At a water hole, on the ground, they left behind a scent or taste that cattle or horses did not like. The lead steer on a cattle drive, coming upon the trail of a band of sheep, might lead the cattle in a stampede. Horses would also leave a spot where they sniffed sheep.

The sheep, like the cattle, would be successful. A pioneer

cattleman of the Big Bend country of Texas, Laurence Haley, in his will specified that his gravestone, near Alpine, have both a cow and a sheep upon it, because he had profited from both. He also specified that there be a likeness of another animal that had helped him: the horse.

Ab Blocker of San Antonio had driven 1,500 cows and heifers to a huge Panhandle ranch—and had suggested the brand that the ranch would use, a brand that would become well known. "Old Barbecue Campbell," Blocker said, "was undecided as to selecting a brand to be used by the ranch syndicate, and when I suggested XIT it pleased him so well he decided to use that brand, and it became known all over Texas, Oklahoma, and New Mexico as the XIT Ranch. I branded the first cow to carry the XIT brand, and after delivering this herd Alex Caspares and myself went to Los Animas, Colorado, where we sold our saddle horses and went by train to Dodge City, Kansas."

The XIT covered all or parts of ten (or nine) counties in the Panhandle. The brand stood for ten—*X*—counties *I*n *T*exas.

Around fifteen hundred miles of its circumference, a barbed-wire fence was strung—the longest in history.

The XIT in the 1890s was under a new manager, Col. Albert G. Boyce. Colonel Boyce, a Texan whose parents had come from Missouri, in 1863 had been the cowboy who walked a long way home after being wounded in the battle of Chickamauga. In 1865 he had been at the last battle of the Civil War at Palmito Hill, Texas. And in 1867 he had begun a two-year trip to drive Texas cattle to California. The XIT Ranch, an incredible eight million acres in area, was the largest ranch in the world. Upon it Colonel Boyce stayed put. He was to be active in its management for eighteen years.

And, while he was there, in 1895, the XIT was to send north to the railroad the very last longhorns that ever plodded north. The XIT, in the Panhandle, almost halfway from the Gulf of Mexico to Canada, anyway, was in a position to send the last cattle along the trail—the distance was far shorter for them to go. The ranch itself continued; its last cattle would be disposed of in 1912. And so large was it, and so many cowboys did it have, that the XIT Trail Drivers to this day retain their own organization.

50

A young man
picks ticks off cattle

TICK FEVER spread from Southern cattle to Northern cattle. It wiped out entire herds of Northern cattle. That much was known. The Kansans and other Northerners who opposed Texas longhorns arriving in their area always had a point.

How tick fever spread was not known. What was the cause of tick fever—or as it was also known, Texas or Spanish fever—was not known. A number of scientists tried to find out.

A young pathologist, Theobald Smith, born in 1859, who had graduated from Cornell University at Ithaca, New York, became concerned about Texas fever. He also had studied medicine in Albany, and he had learned about researches being made on disease-causing agents. The whole idea of germs was new. Smith worked on germs in Washington for the Department of Agriculture's Bureau of Animal Industry.

North or south, always after a month or so of Northern and Southern cattle grazing together, the Northern animals stopped eating, shed red urine, arched their backs, stood around moodily, and drooped their eyelids. They might recover. Often they died. Cattlemen were worried. They pressed Smith's boss, Dr. Salmon, to find the answer.

In 1888, Dr. Salmon had Smith, twenty-nine, on the job. Smith heard that the cattlemen themselves had an idea. They said an insect lived on cattle and sucked blood. They said this insect was a tick, and that it somehow caused Texas fever.

Many people of the day—including doctors and veterinarians —hooted at the very idea of the tick. The cattlemen were ridiculed.

Not by Smith.

Smith in 1889 reasoned that the cattlemen—who lived with cattle the year around, who themselves smelled of the cattle—just might have some reason behind their belief in the tick as the culprit.

On June 27, 1889, seven cows were delivered to Smith from North Carolina farms, then a hotbed of Texas fever.

He looked them over. They were covered with ticks—some microscopic, some half an inch long and full of blood they had sucked.

Smith put four of the tick-infested cattle into a field—along with six uninfected Northern cattle.

From the other three North Caroline cattle, Smith and an assistant named Kilburne tried to pick off—with their fingers—all the ticks.

They sweated. The cattle fidgeted, kicked, ran off. Finally the men thought they had removed the ticks. Into another field went the three tick-free cows—plus four non-tick-infested Northern animals.

Two months passed.

Meanwhile, Smith studied ticks in detail. He learned how the young ticks clambered onto cows, hung onto the hides, sucked blood, mated, dropped off the cows, laid their eggs in the grass on the ground, and died.

Smith also watched the cattle.

In the first field, a little after the middle of August, the Northern cows had acquired ticks—and Texas fever. Their blood turned to water, they grew thin, they began to die. Smith looked through a microscope at the blood of the dead cows. Inside the blood corpuscles, he saw microbes—pear-shaped, tiny, one-celled creatures, among the one-celled beings that are called the protozoa.

In the second field, whenever a few more ticks appeared on the Southern cattle—and they did keep appearing—they were picked off, and the field was kept free of ticks. The Northern cattle in field number two remained healthy. Finally, Smith switched two healthy Northern cattle from field number two to among the tick-infested cattle in field number one. Soon both the Northern cattle had Texas fever.

Next, Smith obtained some grass from North Carolina—grass swarming with ticks. He put the grass with its ticks into field number three—a field where no cattle had ever been penned. Into this field he put four healthy Northern cattle (but no Southern cattle). In four weeks, three had Texas fever. One died, two managed to recover.

It looked certain that it was the tick that caused Texas fever.

The hunch of the cattlemen had been right.

How did ticks do it? In 1890, Smith found out.

He had laboratory-hatched ticks bite a healthy heifer. She developed Texas fever—with the pear-shaped microbes invading her blood corpuscles.

So, Smith reasoned, it was the young of the tick that, biting a cow, gave her Texas fever. The microbes were carried, via the ticks' eggs, to the young tick, and from the young tick to a cow.

The mother ticks had to drop off their cows, lay their eggs in the grass, the young had to hatch and grow, the young had to climb onto new cattle—all this was why it took a month or two for Texas fever to develop in a healthy herd, a month or two after the first contact with ticky cattle.

In 1893, Smith wrote a report on Texas fever.

To reduce the disease, he advised, reduce the ticks. The Bureau of Animal Industry's Dr. Cooper Curtice had studied and further described the life of the tick. Ticks can be destroyed, it was learned, by dipping cattle into a creosote mixture. On Texas' King Ranch, R. J. Kleberg tried many mixtures of creosote. Creosote has a petroleum base. Oil would be found in large amounts at Spindletop, Texas, in 1901, and therefore would become inexpensive. Many dipping mixtures were tried. Tick fever, as a result, was to be brought under control.

Smith himself went on to serve at George Washington University, at Harvard, and with the Rockefeller Institute.

His work went on to serve all men so significantly that it is hard to overestimate its importance.

Smith and the scientists with him did more than identify the tick as a carrier of a disease in cattle. By doing that, they showed that ticks, which are related to mites and spiders, could carry a disease. Ticks, mites, and spiders belong to the phylum Arthropoda, the jointed-legged animals. They are all eight-legged; they are not insects, which are six-legged. The idea that small creatures, either arachnids (ticks, mites, and spiders) or insects could carry disease was gradually being accepted, ever since in 1869 Raimbert had showed that flies could carry the bacteria of anthrax. Smith and his associates showed, also, that an intermediate host or carrier—the tick—could carry a disease from one animal to another; that is, the tick did not itself give the disease, it carried the microbe that did so. This led directly to discoveries that the germs of many diseases of both animals and men—malaria, yellow fever, Rocky Mountain fever, typhus, others—are transmitted by ticks or insects. Ticks themselves specifically spread Rocky Mountain spotted fever, tularemia, and equine encephalitis. And Smith and his colleagues had done work that, as in the case of tick fever, led to solving problems in the spread of many diseases.

51

Heroes on various fronts

His FATHER, Joshua Potter, on January 8, 1815, had been one of the Kentucky sharpshooters who, at the breastworks near New Orleans, helped Andrew Jackson defeat the British. (In 1815, Texas still had six more years to remain in the Spanish Empire.)

Fifteen years later, in 1830, when the longhorns already were roaming in west Texas, then a part of Mexico, the son was born. In view of his dad's veneration of Andrew Jackson, the infant was named Andrew Jackson Potter.

The boy, as he grew up, spent a total of three months in school; he learned to read—barely; he did not learn to write—not even barely. In 1846, sixteen years after his birth, and one year after Baylor University had been established in Waco, Texas—Andrew Jackson Potter volunteered and joined the U.S. Army in the war with Mexico. He was too small to carry a rifle and a pack and so was assigned to drive oxen. He was with a forty-wagon army team when, after the soldiers had ridden on ahead, it was captured by Indians. They took all the provisions, but left in place the drivers' scalps. Once, at an army post, sixteen-year-old Andrew Jackson Potter got camp fever. That winter he made a 300-mile wagon trip through the Raton mountains to Santa Fe.

285

The next year, 1847, he nursed men in a hospital at Santa Fe—men with scurvy, measles, pneumonia, whatever—all packed in narrow bunks crowding each other. Many were delirious and would sit up and shout, "Good-bye, I am going home." Potter went along when those well enough to be moved started home—by one- or two-mile-an-hour ox team across the Rockies. Said he: "I took my last look at the old adobe town of Santa Fe, with eyes dimmed by unshed tears, as I gazed for the last time on the graves of so many brave soldiers. . . . Many of our sick died in the great wilderness and we rolled them up in their blankets and laid them in earth's cold clay. . . ."

Five years later, in 1852, when Texans—at long last Americans—were staging some of their first cow hunts for wild longhorns, Andrew Jackson Potter, just out of the army, landed in San Antonio. He was struck by typhoid fever, almost died, then recovered—broke and with a big doctor bill. He drove oxen, the trade he knew, to pay it off. Then he took a wrong turning: he became a gambler and horse-racing man.

He went to hear a visiting preacher, Rev. I. G. John. At a country religious revival, Potter was converted by John.

Now Potter desired an education. He learned to read better in order to read the Bible. In 1859, a year when Oliver Loving made one of the very early cattle drives, to Colorado, and at twenty-nine years of age, Potter learned to write and began to deliver sermons —to preach. At that same age, twenty-nine, Theobald Smith had been beginning his research on tick fever.

In 1861 Potter wanted to reach his old family home in Missouri. He had no money. He drove cattle part of the way, drove for forty-seven days from Texas to Kansas—this years before the Long Trail was opened. When he reached his Missouri home, only his sister remained alive.

In 1862, with the Civil War on, sixteen years after he had volunteered for the war with Mexico, Potter volunteered as a private in the Confederate army. With it, he went through hunger, sickness, hardship, and battle. He was with it when berries, bread, and sugar were the only food.

Some of those berries were wild ones, and were due to seeds sown by the robin redbreast migrating across the land.

When a battle was about to begin, Andrew Jackson Potter

walked back and forth among the soldiers. He said: "Boys, some of you may fall in this battle; in a few minutes you may be called to meet your Maker. Repent now and give your heart to Christ. He is waiting to receive you. Oh, men, it's a solemn moment! You are facing death and eternity!" And when the order into battle was given, Andrew Jackson Potter seized a rifle and fought with the rest.

After the battle, he comforted and wrote letters home for the wounded and dying, and said prayers for the dead.

After the war, in 1866, the year Jim Daugherty drove his early herd to Kansas, and the year Charles Goodnight invented the chuck wagon, Potter was sent to the mountain frontier near Kerrville, Texas—to preach in an area of Indian raids on nights of the full moon. After a year, in 1867, the year Joseph G. McCoy made Abilene, Kansas, into a cattle town, Potter went on to Uvalde, near the Mexican border, where the Indians didn't wait for the full moon —they raided every day. He fought the Indians. One day he reached an army post just after the soldiers had been paid off.

He was told the only place available for a church service was the local saloon. So he had an announcer, in the manner of the old town crier, announce the place. He preached in the saloon. A crowd assembled outside—ex-gamblers, drunks, and cardsharps; one of the toughest-looking congregations ever. Afterward, they wanted to buy drinks all round. Instead, Potter passed the collection plate—an empty cigar box.

In 1878 or '79, Potter preached at Fort Concho. In 1883, Potter preached at a small frontier village, San Angelo. At about this same time, cowboy A. J. Carajal, at noon saw a swarm of buffaloes; the buffaloes took till 6 P.M. to pass him. Thus buffaloes still teemed only 86 years before, on July 20, 1969, there were men walking on the moon.

In 1895, Potter preached around Lockhart, where so many trail herds had trod. By this time, he was known—from the Gulf to the Panhandle, throughout Texas—as a helpful person. He knew every road, landscape, and cattle trail, and had used them to reach places where he had married and buried and sat by the sickbeds of cowboys and cowmen and their women and children. He had provided religious services and revivals that were so large a part of the social life of the time.

Andrew Jackson Potter had survived the Indian wars, the war with Mexico, and the Civil War—plus disease, hunger, and the hardships of the Long Trail country. He said he wished to end his days with his boots on—for him, that meant in the pulpit. On October 21, 1895, at sixty-five years of age, he rose to preach at Tilden, Texas, south of San Antonio toward the Gulf, in what was to have been the last sermon of the year. That was the year the XIT Ranch sent the last herds up the Long Trail. Andrew Jackson Potter reached a point in his sermon where he lifted his hands over his head, and said, "I believe." And he collapsed and died.

Another preacher died in 1895, George Webb Slaughter, who in 1836 had been a messenger to the Alamo, who had been a preacher with a six-shooter at his side, and who for a long time had been a cowboy and a cowman. He died on March 19. He was at his home near Palo Pinto, Texas, and he was survived by eleven children.

Branch Isbell, who had first gone up the Long Trail in 1871, with Amanda Burks and her husband, and who had had some difficulties in his relationships with girls, had given up the trail: "In the summer of 1898, I came to Odessa, Ector County, Texas, my present home, where I have been engaged in merchandising in a small way ever since. I have never 'hustled' nor been 'up-to-date'. . . . If work kills half the people and worry the other half, my chance should be good to survive indefinitely—for I've quit them both."

In the Spanish-American war of 1898, horsemen—many of them cowboys in two volunteer cavalry regiments—trained and equipped at Fort Sam Houston, San Antonio. They went to Cuba and charged up San Juan Hill: Teddy Roosevelt's Rough Riders. The world-encircling Spanish Empire, which Columbus had begun, which had brought longhorns and mustangs to North America, which had included much of the western United States, which had sent explorers all the way from Mexico into Kansas and perhaps Nebraska—already by 1898 had been greatly reduced in size. The Spanish-American war was the last blow to the once-wide empire. As a result of the war, Spain lost Cuba, Puerto Rico, the Philippines, and the Pacific Ocean island of Guam.

There was in 1898 a follow-up to an event during the Civil War, an event that had involved cowboys back when they were just beginning to be called cowboys. For the Confederate army, on May 23, 1863, the Second Texas Volunteers defended a hilltop near Vicksburg, Mississippi. Some of the Texans were youngsters who had been on the earliest cow hunts, and taken part in early round-ups. The Texans repulsed a Union regiment attacking the hill. During the battle, Pvt. (or Sgt.) Thomas J. Higgins of the Ninety-ninth Illinois Volunteers (Higgins had been born in Canada) tried to carry the American flag to the hilltop in the face of fire from the Second Texas Volunteers. He was shot at, he stumbled, he was again shot at, and he advanced. Finally the Texans stopped shooting. They yelled, "Come on, you brave Yank! Come on!" They reached out and pulled him over their breastworks. With their help, Higgins planted the American flag on a parapet that his comrades-in-arms did not successfully hold. Then, thirty-five years later, in April 1898, came the end of the tale: Thomas J. Higgins was awarded a medal established during the Civil War, the one that is the United States' highest award for valor, the Congressional Medal of Honor.

Among the principal ones who recommended Higgins: His once-upon-a-time enemies, those cowboys, members of the Second Texas Volunteers.

52

Some of the last
of the cowboys

THE 1900s. On September 8, 1900, a hurricane and a tidal wave struck Galveston and took 6,000 lives—the worst toll by such a storm in U.S. history. This led to scientists analyzing hurricanes and learning something about how to predict their paths and thus save human lives. Men's efforts on many fronts in the early 1900s were bringing into existence today's world. On January 10, 1901, on the Texas coastal prairie near Orange and Beaumont, where cattle grazed on the salt grass, and near tropical growths of pines, cypresses, hyacinths, magnolias, and orchids, an oil well was being drilled. A one-armed Sunday School teacher named Patillo Higgins —his first name was Spanish, his last name was Irish—for ten years had thought there might be oil there. He had persuaded Anthony Lucas, from Austria, to drill. Lucas' wife had sold her heirloom furniture—her security—to help raise money. Lucas used techniques previously worked out to drill deep water wells for windmills. At the place called Spindletop, on that tenth of January, a gusher blew in—and mankind for the first time had enough oil to use it for fuel. Liquid fuel. Plenty of it. In 1902, R. E. Olds massproduced the first gasoline auto ("In my Merry Oldsmobile"). It looked exactly like a carriage, but there was no horse in front—so, with perfect logic, it was called a horseless carriage. Olds in 1902 manufactured 420 horseless carriages. On December 17, 1903, at Kitty Hawk, North Carolina, two bicycle mechanics, Wilbur and Orville Wright, flew a glider with a homemade gasoline engine—man's first airplane. After Spindletop came oil for factories, homes, and some generating plants. And gasoline for autos, trucks, buses, farm tractors and machines, planes, and ships (switching from coal) —the energy for the mechanical transportation that replaced the horse and the ox and the mule. And in parts of the world the camel, which before the Civil War had failed in the American Southwest.

Still functioning in 1900 was a Justice of the Peace west of San Antonio named Roy Bean. He was growing old; he had been born in Marion County, Kentucky, in 1815, the year Andrew Jackson had defeated the British at New Orleans. Roy Bean had driven freight wagons. He had been a Pony Express rider. When the San Antonio area became what he thought was crowded, Bean moved out. As railroad tracks were laid across Texas, Bean followed the line as a saloonkeeper.

He reached the Big Bend country—where cattle rustlers often drove stolen cattle ("wet heads")—across the Rio Grande river, the Mexican border. The Big Bend, which the Spaniards had reached in 1583, is the giant curve made by the Rio Grande, among rugged, ragged mountains, where there are cottonwoods, oaks, firs, cedars, junipers, madronas, sotol and century plants, and where in the lonely river channel catfish grow huge, and where there are 500-foot-high cliffs with many caves.

Roy Bean settled at a place right next to the Mexican state of Coahuila, a place called Vinegarroon after the Texas-Mexico scorpion. Counties in that far-western part of Texas then were not even organized.

Cowman John Jacobs said that Bean obtained an appointment as Justice of the Peace, ran a saloon, and became known as the Law West of the Pecos. Once, when a dead body was found, with $150 and a Colt .45 on it, Judge Bean fined the corpse $150 for carrying a concealed weapon. When a slicker from the big city—Austin—came to Judge Bean's saloon, the judge charged him $9 for his liquor. The Austin man complained. The judge fined him $1 for disturbing the peace, and gave him no change from a $10 bill.

Bean often fined a man a round of drinks for the crowd.

Judge Bean also supplemented his income by mending shoes, and, for two bits, cutting a man's hair.

He was an admirer of an English actress, Lillie Langtry, who had been admired also by the Prince of Wales. Bean renamed his location at Vinegarroon on the Rio Grande: Langtry. Lillie, from the English Channel island of Jersey, was called the Jersey Lily. Over the doorway of his saloon, Judge Bean inscribed the name, the Jersey Lily.

Lillie, born in 1851, had toured the United States for the first time in 1881—about the time Bean reached Langtry. Judge Bean wrote her and asked her to visit Langtry. She did. In 1915 she visited the saloon named for her, and the courtroom, while a train hauling her special car waited.

But Roy Bean was not there. He had died in 1903. Cowboy John Jacobs said he willed two pistols to Miss Langtry. He is buried today in Woodlawn Cemetery, on the western side of the Rio Grande town of Del Rio.

As the Long Trail days were fading, there still was an occasional cattle drive. In 1901, William Baxter Slaughter took his wife along with a herd that he moved from Clifton, Arizona, to Liberal, Kansas.

Most cattle, however, now traveled by rail—even to reach Northern ranches. The Matador Land and Cattle Company, managed by Murdo MacKenzie, in May 1904 began moving by train thousands of cattle from Texas to grazing lands in South Dakota. A cowboy, Ike Blasingame, met them at Evarts, South Dakota. Blasingame added some notes to the cowboy's story. His mules, he said, sat down on their haunches like dogs when they did not want to pull a chuck wagon. The mules liked the cook's pies, though, and one day the mules smelled freshly baked pies, and, while the cook was asleep, ate them. The cook, named Walter Krump, had another problem: a dog that lay down on clean dish towels drying on the grass. Krump cured the dog, Blasingame suspected, by a few drops of scalding water whenever the dog stretched out on a towel.

Cowboy Blasingame saw a landmark, a flat-topped butte sticking up high out of the Dakota flatland. It was riddled with crevices and holes. By the middle of September, the butte was alive with thousands of rattlesnakes and other snakes come to hibernate in the holes and cracks.

Even in 1904, Blasingame thought that some of the Indians on reservations still itched to gather a few more scalps.

In the spring of 1905, Blasingame on his horse C Heart fell through thinning ice in the Missouri River. C Heart lunged and clawed, got up on more ice, which in turn gave way. This kept up, over and over, till C Heart brought Blasingame to the bank. C Heart looked back at the river, whistled, and snorted.

Blasingame said night horses, those most trusted of all a cowboy's horses, would somehow know to stop, in the dark, just short of a washout or gully they would otherwise have hurled their riders into. Some night horses, he said, even stopped short and felt ahead with their hoofs and so located the holes ahead.

Horses often received names that labeled them, Blasingame said. Rainbow was a horse that changed color from winter (black) to summer (chestnut sorrel). Ring-eyed showed the whites of his eyes completely around the irises. Bad characters were horses named Widow Maker, Skittish Bill, Rollers, and Danger.

As the Matador and other cattle arrived, Evarts, South Dakota, became an important cattle shipping point, both for cattle coming in and going out. Ten loading chutes loaded ten railroad cattle cars at a time. A trainload of 400 cattle could be loaded in an hour. A trainload left Evarts every hour.

Wild West shows, following the hoofprints of Buffalo Bill's, were held. In New York City's Madison Square Garden one day in 1905, a steer ran wild and into the crowd. Frightened spectators fled. A cowboy, twenty-six, threw his rope over the horns of the steer, dug his boots into the tanbark, hauled on the rope, led the steer back to a corral. That was how the career of Will Rogers started.

Also back east, on June 10, 1867—the year the trail to Abilene had been opened—there had been born to a wealthy New York lawyer a son. N. Howard (Jack) Thorp, as the boy would be called, attended St. Paul's school in Concord, New Hampshire. He first became acquainted with horses when he played polo with Theodore Roosevelt. Cowboys came from all over the United States and the world, so it will not surprise you to learn that Jack Thorp became one. He visited a Nebraska ranch run by his brother, and that helped. In the 1890s, Jack Thorp bought Western ponies, and sent them east to become polo ponies.

In 1889–90 he made a 1,500-mile-long horseback ride through Texas and New Mexico. On the trip, he jotted down the words (not the music) of a number of cowboy songs. In 1908, he had a printer in Estancia, New Mexico, publish the first collection—ever—of cowboy and Western songs. "I paid the printer six cents per copy," Thorp remembered. There were twenty-three songs in the book.

The first song he put down was about "the little steel dust, the color of rust," the fastest cutting-horse in Texas—name of Dodgin' Joe.

In 1921, he published a second, much-expanded edition—101 songs.

Thorp collected and published, along with other songs, "Little Joe, the Wrangler"; "Windy Bill"; "The Tenderfoot"; "California Trail"; "Top Hand"; "Grand Roundup or The Cowboy's Dream" ("I wondered if ever a cowboy . . ." to the tune of "My Bonnie"); "(My) Little Adobe Casa" (on the plains); "The Texas Cowboy"; "Mustang Gray"; "Sam Bass"; "A Cowboy's Lament" ("Once in the saddle I used to go dashing . . ."); "Chase of the O.L.C. Steer"; "The Pecos Stream"; and "Pecos River Queen."

A cowboy who wrote a song often did not sign it, and Thorp did not always know who his authors were. In one song, a cowboy writer included a line that told his reason for remaining anonymous: "My name is nothing extry, so that I will not tell."

Thorp, out west for fifty years, said he never knew a cowboy who could sing. However, he said, sometimes one would open his mouth and words came out.

Since Thorp, there has come a flood of cowboy and Western music, real and phony, that shows no signs of letting up.

Part of the flood in the early 1900s were Mexican songs making their way in the land of the Long Trail. A song of the Mexican *vaquero* (cowboy) that was popular was "La Paloma" (The Dove).

A Mexican folk song heard in cactus country was "El Rancho Grande" (The Big Ranch). Others were "La Cucaracha" (The Cockroach), and "Cielito Lindo" (Beautiful Heaven).

It was 1914. A gasoline-driven railroad car mysteriously started its engine and, driverless, went down the track. Cowboy Hiram Craig, riding a favorite pony, Joshua, chased the railroad car two-and-one-half miles. He caught up with the car, got ahead of it, and threw a plank across the track. This stopped the car.

The horse had won the race.

"The little pony," he said later, "is now playing polo in New York."

That was one of the last times a horse would come out ahead. The machine was taking over.

53

Some of the things they got done

WHEN A man complained, the cowboy had a way to silence him: "If you don't like the world, you have my permission to change it."

Nevertheless, the cowboys themselves can be said to have changed the world about as much as any group of men ever did. For one thing, they put new place names on the map from the Gulf to Canada. Here is a small sampling of the names the cowboy put on the map:

Dead-Horse Mountain, Texas.

Bone Springs, Texas (a town near a marsh where the cattle bogged down and died).

Pommel Peak, Texas (after the pommel of the cowboy's saddle).

Spur Junction.

Rattlesnake Mountains.

Ganado (Spanish or Mexican for cattle; named for wild longhorns that roamed around it, when it was settled in 1882).

Bronco (astride the New Mexico–Texas line).

Crockett County (after the man at the Alamo; the county is larger than the state of Delaware).

Horsethief Crossing.

Grassland.

Sweetwater.

Muleshoe.

Eagle Pass.

And Maverick, Texas.

In Oklahoma: Muddy Boggy Creek, Sod House.

In Kansas: Lone Star, Wolf, Clearwater, Prairie Dog Creek, and Horse Thief Canyon.

In Nebraska: Broken Bow, Redbird, Prairie Center. There are Antelope, Buffalo, Frontier, Custer, and Sioux counties.

North Dakota has a town called Alamo.

South Dakota has Rattlesnake Butte (which cowboy Ike Blasingame saw in 1905), Eagle Butte, White Owl, and Hot Canyon Butte.

Colorado has Red Wing, Powder Wash, Skull Crossing, Texas Creek, Steamboat Springs, Wagon Wheel Gap, and Wild Horse.

Perhaps the most distinctive name from Long Trail days is that of the Y E Mesa, in the Rocky Mountains below where they enter Texas from New Mexico at the thirty-second parallel. The Y E Mesa was named for the brand on the cattle of the Buttrill ranch.

If the cowboy changed the names on the map of the middle of the continent, he also changed the land itself. His Long Trail actually was a series of trails, running south to north, that crossed the east to west routes of the covered wagons—the Overland Trail, the Utah Trail, the California Trail, the Oregon Trail, the Santa Fe Trail, the Pony Express route. The cowboy wove essential threads into the fabric of the U.S.A. His trails linked together the east-west routes and made of the midcontinent a unified whole.

From a wilderness in 1867, the cowboy had helped develop sixteen states and territories: northwest Texas, Utah, Wyoming, Arizona, New Mexico, Washington, Oregon, Nevada, Colorado, North Dakota, South Dakota, Montana, Iowa, Nebraska, western Kansas, and the western section of the Indian Nations (Oklahoma).

The Long Trail with its cowboys, like the Mississippi River with its steamboats, brought South and North together and—in spite of differences between cattlemen and farmers and Kansas Jayhawkers and others—the cowboy helped South and North to understand each other. He gave the Midwest a broader outlook and, living as he did in the horse-and-buggy age—a time when the average American man, woman, or child almost never traveled over 100 or 200 miles from home—he himself rode from the Gulf to Canada. Shaped by limitless space and sky, by a continent instead of a town, he became a man with a continental outlook.

The cowboys provided good, nourishing food—beef—for Americans after the Civil War.

As food, meat has a special value. Says the *Columbia Encyclopedia,* referring to meat of cows, calves, sheep, lambs, and swine: "Its food value is high, the protein contributing to the growth and repair of tissue, the fat being a source of energy." Beef is almost completely digested, the encyclopedia explains, 95 to 98 percent of its fat and almost all its proteins being used by the body. Besides fat and proteins, meat contributes other needed substances.

The cowboys' beef helped the throngs of people in the Northern cities—people who had flocked there to work in the nation's first large-scale factories. The cities grew; the factories flourished; the mass production of all kinds of goods for all kinds of people increased; the standards of living of Americans increased. Among other things, better-fed workers produced autos, planes, railroad cars and locomotives, and all kinds of machines.

The meat provided by cowboys and the Long Trail helped bring about all these things.

Large supplies of beef brought prices down. More people could eat beef. More did eat it. Even laborers in factories could, and did, have more than ever.

Commented Daniel J. Boorstin, the director of the National Museum of History and Technology of the Smithsonian Institution, Washington, D.C. (in his 1973 book *The Americans: The Democratic Experience*): "In the Old World, beef was the diet of lords and men of wealth. For others it was a holiday prize. But Americans would eat like lords—because of the efforts of American Go-Getters [cattlemen and cowboys] in the half-charted west."

The cowboy on the Long Trail and his longhorns caused meat-packing plants to be built—and caused them to be big enough to do a job on the U.S. scale. At Fort Worth, Kansas City, St. Louis, Chicago, and in other cities, new packing plants were constructed that were colossal in size compared to any that had existed before.

The big new plants used every part of a cow except the Moo to provide dozens of products including lard, tallow, sausage, glue, shoes, boots, and purses.

The beef for the nation supplied by the cowboy was even more important than it sounds today. A hundred years ago people did not have nearly the supplies of other meats and fruit and vegetables that we grow today, and had most of them only in season, or immediately after an animal was killed. For many people simply to get enough food to eat was a lifelong struggle; everyone knew how hard it was to keep on hand food enough to get through a winter.

In providing meat on a large scale, the cowboys made it possible, for the first time, for many people to have regular, satisfactory meals the year round.

A San Joaquin, California, farm woman, as she leaned on a fence under a mulberry tree, told a *U.S. News & World Report* journalist in 1974: "I've never been hungry in 80 years in this country."

Not many eighty-year-olds of any previous generation anywhere could have said that.

Food, enough food, is so taken for granted today that it is hard to realize what the elimination of hunger pangs means. But it was a tremendous thing. And the cowboys and ranchers and farmers and transportation people and businessmen and grocers and scientists who all contributed to an end of frequent hunger in North America —plus the universities and the agricultural research stations and the Department of Agriculture—can scarcely get too much credit. The elimination of hunger in North America was one of man's great achievements.

Men in other continents would love to duplicate it.

The cowboys helped bring it about.

The cowboy helped to establish a big business: in the late 1970s, the largest food industry in the United States is meat packing and processing. By 1975, there were on U.S. ranches and farms about 132 million cattle and calves. Fewer than 12 million of these were milk cows. The rest were beef animals. Thus there was more than one beef animal for every two Americans. There were more cattle in the United States than total motor vehicles—more than the almost 130 million autos plus buses plus trucks. In the future, the

Department of Agriculture expects beef cattle on American ranches to climb in number.

The cowboys of the Long Trail reached—and the ranchers helped to build—most of today's cattle-raising states. Principal cattle states include Texas (first), Nebraska (second), Iowa, Kansas, Oklahoma, South Dakota, Missouri, Minnesota, Montana, Colorado, Ohio, Illinois, Indiana, North Dakota, Wyoming, Wisconsin, Arkansas, Idaho, California, Kentucky, Tennessee, Mississippi, Louisiana, Florida, Georgia, and Alabama.

The Long Trail started a number of cities on their way to growing large: San Antonio, Austin, Houston, Waco, Fort Worth, Dallas, Oklahoma City, Tulsa, Omaha, and Calgary, Canada (whose population is 403,319) all are examples.

The towns that were temporary goals of the Long Trail today are mostly small: Abilene, Kansas, population (in 1970) 6,661; Baxter Springs, 4,489; Dodge City, 14,127; Newton, 15,439; Ogallala, Nebraska, 4,976; Cheyenne, Wyoming, 40,914.

In addition to affecting names on the map, and the land, and factory workers in cities, the cowboy affected someone else: you. You eat what you eat because of him.

In one recent year, Americans consumed 4,421,648,000 hamburgers!

54

A vanishing animal makes a comeback

IN THE 1920s, the longhorn had all but disappeared. Anguses, Herefords, Brahmas, Jerseys, and others had almost entirely replaced it. "At low ebb," David Snell wrote in the June 1974 *Smithsonian Magazine,* "their numbers were far fewer than buffalo (bison) of the Great Plains had ever diminished to."

Will C. Barnes and John Hatton of the Forest Service became concerned and worked on preservation of the longhorns. Urged by a cattleman from Wyoming, U.S. Sen. John B. Kendrick, the Congress appropriated $3,000 to save the longhorns. Forest rangers and a former Texas Ranger, Graves Peeler, located twenty cows, four calves, three bulls, and three steers, and sent them to the Wichita Mountain Wildlife Refuge in Oklahoma. At about this time men had begun to come upon longhorns—free and wild—in thickets in east Texas, foraging by night, eating tree leaves if necessary, hardy, scraggly, and identical to the longhorns of Long Trail days seventy years earlier. In the same thicket, also wild and free, were razorback hogs—both the cattle and hogs were descendants of animals the Spanish had brought 400 years earlier.

The cattle at the Wichita Mountain refuge multiplied, and some of its animals made a second herd at the Fort Niobrara National Wildlife Refuge, Nebraska.

In the 1930s, cowboy historian J. Frank Dobie and oilman Sid Richardson encouraged Graves Peeler to search for more longhorns. Peeler found thirty cows and two bulls this time. Twenty of the cows and two of the bulls, donated to the state of Texas, produced descendants alive today. One place you can find them is in the Lyndon B. Johnson State Park.

Near Goliad, Texas, today, on the Capo de Vino Ranch, Walter B. Scott raises Texas longhorns. He is a past president of the Texas Longhorn Breeders Association of America, a new (founded in 1964), small (325 members in 1974) group. This group tried to define a Texas longhorn, and agreed that the longhorns had long horns and strong, long legs. And that each one also had a "rafter" slope to the hips like the sides of a gable roof. And a small (three or four inches long) dip in the back just above the tail. The rafter slope and the dip, David Snell reported, are believed to help the longhorns give birth easily to their lightweight, string-bean calves.

By 1974, the Longhorn Breeders Association knew of 5,380 longhorn cows, 1,151 bulls, and 794 steers. These figures did not include the latest unbranded short yearlings and calves. Nor did it include about a thousand longhorns not registered.

Today longhorns—gen-u-wine, to use a Texas pronunciation—are being raised in Texas, Colorado, California, and other states, even Massachusetts; and, in Canada, in British Columbia and in Montreal. Walter Scott of the Capo de Vino Ranch, a graduate of Baylor University, one day looked from a highway into a pasture. "I saw some Texas longhorns," he remembers. "They were beautiful. Not just beautiful longhorns, but beautiful cattle." He had been having illness among his cattle of other breeds, and he recalled that he never had heard of a longhorn needing a veterinarian —nor any doctoring. "So I told my wife, Mary Elizabeth, it might be interesting to own two or three just to look at." He bought some, branded them with a wineglass brand, and was on his way.

Dr. Stewart H. Fowler, of Louisiana State University, visited Walter Scott's ranch and was impressed by the vigor and looks of his longhorns. Dr. Fowler now is head of an agricultural experimental station at Uvalde, run by Texas A & M University. Dr. Fowler says Texas longhorns resist parasites and diseases. He tells of longhorn cows licking cuts and scratches of their calves to get out the screwworms. Dr. Fowler says that, to obtain something to eat, the longhorns can forage skillfully.

Longhorn meat is red and lean. And in tests today, longhorn bulls put on weight about as rapidly as do other breeds. The long-horn in the late 1970s is in a position where it actually can come back some day as a meat animal. It might once again be on American dining tables, as it was a hundred years ago.

55

After the trail
was over

THE COWBOY knew he had reached the sunset, the end of the Long Trail. The cowboys—twelve hundred of them—banded together in the Old Trail Drivers Association, and proceeded to hold one rip-roaring reunion after another, meeting at least once in Houston and often in October in the Gunter Hotel in San Antonio, right in the center of the area where the Long Trail began.

The Old Trail Drivers Association's members dressed as cowboys, drank boiled black coffee, danced wearing red, blue, or black bandannas, sang cowboy songs, told tall tales, and ate dinner served from chuck wagons.

Their meetings were almost as unique as the Long Trail itself, and as unique as their driving ten million longhorns for thousands of miles—the only time any group of men in all history ever did any such thing.

In the late 1970s they still gather each October in the Gunter Hotel—only now it's their grandchildren and great-grandchildren.

At an early Trail Drivers' meeting in San Antonio, C. S. Broadbent read a verse:

Cowboy, rest, thy labor o'er,
Sleep the sleep that knows no breaking . . .

The cowboy now sang about the farmer. A song said the farmers had taken up all the water and land. But the cowboys hoped they'd "succeed in the future as the cowboys done in the past."

At a 1915 meeting of the trail drivers, one of them, Branch Isbell, met a friend. It had been in 1871 when he first rode north from Texas, along with William Burks and his wife, Amanda. Now, forty-four years afterward, Isbell saw a familiar figure. As you have learned, Isbell had an eye for girls; the figure was female. He said he would have known it in a thousand. It was Amanda Burks. It was the first time he had seen her since 1871.

Members of the Old Trail Drivers elected, as their first president, George W. Saunders. Saunders, barely seventeen, with Jim Byler, had first ridden the Long Trail in 1870. He had driven to Abilene and Dodge City and elsewhere. He was to be a cattleman for over fifty years.

At the Trail Drivers' 1917 meeting, George Saunders did some summing up. He figured that, altogether, 9,800,000 cattle had slowly walked north on the Long Trail. This was an average of 350,000 a year for each of twenty-eight years, from 1868 to 1895. He figured this brought to Texas $10 per cow, or $98 million, in those days a tremendous sum. Saunders thought that, in addition, a million horses had been driven north, also at $10 a head, for $10 million more. In other words, the cowboys and cowmen of the Long Trail brought to Texas $108 million.

The *Texas Almanac* of 1947–48 had an estimate of how much money the cattle trails had brought to Texas: not Saunders' $108 million, but $200 million.

Other figures for the total number of cattle driven north run far above 10 million to as high as 15 million.

Texans, desperately poor, took to driving cattle to get a fairer shake—a better living—for their women and children and themselves.

This they achieved.

When the trail driving ended, there were more cattle in Texas than there had been when trail driving began. There had been more calves in the state each year, on the average, than there had been cattle sent up the trail.

There still are more cattle in Texas than there were in 1866. There often are more cattle than people in Texas. And the state often receives more income from cattle than it does from all other farm products.

The trail drivers, Saunders said, between 1868 and 1895 totaled around thirty-five thousand. One-third of them made more than one trip.

That's how many cowboys—35,000—rode the Long Trail.

In other words, the accomplishments of the cowboys were the accomplishments of a number of men about as large as the 1970 population of Temple, Texas.

At the 1919 meeting of the Old Time Trail Drivers Association, Luther A. Lawhon recited a poem that mentioned another change taking place. It included the name of a fairly new drink that had become available: Coke.

At about this time, *The Trail Drivers of Texas* commented, "many" old-time drivers had achieved a distinction, which might have come from cattle or from oil or natural gas: they were rated in Dun and Bradstreet's "in the seven-figure class."

Other cowboys, less fortunate, were running gas stations.

Fred Sutton in 1881 had lived through the day when he was not killed by Billy the Kid.

Sutton in 1919 met Charley Colcord, the man who had brought the first toothbrush to Medicine Lodge, Kansas. As a small boy, you remember, a cowboy often had a wardrobe that consisted of one shirt. His mother had sewed the shirt with thread she herself had spun on the old spinning wheel. And a cowboy, you remember, often started up the Long Trail with a single pair of trousers.

Sutton said he had seen Colcord, wealthy from oil one of Dun and Bradstreet's "seven-figure" men, in a full-dress suit. It gave him a shock to see a former cowboy in formal clothes.

Sutton said that other cowmen had changed Dodge City, Kansas, from a "wide-open town with its Indian fighters, buffalo hunters, cowboys, dance halls, honkytonks, and gambling houses into the modern city of today, where a beautiful high-school building ornaments the summit of notorious Boot Hill, where many a mother's boy who left the East so suddenly that he forgot to take his name with him was laid away by the followers of the Chisholm Trail.''

Another trail driver who benefited from oil was Robert Samuel Dalton, the son of Marcus L., the man who had almost reached home but on November 4, 1870, was killed by Indians twenty miles from the end of his journey. The younger Dalton received oil royalties of as much as $800 a day, and his ranch became an oil field.

To cowboy John G. Jacobs it was as though it never had happened. "It seems now," he said in 1921, "as though it was all in some other world, and under fairer skies.''

But it had happened—quickly.

The cowboy had not had much time to write his name in history. He had less than thirty years, from 1868 through 1895, when the Long Trail was busy, and in the last of those years the trail was petering out. In less than a single generation (thirty-three years), the young man on horseback had opened the trail, made it important, made his contribution to the nation, made Americans eaters of beef, and then departed.

Less than thirty years. And yet it took the Cossacks, perhaps the most famous horsemen in history, over four hundred years to make their reputation for fearless horsemanship on the steppes of Russia. The Spaniards, some of them on horseback, the men who brought longhorns and mustangs to the Great Plains, and who explored or established outposts in Mexico, Texas, New Mexico, Arizona, California, parts of Utah and Colorado plus Latin America (which they made *Latin* America), were in Mexico from 1519 to 1821—or over ten times as long as the cowboy was on the Long Trail. And Spanish horsemen traced their ancestry back to the Moors with their Arabian horses 700 years before 1519.

Cowboy W. T. (Bill) Brite of Leming, Texas, on December 24, 1921, commented on the progress of his family. "I married in 1879. There are 15 children in our family, nine boys and six girls, all

living, and my wife and I are still hale and hearty. Including grandchildren, there are about 45 members of our family, and there has
been only one death. None of my boys have ever been sent to the
penitentiary or elected to the legislature, and I think that is a pretty
good showing."

"I suppose I had more experience, good and bad, than any one
man on the trail," said Gus Black of Eagle Pass. He was the one
who, in 1882, had put an adult longhorn's horns onto a dogie and
fooled Wyoming Governor Bush about its age. Said Gus Black: "I
worked 18 hours out of every 24. Wound up in 1882 without a
dollar in hand, but in possession of several thousand dollars' worth
of fun."

In 1920, Branch Isbell, who after having been twice rebuked
by girls had first married at age forty, and then had lost his wife
after seven happy years, was married a second time. To Mrs.
Nettie S. Hicks, widow of Dr. J. M. Hicks. Isbell was sixty-nine,
or thereabouts.
   Isbell, still of Odessa, Ector County, Texas, wrote a four-line
poem he entitled "The Old Trail Driver":

May life's future pathway with roses be strewn,
Whose thorns have all been pruned away;
May sunshine abide when its shadows have flown—
Is the blessing I wish him today.

The Gonzales, Texas, city hall benefited from cowman R. A.
Houston. He had made a large copper steer, and he had it erected
over the city hall. Upon it was his trail-driving brand, 141.

William J. Bennett looked backward—and forward: "It usually required three months to take a herd to the Red River. Only a
few days ago the papers gave an account of an aviator flying from
San Antonio to Oklahoma City, a distance of over six hundred
miles, in the short space of three hours. . . . May we not venture to
predict that in another sixty years somebody will have established
a trail to Mars or other planets?" The Apollo landings on the moon
from 1969 onward would not have surprised him.

Oscar J. Fox of San Antonio never did stop composing cow-boy songs, not even after the trail-driving days were over, and he was still at it in the 1920s. Born in Burnet County, Texas, in 1879, he had published "A Cowboy's Lament" ("Oh, bury me not on the lone prairie . . .") and "Rounded Up in Glory." He kept right on writing verses that were sung at Old Trail Drivers' meetings.

At the San Antonio meeting in October 1922, Elizabeth Slaughter, the daughter of Mr. and Mrs. W. B. Slaughter, was a hit. W. B. Slaughter was the cowman who, in 1885, with the aid of an alarm clock, had peacefully driven 104 buffaloes along the trail.
    Elizabeth sang "The Old Chisholm Trail": "Come along boys, and listen to my tale . . ."

In 1922, Ira C. Jennings, who as a youth had driven to Kansas, died at Laredo. He was sixty-five years old when a heart attack struck him and he fell over holding a hot branding iron in his hand. Jennings, who had been one of the last men to depend on the horse for transportation, had a son who was a railway conductor.

As the men who rode the Long Trail headed for the last round-up and eternity's dawn, they told stories about themselves: A cowboy newly arrived in Heaven saw other cowboys staked out. St. Peter explained, "They are old cowboys from the Panhandle of Texas. If we turn 'em loose, they will every last one go back."
    Another cowboy reached the gates of Heaven and approached St. Peter. Said the saint, "Well, come on in, but you won't like it."

At the age of ninety, in 1926, Charles Goodnight had lived three-fifths of the years the United States had existed—the nation then was 150 years old. That year Goodnight retold the story—accurately—of the trip by him and Oliver Loving and the one-armed Bill Wilson on what would become known as the Goodnight-Loving Trail. He told it to J. Frank Dobie of the University of Texas. Goodnight retold the story fifty-nine years after he and Loving and Wilson had traveled the trail, and Loving had been wounded by the Comanches and had died as a result.
    There had been no schools in the Texas Panhandle when Goodnight, in 1876, with John G. Adair, had owned the JA Ranch,

so he had established Goodnight Academy. The town of Goodnight, almost in the center of the Texas Panhandle between Oklahoma and New Mexico, was named for him. Goodnight eventually
was called the father of the Texas Panhandle.

Said Goodnight:

"All in all my years on the trail were the happiest I have lived.
There were many hardships and dangers, of course, that called on
all a man had of endurance and bravery, but when all went well
there was no other life so pleasant."

And:

"Most of the time we were solitary adventurers in a great land
as fresh and new as a spring morning, and we were free and full of
the zest of darers."

Goodnight all his life believed in remedies used on the frontier: prickly pear (cactus) poultices for wounds; salt and buffalo
tallow for piles (hemorrhoids—a common cowboy complaint), and
prairie-dog soup. Whatever remedies he used, they worked well
for him.

Goodnight remained married to his first wife for fifty-five
years. After she died, he remarried—in 1927, when he was ninety-
one years old. On December 12, 1929, at ninety-three, Charles
Goodnight, one of the last of the pioneers of the Long Trail, died.

Born in 1865, the year before Jim Daughterty drove one of the
first herds of longhorns to Kansas, J. Frank Norfleet grew up to be
small in height (a little over five feet), and light in weight, as were
many cowboys. He became one. He later became a rancher on his
own on the south Texas plains. When, in the early 1900s, he was
swindled out of $45,000, he tracked the swindlers to New York
City. A deputy sheriff in Texas, he was treated by the New York
police as a visiting lawman, and his .45 was licensed. In time, Norfleet located the eight swindlers in Canada and caused their arrest
and conviction. At his home in Hale Center, Texas, he died on
October 16, 1967. One of the last of the cowboys of the Long Trail,
he was 102 years old.

Born when the Long Trail was crowded with cattle, about the
time William and Amanda Burks in 1871 went up the trail with
tenderfoot Branch Isbell, Jack Hart became a cowboy. Years later,

as he followed the circuit of rodeos (it starts in south Texas and ends in Calgary, Canada), he could say, "I've been a cowboy all my life. I can still handle horses, and I still ride some." So he refused to retire. That was in January 1971, and he was ninety-nine.

John G. Jacobs, who had told of cowboys on night herd humming lullabies to their cattle, was one of the many men who in later years testified as to how the cowboys protected women: "They were to a man defenders of women and children."

There were reasons for the cowboy's chivalry. George Saunders, who thought highly of his fellow cowboys, really let himself go on the subject of their women. "They are more deserving of praise," he said, "than all of the men combined. Consider the pioneer mothers and wives . . . and think of the hardships and privations they endured for the sake of being near and helping husband or father to make a home in the new country. Their social pleasures were few, their work heavy. Dangers lurked on every hand, but bravely and uncomplainingly these women endured their hard lot, cheering and encouraging the men who were their protectors. God bless them!"

He quoted another man, J. M. Hunter, to back up his description of the cowman's woman: "Bravely has she gone to the unprotected frontier, with no shelter but the crude cabin, the dugout, or open camp, where winds whistled, wolves howled, where Indians yelled, and yet within that rude domicile, burning like a lamp, was . . . faith, love, fortitude and heroism."

Although he had the help of his women, the cowboy, from the time he first rode the Long Trail, till he married the farmer's daughter, till it was time for him to sleep the sleep that knows no breaking, was beset with difficulties.

Oliver Loving lost his life driving cattle. So did many a cowboy, buried on the lone prairie. Other trail drivers lost cattle to Indians, stampedes, rustlers, flooded creeks and rivers, hail, blizzards, and drought. But when the results of the less than thirty years of driving on the Long Trail were totaled up, and the tales of the Long Trail had been gathered, and the songs of the Long Trail had been sung, one remarkable thing about the bowlegged human being who was the cowboy stood out: No matter what the difficulties, no herd that started north ever turned back.

Not one.

On separate occasions, two men—both cowboys—uttered identical sentences that summed up the importance of the cowboy. One man who said it was A. N. Eustace. Another was J. M. Custer, who had G.T.T. (Gone to Texas) hurriedly, needed to avoid the law for twelve years, neglected to remember his name, and called himself Bill Wilson.

What each man said about the cowboys was: "We had our day, and the world is better for it."

56

Postscript:
Memories and Reminders

TODAY YOU can see a statue of the pioneer woman, the farmer's wife—the mother of the girl who married the cowboy—at Ponca City, Oklahoma; the statue is by Bryant Baker. Another statue of her, by Robert Merrill Gage, you can see at Topeka, Kansas.

A one-room schoolhouse—where her children were educated—is at Emporia, Kansas.

You can see the dirt house the pioneer woman lived in at Sod Town, Kansas, two miles east of Colby. Still standing are two of the original sod houses of the first homesteaders.

A renovated sod house and windmill are at Oberlin, Kansas.

The Texas Cowboy Monument by Constance Whitney Warren is on the lawn of the state capital at Austin. It is a sculpture of a cowboy on a rearing horse. The sculptor herself presented it to the state in 1925.

A statue of a cowboy 100 feet tall, Big Tex, towers over the annual Texas State Fair in Dallas, biggest in the United States.

A life-size statue of a mule is in the middle of the town of Muleshoe, Texas.

You can see the tall grass of the prairies, the grass that the cattle and horses grazed on, the Sea of Grass that made the Long

317

Trail possible, at the Caddo National Grassland, near Honey Grove, on the Texas side of the Red River. Or, north of Dalhart, on the High Plains in both Texas and Oklahoma, at the Rita Blanca National Grassland. Or, near Sweetwater, Oklahoma, in the Black Kettle National Grassland. Or, southwest of Dallas, around Alvarado, at the Cross Timbers National Grassland.

You can see longhorns today at a number of places, including an exhibition park at Six Flags Over Texas, Dallas. A faithful reader may count up five flags that have flown over Texas that I have mentioned: Spanish, Mexican, Republic of Texas, United States, Confederate, and United States again. The sixth flag was that of France. The French regarded their territory of Louisiana as extending all the way to the Rio Grande.

You can see buffaloes—in addition to those in many zoos—at Cedar State Park, South Dakota; Yellowstone National Park, on the continental divide in Wyoming, Montana, and Idaho; the Fort Niobrara National Wildlife Refuge, Nebraska; the 50,000-acre Wichita Mountain Wildlife Refuge, Oklahoma; Sullys Hill National Game Preserve and Theodore Roosevelt National Memorial Park, North Dakota; and in 700 smaller herds in parks, on ranches, and on ranges all across the United States, including the East. Private individuals today own 15,000 buffaloes, most of them among those on ranches.

In Canada, there are 16,000 buffaloes on the 17,000-square-mile wilderness that makes up the Wood Buffalo National Park, on the Alberta–Northwest Territories boundary.

Mounted buffaloes are at the Dyche Museum of the University of Kansas at Lawrence. There is also—mounted—the only survivor of Gen. George A. Custer's last stand, a horse, Comanche. There are also mounted elk and prairie falcon, a bird of the Long Trail with eyes so sharp—eight times as acute as human eyes—it can see a mouse move a mile away.

You can also buy buffalo meat today—as a gourmet food.

A rattlesnake roundup is held annually in April at Okeene, Oklahoma.

At De Lon Plaza, in Victoria, Texas, each June, a local wild animal is honored: the armadillo. Highlights include a beauty pageant for armadilloes, and the world's champion armadillo race.

Barbed wire today is the object of collectors—for whom one

name is barbarians. There are different varieties of barbed wire—
the fence that tamed the West—and at least sixty thousand barbarians are after them. Names of kinds of the wire: Dodge Star,
the Winner, Ross's Four-Point, Ellwood Ribbon, Lazy Plate,
Scutt's Clip, and Sunderland Kink.

You can drive the Chisholm Trail on U.S. 81—the northern
section through Oklahoma wheat fields. Northwest of Boise City in
the Panhandle of Oklahoma, you can find wagon ruts of the Santa
Fe Trail.

On Interstate Highway 76 in Kansas is a historical marker
saying that the Chisholm Trail was roughly parallel to the turnpike
from Oklahoma to Wichita. A mile south of Caldwell a marker
shows where the Chisholm Trail reached Kansas. And at Abilene,
a boulder on the post office lawn marks the end of the Chisholm
Trail.

A mule train, just like in 1870, leaves Spearman in the Texas
Panhandle every July 4. Women with it wear 1870-style dresses
(but have not had to make their own thread, cloth, and clothes),
and drive their own mules. Earl Riley, wagonmaster, pointed out
that the mule train goes to New Mexico and Colorado, parts of
which are cooler than Texas in July.

You can today be a temporary cowboy and ride the trail—
without actually having to drive cattle. You can follow the Old
Spanish Trail from Logansport, Louisiana, to Houston. At least a
few hundred cowboys—what the *Houston Post* calls "the real and
the drugstore kind"—make the trek each February. More than 600,
the *Post* said, recently started out in Logansport. About half of
them rode as far as the city limits, while the others went on at least
part of the way to Houston.

The Old Spanish Trail originally ran from the oldest city in the
United States, St. Augustine, Florida (established by the Spaniards
in 1565), through the locations of Mobile, Alabama; New Orleans;
Houston, San Antonio, El Paso; Tucson and Phoenix; to San
Diego, California (its coast was first discovered by European man,
Spain's Juan Rodríguez Cabrillo, on September 28, 1542). Running
along the southern border of today's United States, the Old Spanish Trail passes through the parts of the United States first settled
by European man. And the parts where he first drove cattle.

At Johnson City, Texas, near the Pedernales River, you can visit the working ranch of former President Lyndon Baines Johnson. You can see the small country school that Johnson attended, as well as restorations of his grandfather's corrals, barns, and blacksmith shop. Johnson's grandfather and a great-uncle drove thousands of cattle to Abilene, Kansas, in 1870.

At Abilene itself, you can see Old Abilene Town, reconstructed as it was in the days of the Long Trail, with the Merchants Hotel, the Alamo Saloon, boardwalks, hitching posts, and the depot of the Kansas Pacific.

Dodge City, Kansas, has a gun collection, and a reconstruction of Front Street with the Long Branch Saloon, the Rath and Wright General Store, and the Beatty and Kelly Restaurant. In summer, gunfights are staged every night in front of the Long Branch Saloon.

Dodge City's most unusual exhibit: At Boot Hill, an open grave.

The 1872 Cow Town of Wichita, Kansas, has been restored, with Munger House, a hotel built in 1869 by D. W. Munger; a Wells Fargo express, the Cannon Ball Stage Line office, a handcar in front of the depot, the general store, the city jail, the first log house, the first church, and the sod-roofed school.

At Stamford, Texas, each July 4 there is held the Texas Cowboy Reunion and Western Art show, with chuck wagons serving food and over three hundred cowboys in the world's biggest amateur rodeo.

You can, every year, join twelve million spectators in four provinces of Canada and in the United States, who attend over a thousand rodeos. The 3,400 cowboys in them, most of them members of the Rodeo Cowboys Association, ride bulls, ride broncos with saddles, ride broncos bareback, and rope calves. The cowboys compete for $41 million in prizes. A hazard for them, as it was for riders on the Long Trail, is broken bones. The rodeos start, as did the first roundups, in Texas in the spring—January and February—in San Antonio, Houston, and Fort Worth. The rodeos progress northward till in July they reach Cheyenne, Wyoming, and Calgary, Alberta, Canada (the Calgary Stampede), and in September the Pendleton Roundup, Oregon.

In a dozen states in the 1970s, rodeos are an intercollegiate sport. An all-girl rodeo is held each summer in Duncan, Oklahoma.

Each summer at the Palo Duro Canyon State Park you can see a cowboys-and-Indians show complete with thunder and lightning so real that audiences duck for cover.

At Ennis, Texas, in April, you can take the trail through blue-bonnets.

Emerson Hough (1857–1923), an Iowan, the author of *The Covered Wagon*, also wrote *The Story of the Cowboy* (1897), and about the cowboy in *North of '36* and in historical novels. Eugene Manlove Rhodes (1869–1934), a Nebraskan, was a cowboy in New Mexico and author of the poem, "The Hired Man on Horseback," considered the outstanding poem about the cowboy. A *Saturday Evening Post* writer, Rhodes also wrote fourteen novels and short stories about the cowboy and/or the people the cowboy knew. His books include *Good Men and True* (1910) and *Once in the Saddle* (1927). His books, says the *Oxford Companion to American Literature*, "are considered to be among the best literary interpretations of cowboy life. His subject was consistently the romance of the cattle industry during the late 19th century." His accuracy places his books above most Western tales. Owen Wister (1860–1938), a Pennsylvanian, wrote of the cattle country. Perhaps his most famous book, *The Virginian* is about the Wyoming cowboys during the Long Trail era, the 1870s and 1880s. In the book, the Virginian is a cowboy who woos and wins a schoolteacher. A sentence from the book: "When you call me that, smile!"

The Amon Carter Museum of Western Art, Fort Worth, contains paintings, drawings, and sculpture by Charles Marion Russell. Many are shown and described in a book by Frederic A. Renner. Artist Russell's bronzes include "The Texas Steer," a saddled cow pony, and wolves. His artwork includes a wax rattlesnake, coiled—the very one that Russell used to slip up beside the elbow of a cowboy at a bar. The Amon Carter Museum also has paintings by Frederic Remington, a Yale student who in 1879 played football against Princeton with Walter Camp, and then went west to paint. A book on the Frederic Remington paintings in the museum is by Peter H. Hessrick. The museum has also published a book by Gordon Hendricks on another Western artist, Albert Bierstadt.

Another cowboy artist was Joe de Yong (Joe D. Young). A sort of Grandma Moses of the longhorns and cattle-trail days was Clara McDonald Williamson, that is, a primitive painter of barber-shops, one-room schoolhouses, harvest hands at dinner—and the longhorns. Her work may be seen at the Amon Carter Museum. Other museums that have works of these and other Western artists are, at Tulsa, Oklahoma, the Thomas Gilcrease Institute of American History and Art; at Houston, the Museum of Fine Arts; at Ogdensburg, New York, the Remington Memorial Museum; at Great Falls, Montana, the C. M. Russell Gallery; at El Dorado, Kansas, the Warren Hall Coutts III Memorial Gallery; and, in the Buffalo Bill Historical Center at Cody, Wyoming, the Whitney Gallery of Western Art.

An unusual collection includes the sketches and paintings of a native artist of the Texas Panhandle, Harold Dow Bugbee, a man who set out at the end of the Long Trail days to record as much of it as possible in pen and ink and in paintings. His work may be seen in the Panhandle-Plains Historical Museum, in the country where Charles Goodnight ranched, at Canyon, Texas. Some photographs of dugouts, chuck wagons, cattle herds belong to the Crosbyton, Texas, Crosby County Pioneer Memorial Museum & Civic Center.

Two photographers who recorded the cowboys were Erwin Smith, who worked on Texas ranches as the century turned, and whose pictures now are in the Library of Congress, and Charles J. Belden, who began to picture the cowboys in Wyoming about 1907. Other photographs may be seen at the historical societies of many of the states of the Long Trail, in particular Oklahoma, Kansas, and North Dakota.

Some artists are at work today recording the Long Trail. At Lindsborg, Kansas, Frank W. Reese, Sr., is an unusual kind. By profession a welder, he repairs farm implements. His hobby is sculpture in steel. Working from photographs sent him by the Cowboy Hall of Fame, he fashioned a steel longhorn steer. He has made a buffalo, a horse, and an elk. His animals are small, about a foot high, accurate in detail, and are made of cold-rolled steel that is shaped by the arcs of his acetylene and electric cutting torches.

At Fort Hays Kansas State Teachers College, Pete F. (Fritz) Felten, Jr., studied art, and today he is a sculptor in Indiana limestone, Kansas limestone, Colorado yule marble, Vermont blue marble, Texas limestone, fence-post limestone, alabaster, or Carthage marble. His subjects: a buffalo (life-size), a black Angus bull, a bust of Buffalo Bill, and an Indiana limestone statue, entitled "Early Settler," of the father of the farmer's daughter who married the cowboy.

The National Cowboy Hall of Fame and Western Heritage Center is at Oklahoma City. The museum includes the National Rodeo Hall of Fame. Near the foot of Persimmon Hill, on which the museum is located, there was a branch of the Chisholm Trail.

Conceived by Chester A. Reynolds, a Kansas City manufacturer, when he visited the Will Rogers Memorial in Claremore, Oklahoma, the Cowboy Hall of Fame opened in 1965. It is sponsored by people of seventeen Western states, and it attracts millions of visitors to its displays of great Western art, listed by the museum as by Frederic Remington, Charles Schreyvogel, Thomas Moran, Henry Farny, William Leigh, Irving Couse, Frank Tenney Johnson, Alfred Jacob Miller, Joseph Sharp, Carl Rungius, Albert Bierstadt, Thomas Hill, and Nicolai Fechin and others. The Hall of Fame also shows exhibits about cattlemen, range cowboys and rodeo cowboys, and about homesteaders (and the farmer's daughter), Indians, soldiers, and other Western pioneers. A major exhibit is James Earle Fraser's "End of the Trail": a statue of a defeated Indian warrior slumping on his pony. The museum labels it "the west's most famous statue." Fraser sculpted with his wife, Laura Gardin Fraser.

Another major exhibit: the original model for a coin, a nickel, that had a buffalo on one side and the head of an Indian on the other. Still other exhibits: saddles, spurs, and a chuck wagon.

The men named to the Cowboy Hall of Fame include John Warne Gates (the barbed-wire salesman), Charles Goodnight, Sam Houston, Richard King (the King Ranch), John W. Iliff (the early Colorado rancher), Edward Creighton (a rancher who also built the first transcontinental telegraph line), John S. Chisum, Charles F. Colcord, Stephen F. Austin (the colonizer of Texas), Mifflin Kenedy, Oliver Loving, and William F. (Buffalo Bill) Cody.

You can sit and watch a theater production that, on a huge

relief map of the United States, shows in moving lights the trail of the Spaniard Coronado (the first European in much of the Long Trail country), the covered-wagon routes, and the Long Trail and its branches and the railroads that came out to meet it.

Indian City, U.S.A.—Andarko, Oklahoma, southwest of Oklahoma City—has the Southern Plains Indian Museum and the National Hall of Fame for Famous American Indians. Among those named to the Hall of Fame: Sacagawea, the Bird Woman, who was a Shoshone guide of the Lewis and Clark expedition.

There is at Smith Center, Kansas, the one-room home—a log cabin—of the man who wrote "A Home on the Range," Dr. Brewster M. Higley.

Three miles northwest of Lindsborg, Kansas, you can visit a spot where Coronado is believed to have camped.

At Oberlin, Kansas, a monument commemorates the last Indian raid in Kansas—in 1878, by the Cheyennes.

At Atchison, a monument commemorates the beginning of the Santa Fe Railway. In a number of midcontinent towns there stand as monuments actual steam locomotives—the first mechanical transportation that replaced the horse.

In San Antonio, Texas, there is the Witte Museum, with the Pioneer Memorial Building devoted to the Texas Rangers, Texas Pioneers, and the Old Time Trail Drivers Association.

In San Antonio, for three days every April, citizens celebrate the Battle of San Jacinto, which avenged the killing to the last man of the defenders of the Alamo. You can visit the Alamo while you're in San Antonio. The San Antonio fiesta includes Mexican food and customs: tamales and tacos and hot buttered corn; singing mariachis; and cracking on people's heads decorated eggshells filled with confetti.

The fiesta includes the landings of Columbus—which brought to the New World longhorns and mustangs, and which also brought to the New World European man. The fiesta also includes the landing on the moon.

At Houston, there is a horseback statue of Sam Houston, the man who won the battle of San Jacinto, and so helped win the West and much of the Long Trail country. The statue stands in front of the Warwick Hotel and the Houston Museum of Fine Arts, near Rice University and the Houston Medical Center, in the United States' sixth largest city. One of the statue's hands points to a place beyond the horizon: the San Jacinto battleground.

At Huntsville, Texas, there is the Sam Houston Memorial Museum. At Waco, the Fort Fisher Texas Ranger Museum. At Del Rio, the Judge Roy Bean Museum. At Bandera, the Frontier Texas Museum.

Abilene, west of Fort Worth, each October has the International Cowboy Campfire Cook-off.

Gun collections are pervasive as ticks in the bad old days. Texas A & M University has one. There is a fine one in Kansas' Ottawa Historical Society Museum.

At Bonner Springs, Kansas, the story of the homesteader, his wife and daughter, and how farmers replaced cattle drives as wheat replaced grass, is told in the Agricultural Hall of Fame and National Center.

Across a golf course at Wellington, Kansas, is perhaps one of the most impressive memorials of the cowboys and the longhorns. Here you can see, crossing the course, tracks made by the animals driven up the Long Trail, still visible after a hundred years.

In the land of the Long Trail, today people remember.

Annotated bibliography

Here are the principal books I have used for information and as references for *The Long Trail*. Other useful reading lists: starting on page 677 of *Texas: A Guide to the Lone Star State* (Federal Writers' Project, 1940) and starting on page 265 of Wayne Gard's *The Chisholm Trail*.

Abbott, E. C. (Teddy Blue), and Smith, Helena Huntington. *We Pointed Them North.* New York: Farrar & Rinehart, Inc., 1939. Later reprinted—Norman: University of Oklahoma Press. Abbott was a cowboy; this tells of his life on the trail, and some of my stories about Abbott are from this book.

Adams, Andy. *The Log of a Cowboy.* Boston: Houghton Mifflin Company, in 1903. Adams, a Texas cowboy from Indiana, in this semiautobiographical novel tells of a Long Trail drive from Texas to Montana, and describes a night of celebration in Dodge City, Kansas. Adams also wrote *The Outlet* (1905), a novel of cowboys and railroads; *Cattle Brands* (1906), short stories; and *Reed Anthony, Cowman,* a biography (1907) about a Texas cowman out of the Confederate army.

Boorstin, Daniel J. *The Americans: The Democratic Experience.* New York: Random House, Inc., 1973. Has a section on the Long Trail and the cattle business and their effects on the American people.

Botkin, Benjamin Albert. *A Treasury of American Folklore.* New York: Crown Publishers, Inc., 1944. 930 pages. Index. Botkin in his footnotes lists many little-known source books about the West and Western ways.

Botkin, Benjamin Albert. *A Treasury of Western Folklore*. New York: Crown Publishers, Inc., 1951. 806 pages. Index.

Bowie, Alexander. "The Cow Walks Neatly." *Southwest Review,* winter 1959. Texas in 1876.

Branch, Douglas. *The Cowboy and His Interpreters*. Illustrated by Will James, Joe D. Young, and Charles M. Russell. New York: D. Appleton & Company, Inc., 1926. Mentioned by *Columbia Encyclopedia*, page 435.

Calder, William A. "There Really Is a Roadrunner." *Natural History,* November 1968. This magazine is published by the American Museum of Natural History, New York City.

The Columbia Encyclopedia. New York: Columbia University Press, 1935. A one-volume encyclopedia.

Costello, David F. *The Prairie World*. New York: Thomas Y. Crowell Company, 1969. Available at Mercantile Library, New York City. Plants and animals of the grassland sea.

Crompton, John. *Snake Lore*. Garden City, N.Y.: Doubleday & Company, Inc., 1964.

Dale, Edward Everett. *Cow Country*. Norman: University of Oklahoma Press, 1942—reprinted 1965. Born in Keller, Texas, the University of Oklahoma history professor also wrote (with James Shannon Buchanan) *A History of Oklahoma in* 1924.

Dobie, J. Frank. *Cow People*. Boston: Little, Brown and Company, 1964. Mentions many books helpful on the subject of the Long Trail, and includes material on Charles Goodnight.

Dobie, J. Frank. *The Longhorns*. Boston: Little, Brown and Company, 1941. The cattle and life on the range.

Dobie, J. Frank. *The Mustangs*. Boston: Little, Brown and Company, 1952. A companion volume to Dobie's *The Longhorns*.

Dobie, J. Frank. *Tales of Old-time Texas*. Tells of everything from Bowie knives to how cowboys sang to Sam Bass' cattle.

Dobie, J. Frank. *Up the Trail from Texas*. New York: Random House, Inc., 1955. A summary of the cattle trail.

Dykstra, Robert T. *The Cattle Towns*. New York: Alfred A. Knopf, Inc., 1968. Abilene, Ellsworth, Wichita, Dodge City, and Caldwell, 1867 to 1885.

Ebbutt, Percy G. *Emigrant Life in Kansas*. London: Sonnenschein and Co., 1886.

Federal Writers' Project. *Texas: A Guide to the Lone Star State*. Sponsored by the Texas State Highway Commission. New York: Hastings House, 1940. Illustrated. 718 pages. Index. This WPA guide has a Selected Reading List full of books about Texas history.

Gabriel, Ralph Henry (editor). *The Pageant of America*. New Haven: Yale University Press, 1926. Ten volumes. Volume III, Chapter 8: Cattleman and Nester.

Gard, Wayne. *The Chisholm Trail*. Norman: University of Oklahoma Press, 1954. One of the best books on the cattle drives to Kansas. Contains an excellent and detailed bibliography.

Grant, Bruce. *The Cowboy Encyclopedia*. Chicago: Rand McNally & Company, 1951. Includes a bibliography arranged by subject and drawings.

Hughes, Thomas (editor). *G.T.T.—Gone to Texas, Letters from Our Boys*. New York: Macmillan and Co., 1884. 228 pages. Tales of young men—William (Willy), Gerard, and Henry Hughes—who went out to Texas from Great Britain in the 1870s and 1880s. A copy is in the New York Society Library.

Hunter, J. Marvin (editor). *The Trail Drivers of Texas*. Nashville, Tenn.: The Cokesbury Press, 1925. (Volume I, 1920; Volume II, 1922; two volumes in one, 1925.) Compiled and edited by Hunter; published under the direction of George W. Saunders, President of the Old Time Trail Drivers Association. I found it in the Roland Tisinger Memorial Library, Shepherd, Texas; and in the Mechanics Institute Library, New York City. It is both the principal source of material for this book, and the principal source of checking any facts or information that may be reported differently elsewhere. It is over one thousand pages long, is not in chronological order, and has no index. Yet it is the actual experiences of hundreds of cowboys, in their own words.

Illustrated Catalogue of the Masterpieces of the International Exhibition 1876. Philadelphia: Gebbie & Barrie, Publishers, 1876. Three volumes, about four hundred pages each, basically illustrated with steel engravings. My main source for information on the world's fair that celebrated the 100th anniversary of the United States, and that included so many exhibits of machines that were ending the world of horse-drawn man.

Kansas! An illustrated quarterly magazine. Kansas Economic Development Commission, State Office Building, Topeka, Kansas 66612. Many articles bear on the cattle trails. In the second issue of 1964 there is an article on George Grant and his Angus bulls. The third issue of 1970, the geologic issue, contains information on the terrain.

Klauber, Laurence M. *Rattlesnakes: Their Habits, Life Histories, and Influence on Mankind*. Berkeley: University of California Press, 1958, 1973. Also see *Scientific American*, March 1973, page 126.

Le May, Alan. *The Searchers*. New York: Harper & Brothers, 1954. About the Texas frontier.

Lesly, Philip, and the Crane Company: *Everything and the Kitchen Sink*. New York: Farrar, Straus, & Cudahy, Inc., 1955. 160 pages. Illustrated. How the century of machines and factories that largely followed the cowboys contributed to good living for all men. One of the best books on how the standard of living was raised by, among others, the children of the cowboy and the farmer's daughter.

Olmsted, Frederick Law. *A Journey through Texas.* New York: Burt Franklin. Originally published 1860. Reprinted 1969. 516 pages. No index. A copy is in the New York Society Library. Texas before the War Between the States. Includes information on the Old Spanish Trail, and the Spaniards' march from Mexico to Kansas. Olmsted was a New York architect and landscape artist.

Oppenheimer, Harold L. *Cowboy Arithmetic.* Danville, Ill.: The Interstate Printers & Publishers, Inc., 1961.

Porterfield, Bill. *LBJ Country.* Garden City, N.Y.: Doubleday & Company, Inc., 1965. A description of the section of Texas where Lyndon Baines Johnson was born, lived, and died.

Rhodes, Eugene Manlove. *Pasó por aqui.*

Rhodes, Eugene Manlove. *The Rhodes Reader.* Stories of virgins, villains, and varmints by Eugene Manlove Rhodes. Selected by W. H. Hutchinson. Norman: University of Oklahoma Press.

Rhodes, Eugene Manlove. *Sunset Land.* A paperback. New York: Dell Publishing Co., Inc. Three novels, originally published by Houghton Mifflin Company, Boston; and in the *Saturday Evening Post,* the Curtis Publishing Company, Philadelphia. The novels are *Good Men and True, Branford of Rainbow Range (The Little Eohippus),* and *The Trusty Knaves.*

Rister, Carl Coke. *Oil! Titan of the Southwest.* Norman: University of Oklahoma Press, 1949.

Sackett, Samuel J. *Cowboys and the Songs They Sang.* New York: William R. Scott, Inc., 1967. Words and music. Has its own bibliography at the back.

Sandburg, Carl. *The American Songbag.* New York: Harcourt, Brace and Company, Inc., 1927. Words and music to American pioneer songs, including Mexican and cowboy songs.

Stowers, Carlton. "From Charlie Goodnight to Computers on the Range." Today's feed-lot fattening of cattle. In the May 28, 1974, Sunday newspaper supplement *Scene,* sent to me by Mrs. Ben Grimes.

Texas: A Guide to the Lone Star State. See Federal Writers' Project.

Texas Almanac and State Industrial Guide, 1947–48. Published by A. H. Belo Corporation and the *Dallas Morning News.* An encyclopedia of Texas. 608 pages. Illustrations. Index.

Thorp, N. Howard (Jack). *Songs of the Cowboys.* Boston: Houghton Mifflin Company, 1921. Another edition with variants, commentary, notes, and lexicon by Austin E. and Alta S. Fife. Music editor, Naunie Gardner. New York: Clarkson N. Potter, Inc., Publisher, 1966. The original collection of cowboy songs.

U.S. Department of Agriculture. *Food for Us All, The Yearbook of Agriculture,* 1969. Washington: U.S. Government Printing Office.

U.S. Department of Agriculture. *Grass, The Yearbook of Agriculture,* 1948. Washington: U.S. Government Printing Office. Encyclopedic information on grass. Other Department of Agriculture yearbooks cover much about cattle.

U.S. Department of Agriculture. *Keeping Livestock Healthy, The Yearbook of Agriculture,* 1942. Washington: U.S. Government Printing Office.

U.S. Department of the Interior, Fish and Wildlife Service. "Migration of Birds." Circular 16. By Frederick C. Lincoln, biologist. Illustrated by Bob Hines.

U.S. Department of the Interior, National Park Service. *Prospector, Cowhand, and Sodbuster.* Washington: U.S. Government Printing Office, 1967. Historic places associated with mining, ranching, and farming frontiers of the trans-Mississippi West. Illustrated with photographs, maps, and a Charles M. Russell oil painting in color.

Vielé, Mrs. *Following the Drum: A Glimpse of Frontier Life.* New York: Rudd & Carleton, 1858. (Mrs. Vielé's first name is not given on the title page, but the book was copyrighted by Egbert L. Vielé.) 256 pages. Life with the army as Texas and the West were won.

Webb, Walter Prescott. *1888–1963: The Great Frontier.* Boston: Houghton Mifflin Company, 1952.

Webb, Walter Prescott. *The Great Plains.* Originally published in Boston in two volumes by Ginn and Company, 1931. Paperback edition by Grosset & Dunlap, Inc., New York. A history of the Great Plains and how they were settled by European man. Webb, born in Panola County, Texas (near Longview, Texas, and Shreveport, Louisiana), was a history professor at the University of Texas and editor of the *Southwestern Historical Quarterly.* He discusses the climate, geography, fencing, and water (or lack of it) on the Great Plains.

Webb, Walter Prescott. *The Texas Rangers.* Boston: Houghton Mifflin Company, 1935. New edition: Austin: University of Texas Press, 1965. Foreword by Lyndon B. Johnson.

Wellman, Paul I. *Glory, God and Gold.* New York: Doubleday & Company, Inc., 1954.

Index

Abbott, E. C. (Teddy Blue), 118, 141, 159, 162, 184, 232, 257, 271
Abbott, J. S., 275
Aberdeen Angus, 256, 303
Abilene, Kansas, 53, 61–64, 70, 144, 320
Ackermann, C. W., 159, 160
Adair, John G., 175, 235, 312
Adams, a trail boss, 138
Adams, Ramon F., 200
Adams, Robert, 220
Adams, William, 220
Agricultural Hall of Fame, 325
Aiken, 47
Alamo, 19, 21, 42–43, 324
Alarcón, Don Martín de, 13
Alkali, 60, 257
Allen, rancher, 41
Allen, Horatio, 17
Altman, Emma, 205, 274
Amarillo, Texas, 177
American Library Association, 195
Anderson, L. B., 37, 112–113, 122, 137, 144, 159, 211, 245–247
Animals, 167, 179–187
  imported, 87
Anthrax, 80
Apollo landings, 311
Armadillo, 182, 318
Armour, P. D., 43

Arthur, Chester A., Pres., 232
Auroch, 16
Austin, Texas, 15
Austin, Moses, 15
Austin, Stephen F., 15, 323
Automobile, 191, 229, 291–292

Baldwin Locomotive Works, 191
Baker, Bryant, 317
Bandera Pass, 248
Banks, Marcus, 149
Barbed wire, 167, 168, 252, 253, 255, 259, 270, 271, 318–319
Barnes, Will C., 303
Barsley, Charlie, 112
Bass, Sam, 130
Bassett, Julian M., 220
Bate, John L., 236
Bates, W. H., 196
Bats, 181
Baylor, Tom, 113
Baylor Univ., 28, 43, 273, 304
Beals, David T., 196
Bean, Roy, Judge, 292
Becholdt, Frederick R., 27
Beckwith, John, 219
Beef, food value of, 299–300
Bees, 132
Belden, Charles J., 322

Bell, W. C., 47
Belli, Nicholas, Padre, 102
Bennett, William J., 311
Benz, Karl, 191, 229
Berry, John, 47
Bicycle, 136, 190, 191, 229
Bierstadt, Albert, 322, 323
Big Tex, 317
Billy the Kid, 237–239
Birds, 128, 209–216
Black, Gus, 244, 311
Black Kettle National Grassland, 318
Blacksmith, 104
Blakely, Bassett, 219
Blasingame, Ike, 293–294
Blocker, owners, 196
Blocker, Ab, 279
Blocker, Bill, 112
Blocker, John, 112, 251, 252, 253
Blue, Teddy: See Abbott, E. C.
Bluebonnets, 93, 107
Boatright, L. S., 116
Bonney, Wm.: See Billy the Kid
Bonnie Blue flag, 23
Boorstin, Daniel J., 299
Boot Hill, 170, 310, 320
Borden, A. P., 219
Borden, Gail, 20, 33
Borroum, B. A., 44, 136
Bowie, James, 20, 103
Bowie, Robert, 20, 103
Bowie knife, 20, 21, 103, 130, 217
Boyce, Albert G., 42, 279
Boyce brothers, 254
Bradley, William, 238
Brahmas, 87, 192, 303
Branding, 38, 99
Brands, 85
Branner, Nath, 51
Brazel, Wayne, 238
Breland, Osmond P., 211
Brennan, cowman, 203
Briscoe, Comrade, 162
Brite, L. C., 220
Brite, S. B., 100
Brite, W. T., 90, 310–311
Britton, A. M., 203
Broadbent, C. S., 106, 307
Brock, George W., 204, 270
Brunson, Dave, 270
Brunson, W. H., 270
Bryan, John Pat, 160
Buckner, Joe, 113
Buffalo, 13, 71, 105, 135, 253, 318
    bred with cattle, 176, 195
    saved, 177
    numbers today, 318
    swarm, 120, 121, 136, 176–177, 206
Buffalo flies, 80
Bugbee, Thomas A., 196
Bugbee, Harold Dow, 322
Bullfrog, 181
Bullock, William A., 120

Burge, Connie, 273
Burkett, W. J., 170
Burks, Amanda, 149, 150, 151, 308, 313
Burks, Jim, 153
Burks, W. F., 149–151, 308, 313
Burleson, Ed, 46, 47
Burleson, John, 90
Burnett, S. B., 137
Burro, 182
Burrows, G. O., 118
Bush, Governor, 244, 311
Butler, Pleasant B., 121
Byler, E. P., 66, 107, 121, 146, 153
Byler, Frank, 254
Byler, Jim, 66, 121, 143, 146

Cabrillo, Juan R., 319
Cactus, 100, 159
Caddo National Grassland, 318
Calamity Jane, 232
Calgary, Canada, 81, 108, 233
Callen, James, 220
Camel, 40
Cameron, Ewen, 27
Camp, Walter, 321
Campbell, Barbecue, 279
Campbell, Billy, 71
Campbell, H. H., 219
Campion, William James, 248
Capo de Vino Ranch, 304
Capt, Arnold W., 137
Caraval, A. F., 271
Carlyle, Jimmy, 237–238
Carroll, Jake, 71
Caspares, Alex, 279
Catfish, 35, 89, 292
Cather, Willa, 32
Cattalo, 176, 195
Cattle, crossbreeding, 86, 87, 176, 195
    numbers today, 300
    numbers trailed, 308
    singing to, 129 ff
Cattle thieves, 249–250
Chamberlain, Henrietta M., 86–87
Chapman, Joe, 90, 91, 92
Chaparral cock, 210
Childers, T. A., 270
Chisholm, Jesse, 41, 54, 75–78, 156
Chisum, John, 77, 187, 197, 323
Choate, Monroe, 44
Chuckwagon, 50–51, 114, 127
Clark, Red, 169
Clark Thread Company, 192
Clay, John, Jr., 234
Clemens, Samuel Langhorne, 120
Clocks, 139, 192, 253
Cloth, woven at home, 89
Clothes of 1870s, 91
Coble, W. T., 203
Cody, Arta, 65
Cody, Wm. F. (Buffalo Bill), 65, 245, 323
Coffee, Rich, 41
Coggin, 219

Coggin, M. J., 195
Coggin, S. R., 195
Colcord, Charley, 245, 309, 323
Colt, Samuel, 26–29, 166
Colt, six-shooters, 15 ff, 82, 163 ff, 216–229, 251, 257
Columbus, Christopher, 11, 39, 116, 288, 324
Combs, D. S., 43, 44, 138, 173, 206
Connell, W. E., 270
Conner, John B., 128, 254
Cook, the life of the, 125–259
Cook, Harold J., 206
Cook, James, 206
Cook, Margaret, 206
Cooper, Peter, 17, 190
Cope, Edward D., 135
Cornelius, F., 118
Cornell University, 281
Coronado, Francisco, 13, 324
Corpus Christi, Texas, 12, 85
Cortez, Hernando, 12, 39, 128
Cotulla, Joseph, 90
Courley, Mrs. S. W. (Mrs. Branch Isbell), 275
Course, Irving, 323
Cowboys:
    clothing evolves, 251
    number, 309
    origin of name, 27
Cowden, Buck, 270
Cowden, Fred, 270
Cowden, George E., 270
Cowden, John M., 270
Cowden, W. H., 270
Cowley, J. M., 80
Cowpoke, 265
Cowpuncher, 265
Cox, J. P., 138
Cox, Mary Kate (Mrs. Mary Kate Cruze), 151 ff
Coyotes, 180
Craig, Hiram, 91, 95–97, 111, 132, 139, 140, 162, 187, 244, 278, 296
Craig, John, 91, 95
Craig, Mrs. John (Caroline), 291
Craig, Walter A., 278
Creighton, Edward, 230, 323
Cresswell, Hank V., 196
Crockett, David (Davy), 14, 19
Crompton, John, 184
Cross Timbers National Grassland, 318
Crossley, Fannie M., 153
Crosson, George, 203
Crowley, Ed, 270
Crowley, Frank, 270
Crowley, W. E., 198
Cruze, Joseph, 152, 153
Cruze, Mary Kate (Mrs. Joseph Cruze), 151–153
Cude, W. F., 22, 66, 80, 95, 127
Cureton, W. E., 108, 157
Curtice, Dr. Cooper, 283
Custer, George A., Gen., 65, 135, 171, 318
Custer, J. M., 315

Daggett & Hatcher, store, 121

Daimler, Gottlieb, 191, 229
Dale, Edward Everett, 105, 107, 231, 233
Dallas Public Library, 273
Dalton, Marcus L., 121, 122, 310
Dalton, Robert Samuel, 310
Dam, stone, 196
Dancing, 153
Daugherty, G. W., 46
Daugherty, James M., 2–5, 44, 246, 313
Davis, John, 33
Davis, J. H. P., 220
Dawson, John, 175, 219
Day, Dock, 138
De Long, G. W., 42
De Vaca, Cabeza, 12, 13
Deer, red, 180
Deets, Louis, 112
Denim (cloth), 116
Dickerson, Mrs. Susanna, 21
Dillon, 227
Dillon Ranch, 224
Dinosaurs, 135
Disease, cholera, 80
Diseases, Gulf Coast, 35
Doan, C. F., 104, 277
Doan's Crossing, 104
Doan's Store, 103–104, 172 , 277
Dobbins, John, 3, 5
Dobie, J. Frank, 304 , 312
Dobie, J. M., 220
Dobie, Jim, 115–116, 254
Dodge City, Kansas, 169–170, 309
Dogs, Mexican hairless, 181
Donald Lawson & Co., 71
Downie, Charles, 270
Drake, Ben, 136, 196, 220
Driscoll, a bad man, 238–239
Driscoll, Jerry, 220
Driscoll, Robert, 220
Drovers' Cottage, 63, 70, 145
Dun and Bradstreet, 309
Dunn, A. W., 270
Dunraven, Lord, 234
Dunsmore, Lord, 234
Durham cattle, 86, 256
Dyer, Leigh, 203

Eads, S. W., 80
Earp, Wyatt, 165
Edison, Thomas A., 219, 269
Eisenhower, Dwight David, 4, 103
Ellison, J. F., Jr., 8, 172
Ellison, Jim, Col., 220, 245
Elwood, I. L., 168, 270
El Paso, Texas, 13
English, Bud, 46, 47
English, Levi, 46
Espuela Land & Cattle Company, Ltd., 204, 235
Estebán, Juan, 248
Eustace, A. N., 315
Eustace, George, 80
Evans, George W., 220

Evans, Jesse, 237
Evans, Oliver, 14–15, 190

Fant, Dillard R., Col., 251
Farmer, R. C., 4
Farmers, Kansas, 144
Farny, Henry, 323
Farris, Jeff D., 245
Faver, Milton, 32
Fechin, Nicolai, 323
Felten, Pete F. (Fritz), 323
Fences, first, 86
Fest, Henry, 91, 118
Field, Cyrus W., 1, 5
Fielder, W. C., 132, 156, 196–197
Figure 2 ranch, 246
Fish, 35, 89
Fitch, John, 190
Fitzhenry, John, 42, 94, 210
Flags, six, over Texas, 338
Food, bread, flour, 90
Food on trail, 89, 125 ff
Football, first game, 79
Forest, brothers, 90
Fort Niobrara National Wildlife Refuge, 303
Forth Worth, Texas, 102–103, 119, 121, 187
Foster, Stephen Collins, 130–131
Foster, W. B., 157, 159
Fowler, Dr. Stewart H., 304, 305
Fox, Oscar J., 312
Frank, Joseph, 234
Franks, L. A., 46, 47
Fraser, James Earle, 323
Frémont, John C., 61
French, C. C., 221
Fulton, Robert, 190

Gage, A. S., 270
Gage, Robert Merrill, 317
Galveston flood of 1900, 291
Game animals, 89
Garay, Francisco, 12
Gardner, D. W., 119
Garner, James Marion, 118, 139
Garrett, Pat, 237–238
Gates, John Warne, 167–168, 323
Gerdes, George, 254, 255
Geronimo, 252
Glenn, Jones, 248
Glidden, Joseph Farwell, 167–168, 270
Godwin, D. W., 119, 220
Godwin, J. W., 119, 220
Goliad, Texas, 19
Goodnight, Charles, 41, 49–60, 76, 77, 118, 158,
    175–177, 185, 193, 195, 197, 230, 235,
    249, 250, 312, 313, 323
Gore, J. W., 145
Gore, Louisa, Mrs. Lou, 70, 145
Gore, Margaret, 70
Grant, Ulysses S., President, 31, 83
Grass, 107, 132, 317
Grasshoppers, 136
Gravis, Buck, 162

Gray, Mustang, 130
Greathouse, Bill, 80
Griffing, Thomas, 119
Gruene, H. D., 121
Guadalupe Hidalgo, treaty of, 32
Gunter Hotel, 203, 307
Gunter, Jot, 203
Gunter, Mumson & Summerfield, 203
Guthrie, A. B., Jr., 117
Guzman, Nuño de, 12

Hagenbeck, Carl, 192
Haley, Laurence, 279
Halff, M., 203
Hall, Asaph, 195
Hall, J. M., 204
Hall, W. S., 256
Halsell, John Glenn, 119
Hamer, Frank, 29
Hamilton, Mary, 170
Hankins, J. M., 66, 140
Hardeman, Bill, 80
Hardeman, W. B., 113
Hargus, Dr. J. W., 4, 130
Harmon, Al, 141
Harold Brothers, 196
Harrell, Monte, 82, 83
Harris, Leasial B., 195
Harris, Lee, 90
Hart, Jack, 313, 314
Harte, Bret, 120, 171, 172
Hartzo, Daniel, 95–96
Hastings, Frank, 219
Hatton, John, 303
Hawks, William E., 63
Haynes, John James, 201
Hazelwood, J. T., 45, 91, 92
Hazlett, H. H., 145
Head, R. G. (Dick), 64, 174
Heaton, Albert, 151–152
Henderson, J. D., 230, 231
Henderson, J. E., 119
Henderson, John W., 270
Hendricks, Gordon, 322
Henry rifle, 56
Herbert, Martin, 31
Herefords, 176, 193, 224, 256, 303
Hessrick, Peter H., 321
Heyl, Henry R., 120
Higley, Dr. Brewster M., 324
Hickok, James Butler (Wild Bill), 145, 165,
    171–172
Hicks, Dr. J. M., 311
Hicks, Mrs. Nettie S., 311
Higgins, Patillo, 291
Higgins, Thomas J., 289
Hill, George, 122
Hill, Thomas, 323
Hilliard, W. F. (Zeke), 196
Hindes, George F., 40, 118, 173
Hindman, George, 238
Hinnant, Lizzie, 153, 274
Hobart, T. D., 219

Hogs, javelinas or peccaries, 87, 89, 181
Hogs, razorbacks, 85, 182, 303
Holoway, Sam, 270
Holt, C. B., 270
Holt Live Stock Company, 261
Homer, Winslow, 171–172
Horned toad, 181
Horse, 39, 160–161, 294
Horse thieves, 96–97
Horses, cutting, 161–162
　trailed north, 139, 254
　total, 308
　wild, 130, 241–242
Horseless carriage, 292
Hough, Emerson, 321
Hough, Mrs. Jim, 38
Hough, Joe, 183
Houston Post, 319
Houston, R. A., 311
Houston, Sam, 20, 21, 217, 323, 324
Houston, Samuel Dunn, 223–227, 261–263
Howell, George, 66
Hudspeth, Claude, 112, 117
Huffmeyer, A., 186, 205
Hughes, 207–208
Hughes, Bill, 93
Hughes, Tim, 158, 182
Hughes, William E., 220
Hughes, Willy, 181, 186, 215
Humphries, J. R., 112
Hunter, J. M., 314
Hyatt, John Wesley, 65

Ikard, Bose, 51
Ikard, E. F., 135
Ikard, W. B., 135, 193
Iliff, J. W., 230, 231, 323
Indian City, U.S.A., 324
Indianola, Texas, 28
Indians:
　Cheyennes, 174, 324
　Choctaw, 75
　Apaches, 252
　Comanches, 26–27, 35, 46, 54–57, 83, 121,
　　139, 176
　in Oklahoma, 105 ff
　Osage, 67, 69, 137
　Pima, 81
　Plains, 25 ff.
　Sioux, 122, 174, 269
　Wichita, 76
Insects in Texas, 185
Iron horse, 16, 190, 191
Isbell, Branch, 112, 138, 153, 154, 205, 274,
　288, 308, 311, 313

JA Ranch, 175–177, 197–198, 235
J. B. Hunter & Company, 138
Jackman, Bill, 132, 207
Jackrabbit roped, 245
Jackson, Andrew, President, 26, 285
Jackson, J. D., 219
Jackson, J. W., 42

Jacobs, John, 292, 293
Jacobs, John G., 99, 100–101, 108, 129, 158, 310,
　314
James, Jesse, 130
Jenkins, D. J., 230
Jennings, Ira C., 312
Jennings, R. J., 160
Jersey cattle, 204, 256, 303
John, Rev. I. G., 236
Johns, H. W., 192
Johnson, Frank Tenney, 323
Johnson, Gus, 244
Johnson, J. Willis, 119
Johnson, Lyndon Baines, President, 320
Johnson, Tom, 71
Johnson, Virgil, 186, 205
Jones, A. C., 220
Jones, Andrew D., 40
Jones, C. J. (Buffalo), 195
Jones, W. W., 220
Juchereau, Louis, 13

Karatofsky, Jake, 145
Kaynaird, 2
Kendrick, John B., Senator, 303
Kenedy, Mifflin, Captain, 86, 87, 192, 252, 323
Kenedy Pasture Co., 252
Kentucky Derby, 136
Kepler, Johannes, 195
Keys, Ben, 3, 5
Kilburne, 282
Kilgore, Jesse M., 90
King, Frank M., 129
King Ranch, 85–88, 223, 283
King, Richard, Captain, 85–87, 192, 323
Kleberg, R. J., 87, 283
Kleberg, Robert J., Jr., 87
Koch, Robert, 80
Kokernot herd, 206
Kokernot, J. W., 270
Kokernot, L. W., 270
Krempkau, William B., 40
Kritzer, John S., 137
Krump, Walter, 293
Kuykendall, Abner, 15
Kuykendall, Joseph, 15
Kuykendall, Robert, 15

LIT Ranch, 197
LX Ranch, 235
La Salle, René Robert, 13
Lake Texoma, 103
Lamar, Mirabeau Buonaparte, 22
Lambert, English tenderfoot, 246
Landergin, John, 220
Landergin, Pat, 220
Lane, 4
Langtry, Lily, 293
Lasater, Ed C., 220
Lauderdale, Jasper (Bob), 139, 173, 174
Law enforcement, 94, 96
Lawhon, Luther A., 93, 309
Lead steers, 100, 187, 197

Lee, Phil C., 119
Lee, Robert E., 31, 42, 120
Lee, William, D., 269
Leigh, William, 323
León, Alonso de, Gen., 13
León, Martin, 16
León, Ponce de, 11
Lewis, Joe, 221
Lewis, W. J., 204, 269
Library Journal, 195
Lice, 121, 175
Light, John W., 247
Littlefield, George W., 197
Livingstone, Dr. David, 136
Lockhart, A. B. (Arch), 138
Locomotive, 16, 17, 107, 136, 190, 191, 204, 256, 324
Locusts, 136
Lone Star flag, 22
Long Trail, name, 109
    route, 101–109
Longhorn, description, 7–9, 27, 33, 99 ff
    for food, 91
    replaced, 193, 204, 303, 304
Longhorn, Warwick, 16
Lord & Nelson, 269
Louisiana State University, 304
Love, T. D., 220
Loving, Oliver, 41, 49–60, 76, 312, 314, 323
Lowe, J. G., 220
Lucas, Anthony, 291
Lucas, Cyrus, 220, 270
Lumm, 226
Lyndon B. Johnson State Park, 304
Lytle, John T., Captain, 141, 247–248
Lytle, William, 247

McAdams, Douglas, 118
McAdams, W. C., 42, 62
McAdams, William Carroll, Captain, 118
McCaleb, J. L., 66, 67, 68, 273
McCall, Jack, 171
McCormick, Peggy, 21
McCoy, Joseph G., 61–64, 131, 145
McCutcheon, Willis, 32
McDaniel, T. M., 247
McFaddin, A. M., 192, 220
McFaddin, James Alfred, Col., 32, 40, 41, 139, 192
McFaddin, Mrs. James Alfred, 192–193
McGehee, A. D., 173
McGill, H. F., 219
McGill, J. C., 219
MacKenzie, Murdo, 219, 234, 293
McNulty, R. L., 203
Machines, 21, 135, 136, 139, 190, 191, 192, 193, 219, 296
Magellan, Ferdinand, 214
Magiller, W. M., 244
Mann, Clay W., 270
Mann, William, 86
Marconi, Guglielmo, 269
Mars (planet), 311

Marsh, Othniel Charles, 135
Marsh, R. B., Capt., 176
Martin, Bob, 206
Martin, T. J., 270
Mason, Sarah (Sallie), Mrs. George Webb
    Slaughter, 21, 138
Massanet, Father Damién, 13
Massengale, W. R., 120
Masterson, R. B., 220
Matador Cattle Company, 204
Matador Land and Cattle Company, 204, 234, 236, 293
Matador Ranch, 197
Matthews, J. A., 135
Matthews, Joe B., 135
Matthews, Willie, 262–263
Maverick, Sam, 93
May, George, 118
Means, John Z., 220
Medicine, 126, 313
Meléndez, Pedro, 13
Menzies, S. J., 235
Merchant, C. W., 220
Merrill, J. W., 270
Meyers, George, 64
Meyers, John J., Col., 4, 61–64, 141, 174
Meyers, John G., 64
Meyers, R. E. L., 64
Meyers, S. E., 64
Miles City, Montana, 231
Miles, John D., Col., 83
Milk, condensed, 20, 33
Miller, Alfred Jacob, 323
Millett, 4
Millett, Alonzo, 112
Millett, Eugene, 112
Millett, Hie, 112
Mills, G. W., 118, 197, 220, 243, 253
Mississippi, Missouri rivers, 172
Mitchell family, 193
Mitchell, C. A., 80
Montgomery, J. W. (Bill), 122
Moody, 90
Mooney, Lump, 80
Moore, Tom, 224
Moran, Thomas, 323
Morris, Nelson, 270
Moses, Tad, 197
Mountain lion, 38, 187, 197
Mud puppy, 181
Munger, D. W., 320
Murchison, R. W., 119
Murphy, J. W., 174
Music, 130–131, 153, 277, 295
Mustang, 39
Muybridge, Edward, 203

Nacogdoches, Texas, 14
Nance, Berta Hart, 220
Nance, Jerry M., 196, 278
National Cowboy Hall of Fame and Western
    Heritage Center, 323
National Geographic Society, 186

National Hall of Fame for Famous American Indians, 324
National Rodeo Hall of Fame, 323
Nelson, O. H., Judge, 193
New Mexico, named, 13
Newman, J. F., 220
Newton, Kansas, 206
Niño, Pedro, 128
No Man's Land, 82, 106
Norfleet, J. Frank, 313
Morris, J. P., 219

O'Connor, Dennis M., 220
O'Connor, Thomas, 33
Oden, Dean, 46, 47
Oden, Sam, 160
Odum, Garland G., 255
Oil: See Petroleum
Old Trail Drivers Association, 307–309
Olds, R. E., 291
O'Leary, Mrs., 136
Olmsted, Frederick Law, 93, 165
Olson, rancher, 234
Oñate, Juan de, 13
Outhouses, first, 92
Owl, snowy, 259
Oxen, 41
Ozment, W. G., 81

Packing plants, 43, 299
Padre island, 12, 102
Palo Duro Canyon, 175
Panhandle of Texas, 175, 176, 312–313
Panhandle Stockmen's Association, 230
Paris, Texas, 77
Parker, Cynthia Ann, 176
Parker, Quanah, 176
Parks, W. C., 195
Parramore, J. H., 220
Pasteur, Louis, 80
Paul, rancher, 41
Paxton, Philip, 36, 38, 183
Pecos Bill, 217–218
Pecos River, 50, 54
Peel, Mrs. John I., 64
Peeler, Graves, 303, 304
Petroleum, 95, 136, 283, 291
Pettus, J. E., 15, 21
Phelps, Burt, 238–239
Pierce, A. R. (Shanghai), Col., 33, 66
Pilgrims, 12, 128
Piñeda, Alonson Alvarez, 12
Piper, Edward H., 31
Plankington, John, 43
Plants, 100–101, 107
Polk, James Knox, President, 28
Polley, Joseph H., 41
Pony Express, 230–231, 248, 292
Poole, J. A., 196
Pope, Albert A., 190
Porcupine, 182
Porter, Lake, 129
Porter, Andrew Jackson, 285–288

Potter, Jack, 146–147, 266–268
Potter, Joshua, 285
Prairie Cattle Company, 197, 235
Prairie dogs, 62, 179, 183
Prairie falcon, 318
Pryor, Ike, 207
Pucket, Dan, 66
Pulliam, M. B., 119
Pumphrey, J. B., 117

Quantrill, William Clarke, Capt., 4, 130

Rabbits, cottontail, 89
Railroad, first across U.S., 79
Rankin, T. L., 137
Rattlesnake, 60, 183
   meat of, 90
   roundup, 318
Read & O'Connor, 146
Red River, 4, 103, 105
Red River Crossing, 105, 277
Reese, Frank W., Sr., 322
Reeves, Jesse, 245
Refrigeration, 135, 137, 236, 258
Remington, Frederic, 321, 323
Renner, Frederic A., 321
Reynolds, Chester A., 323
Reynolds, D. A., 269
Reynolds, George T., 42, 53
Reynolds, W. D., 42
Rhodes, Eugene Manlove, 321
Rice University, 325
Richards, W. Q., 220
Richardson, Sid, 304
Richter, Conrad, 107
Richthofen, Walter, Baron von, 234
Riley, Crockett, 81
Riley, Earl, 319
Ríos, Domingo Terán los, 13
Rita Blanca National Grassland, 318
Rivers, Oklahoma, Kansas, 106
Roadrunner, 210–211
Robertson, A. B. (Sug), 135
Rodeo, 320–321
   first known, 245
Rodeo Cowboys Association, 320
Rodríguez, Augustín, Fray, 54
Roebling, John Augustus, 119
Roebuck, E. A. (Berry), 243
Roentgen, Wilhelm Conrad, 269
Rogers, Will, 294
Roosevelt, Theodore, 234, 260, 288, 295
Rose, Alfred, 269
Rose, Vincent, 269
Roundup, new event, 33, 37
Rountree, Count, 80
Rungius, Carl, 323
Rusk, W. G., 270
Russell, Charles Marion, 260, 321
Russell, Lee, 220
Russell, Majors, and Waddell, 41
Russell, R. R., 220
Rust, C. H., 91, 103, 106, 121, 187

Sacagawea, Indian woman, 324
Sackett, Samuel J., 200
St. Augustine, Florida, 13, 319
Salmon, Dr., 281–282
Samoa Islands, 203
San Jacinto, battle of, 21, 22, 32, 324
Sanford, H. B., 167, 270
Santa Anna, López de, Gen., 20, 21
Santa Gertrudis cattle, 87
Santa Gertrudis Ranch, 86
Saunders, George W., 66, 70, 101–106, 111, 143–147, 169, 246–248, 254, 265, 266, 268, 308, 309, 314
Saunders, Jack, 143
Saunders, Mat, 143
Sawmill, 21
Scharbauer, John, 270
Scheske, A. E., 89, 172
Schorp, Louis, 180
Schreiner, Charles, 247–248
Schreyvogel, Charles, 323
Scobey, Jim, 137
Scott, G. W., 278
Scott, Mary Elizabeth, 304
Scott, Walter B., 304
Scott, Winfield, 135
Sea turtles, 181
Shannon, J. M., 270
Shannon, W. M., 89, 90, 206, 207
Sharp, Joseph, 323
Sheep, 278
Shelby, a cowboy, 186–187
Shelter, 92
Shelton, John M., 220
Shipman, Daniel, 15
Sholes, Christopher L., 136
Shorthorn cattle, 86, 87, 176
Simpson, John N., 220
Siringo, Charles, 130
Slater, Damon, 81
Slaughter, Benjamin, 22, 90
Slaughter, C. C., Col., 162, 193, 219, 244, 269
Slaughter, Elizabeth, 312
Slaughter, George Webb, 20, 21, 138, 163, 164, 288
Slaughter, J. B., 270
Slaughter, John, 90, 138
Slaughter, John B., 195, 269
Slaughter, Minerva, 22
Slaughter, P. E., 198
Slaughter, William Baxter, 120–121, 253, 293, 312
Slaughter, William James, 22
Sleep, lack of, 113, 131, 146–147, 197
Slue-foot Sue, 217, 218
Smith, Dog Face, 268
Smith, Duncan, 235
Smith, Erasmus (Deaf), 21
Smith, Erwin, 322
Smith, Henry, provincial governor, 22
Smith, J. H., 80
Smith, Jedediah, 16
Smith, John, of Virginia, 12

Smith, McCord & Chandler, 63
Smith, Theobald, 281–284
Smithsonian magazine, 303
Snakes, 182 &c
Snell, David, 303, 304
Snyder, D. H., Col., 81, 100, 156, 270
Snyder, J. W., 81, 270
Social life, 93
Sod houses, 92, 317
Songs, western, published, 295
Southern Plains Indian Museum, 324
Spindletop, oil field, 283, 291
Squinch owls, 183
Stagecoach, Concord, 231
Stampedes, 3, 82, 140, 150, 158–160, 196, 206, 211, 278
Stanley, Henry M., 136
Steamboat, 85
Steen, George W., 66
Steer, 41, 201
Stetson, John B., 115
Stetson hat, 104, 115, 243, 251
Stevens, John, 16, 190
Stillman, Charles, 86
Strauss, Levi, 116
Streetcar, 229, 255
Stuart, Granville, 232, 257
Suggs, W. W., 63
Sulfur, 95
Sutton, Fred, 237–239, 245, 309
Swan, Alex H., 234
Swan Land and Cattle Company, 234
Swenson, 204
Swenson, S. W., 195, 270
Swift, G. F., 43

Taft, Charles P., 219
Tanguay, Eva, 269
Taylor, Dan, 81–83
Taylor, George, 81–83
Taylor, L. D., 81–84
Taylor, Zachary, Gen., 42
Telephone, 245
  long distance, 195
Tendersley, R. F., 42
Texas, area, 101
Texas, University of, 130, 211, 230, 274
Texas A&M University, 171, 304, 325
Texas Cowboy Monument, 317
Texas Cowboy Reunion and Western Art Show, 320
Texas (tick) fever, 2, 3, 63, 80, 87, 291 &c
Texas Longhorn Breeders Association of America, 304
Texas Rangers, 19, 26, 27, 29
Thomas, Helena, 155
Thompson, J. C., 63, 156, 204
Thorp, N. Howard (Jack), 294–295
Thread, made at home, 89
  manufactured, 192
Ticks, 26, 281 ff.
Tin cans, 257–258
Tissandier, Gaston, 136

Toothbrush, 245
Towns, 93
Trails:
  Beef, 19
  Chisholm, 75–87, 81 ff., , 319
  Colorado, 133
  Goodnight, 52
  Goodnight-Loving, 52, 53 ff., , 60, 261
  Long, 109
  Loving, 52
  map of, discussed, 324
  Old beef, 15
  Old Spanish, 319
  Overland, 230
  Santa Fe, 319
  U.S. road, 76
  Western, 173
Transportation, 94, 189, 190–191
Travis, William Barret (Buck), Col., 20
Trees, 215
Trimmer, T. J., 31
Troutman, Johanna, 22
Tumbleweed, 135
Turkeys, 91, 128, 213
Twain, Mark, 120
Tweedsdale, Marquis of, 234

U.S. Geological Survey, 219
University of Texas, 130, 211, 230, 274, 312

Vallambrosa, Antoine de, 233–234, 260
Vance, C. P., 31
Venson, Mrs., 22
Vesper, B., 161
Vielé, Mrs., 117, 180, 185
Villalobos, Gregorio de, 12

W. K. McCoy & Bros., 71
Waggoner, Dan, 135
Waggoner, W. T., 135
Walker, James Washington, 40, 81
Walker, Sam, 26
Wallace, Bigfoot, 199
Walsh, C. C., Col., 200
Warren, Constance Whitney, 317

Welder, Thomas, 245
West, George W., 252
West, J. M., 219
West, Sol, 140
Wheeler, Wilson & Hicks, 63
Whisky, 126, 208
White, James Taylor, 15
White, W. B., 196
Whitney, Eli, 28
Wichita, Kansas, 320
Wichita Mountain Wildlife Refuge, 303
Wilbraux, Pierre, 234
Williams, Dan, 46, 47
Williams, E. F., 220
Williams, Frank, 46, 47
Williamson, Clara McDonald, 322
Wilson, Bill, 53–60, 76, 312
Winchester, gun, 104, 164
Windmill, 255, 256, 269, 271, 291
Wister, Owen, 321
Withers, G. B., 244
Withers, Mark A., 69–73, 122, 161, 204, 220, 221, 244, 253
Withers, Richard, 122–123, 160, 220, 246
Witte Museum, 324
Wolcott, Ben, 270
Wolcott, George, 270
Wolves, 146, 180, 224
Wood, John H., 31, 220
Woodland, John, 165
Woods, Jack, 226
Woodward, Mrs. Mont, 155
Woolworth, F. W., 219
Worsham, W. B., 119
Wright, Orville, 292
Wright, Wilbur, 292
Wylie, 219

XIT Ranch, 235, 279

Yale College, 269
Yarger, a gun, 55
Ybarbo, Gil, 14
Yellowstone National Park, 135
Young, Joe D., 322